The
Slavery
Experience
in the
United States

The Slavery Experience in the United States

Irwin Unger
David Reimers

New York University

HOLT, RINEHART AND WINSTON, INC.

New York   Chicago   San Francisco   Atlanta
Dallas   Montreal   Toronto   London   Sydney

To my parents,
Elias and Mary Unger

To my mother,
Ceridwen Reimers,
and the memory of my father,
Arthur Reimers

Bome
Bome

Preface

We have finally begun to recognize that we have neglected the history of black Americans. The neglect by whites has in part been careless, in part deliberate and chauvinistic. The neglect by blacks, although never as extreme, has reflected the cultural imperialism of the white majority and the self-depreciation it all too often produced. But however derived, our historical myopia is clearly coming to an end, and we are now eager to make up the deficiencies and redress the balance.

Within the experience of black Americans slavery was a central element. For two-thirds of the 350 years that people of African stock have lived in the English-speaking New World they were slaves. From 1619 to 1863 the overwhelming majority of blacks served other Americans as exploited, unpaid servants and chattels. Any experience of a people that persists for so long must inevitably affect the subsequent history of that group. And so slavery did. It would be a mistake to ascribe too much of present group characteristics to the experience of the past, but it would also be a serious error to deny that modern men are somehow products of their history.

Indeed, it would not be amiss to say that the American nation as a whole was molded by slavery. The "peculiar institution" had profound effects on the economic, political, and ethical development of the United States. The plantation system, the abolitionist movement, and the Civil War are all products of chattel slavery. And so is the present problem of race relations in the United States, although much else enters into it as well.

In the pages that follow we have attempted to bring together some of the best articles we could find on American slavery. But within that general goal we have sought to emphasize how slavery affected its victims. Much has been written about slavery as an abstract entity. Scholars have discussed it as a moral problem, as an influence on the economic life of the South, and as an instrument of racial control. They have dealt at length with the various forms it has taken in different cultures and societies, and have compared these forms. We have touched on the interesting question of whether slavery retarded southern economic development, but in general we have focused on the human—or perhaps inhuman— aspects of the system. We hope that we have succeeded in assembling for the reader and student a mosaic picture of how slaves lived and how they felt about their bondage.

In the expeditious preparation of this collection we have relied very heavily on the help of Mrs. Jo McNally of the New York University secretarial staff and on Clifford Snyder and his associates at Holt, Rinehart and Winston. For their kindness and aid we are indeed grateful.

New York   I. U.
March 1970   D. R.

Preface

We have finally begun to recognize that we have neglected the history of black Americans. The neglect by whites has in part been careless, in part deliberate and chauvinistic. The neglect by blacks, although never as extreme, has reflected the cultural imperialism of the white majority and the self-depreciation it all too often produced. But however derived, our historical myopia is clearly coming to an end, and we are now eager to make up the deficiencies and redress the balance.

Within the experience of black Americans slavery was a central element. For two-thirds of the 350 years that people of African stock have lived in the English-speaking New World they were slaves. From 1619 to 1863 the overwhelming majority of blacks served other Americans as exploited, unpaid servants and chattels. Any experience of a people that persists for so long must inevitably affect the subsequent history of that group. And so slavery did. It would be a mistake to ascribe too much of present group characteristics to the experience of the past, but it would also be a serious error to deny that modern men are somehow products of their history.

Indeed, it would not be amiss to say that the American nation as a whole was molded by slavery. The "peculiar institution" had profound effects on the economic, political, and ethical development of the United States. The plantation system, the abolitionist movement, and the Civil War are all products of chattel slavery. And so is the present problem of race relations in the United States, although much else enters into it as well.

In the pages that follow we have attempted to bring together some of the best articles we could find on American slavery. But within that general goal we have sought to emphasize how slavery affected its victims. Much has been written about slavery as an abstract entity. Scholars have discussed it as a moral problem, as an influence on the economic life of the South, and as an instrument of racial control. They have dealt at length with the various forms it has taken in different cultures and societies, and have compared these forms. We have touched on the interesting question of whether slavery retarded southern economic development, but in general we have focused on the human—or perhaps inhuman— aspects of the system. We hope that we have succeeded in assembling for the reader and student a mosaic picture of how slaves lived and how they felt about their bondage.

In the expeditious preparation of this collection we have relied very heavily on the help of Mrs. Jo McNally of the New York University secretarial staff and on Clifford Snyder and his associates at Holt, Rinehart and Winston. For their kindness and aid we are indeed grateful.

New York   I. U.
March 1970   D. R.

Contents

If slavery is not wrong, nothing is wrong.
—Abraham Lincoln, 1864

The
Slavery
Experience
in the
United States

part I

Origins of American Slavery

1

The Seventeenth Century
The Emergence of Slavery

Thad Tate

From: *The Negro in Eighteenth Century Williamsburg* (Williamsburg, Va.: Colonial Williamsburg, Inc., 1965), pp. 1–22. Footnotes deleted. Reprinted by permission.

The first Africans who came to Virginia were not slaves, nor was slavery well entrenched until late in the seventeenth century. As Thad Tate points out, in the last third of that century there was a small but steady growth of the black population in Virginia; the plantation system was taking root, ready for the great expansion of the eighteenth century.

The black population of Virginia was at first small and not vital to the economy. Some of the first blacks were probably indentured servants who became freemen after serving a term of years. Slavery in Virginia only became a fixed institution in the 1600s when the first slave codes were enacted, though occasionally blacks were enslaved before then. Maryland followed the same evolutionary pattern, but the founders of the Carolinas from the beginning made provision for slavery. The trustees of Georgia banned slavery and hoped to avoid the growth of a slave society. In the end, however, the pro-slavery forces won there as elsewhere in colonial America. In general economic factors were critical; as the southern colonies developed tobacco, rice, and indigo, they turned to Africans for a labor force that was fixed and permanent and would not depart at the end of a brief period of service.

The slave codes generally became tighter in the seventeenth and eighteenth centuries. Then, during the American Revolution,

3

under the influence of the colonial fight for freedom from Britain, southern slave codes became more lenient. However, in the nineteenth century they became tighter once again. In the antebellum South, slaves had few rights and were controlled by special curfews, courts, and numerous restrictions. It was illegal, for example, to teach slaves to read and write, and they were not allowed to assemble together unless a white man was present. These and other restrictions were designed to subjugate the four million black slaves of 1860 to white domination. Thus what had begun rather casually in seventeenth-century Virginia became the main black experience in America for over two hundred years. The tragedy was compounded by the development of the doctrine of white supremacy, in part to justify slavery, a doctrine that has persisted long after the death of slavery.

Almost everyone who has even the slightest knowledge of the history of colonial Virginia inevitably recalls the year 1619 for three events. In addition to the first meeting of a representative assembly in the New World and the arrival of a shipload of marriageable maidens, the third occurrence was, of course, the landing of a cargo of Negroes in the James River, the first to be imported to the North American continent. The coming of these Negroes, twenty in all, was almost certainly accidental. They were aboard a Dutch frigate which touched Virginia in late August after a plundering expedition in West Indian waters. Arriving at Point Comfort, the Dutch captain struck a bargain with the Governor and the Cape Merchant to leave the twenty in exchange for sorely needed food. Not much later the *Treasurer,* a vessel fitted out in Virginia, left a single Negro in the colony. In all, then, twenty-one Negroes came in that first eventful year.

Although scholars have in some cases been insisting on the opposite for better than a half century, popular understanding has all too often continued to embrace some questionable assumptions about these first Negroes. It has been all but impossible to correct the impressions that slavery immediately became a precise, legally defined institution; that the white colonists just as quickly saw the Africans as a solution to the pressing labor shortage of the colony; and that, as a consequence, a rapidly swelling wave of slave labor began to flow into Virginia from 1619 on. Such viewpoints deserve to be suspect for their insistent note of immediacy, if nothing else. The processes of history normally move more slowly, and the emergence of slavery in Virginia is no exception. Awareness of the economic usefulness of slave labor, the importation of Negroes in quantity, and the legal recognition of slavery were not instantaneous consequences of what happened in the year 1619.

These first Negroes came into a society in which an unfree status, that of the indentured servant, was already well known. Since the twenty on board the Dutch frigate were acquired by the Governor and the Cape Merchant in exchange for public stores, they presumably took their place alongside the other servants of the London Company. Over the next four years these twenty, plus three or four others who were brought in on other ships, became scattered out to several of the settlements in the colony, where they were in the possession of some seven different men, most of whom were officers in the government.

Thus was established a pattern of indentured servitude for Negroes which continued until about mid-century. Like other servants the Negroes completed a period of service and became freemen. Some of them became landowners and masters of other servants. One of the best known of these was Anthony Johnson, who had apparently reached Virginia in 1621 and had within a year or two gained his freedom. Johnson then married Mary, a Negro woman who came on the *Margrett and John* in 1622. He began to acquire property and to import Negro servants of his own, until he had developed a small African community in Northampton County. One of Anthony Johnson's former Negro servants, Richard Johnson, a carpenter, was even able to import two white servants for whom he received the customary headrights of fifty acres. There are a number of other instances of Negroes who before 1660 acquired land on headrights, by lease, or through purchase.

The word "slave" does appear from time to time before the 1660s, but there is no way to prove that it had a meaning in law. Rather, it was a popular expression of the rigorous demands of servitude, applied to Negro and white alike, as in the case of the poor planters who complained that their children were being held as "slaues or drudges" for the debts of their parents.

Gradually, however, in the period roughly between 1640 and 1660 the Negro's status in Virginia society began to decline and white and Negro servants were no longer approximate equals. In time the Negro found himself in lifetime bondage. The precise rate at which this subjection of the black man occurred as well as the reasons why it happened are subjects of dispute among historians. In large part the disagreement becomes one over whether slavery followed from racial prejudice or whether racial prejudice gripped whites only as a consequence of the enslavement of the Negro.

Those who place the appearance of legalized slavery comparatively late, that is, no earlier than 1660, argue that the white colonists were originally without prejudice, developing it only when they came to know the Negro in bondage. On the other hand, those who believe that slavery developed more rapidly, existing in custom and recognized by the courts in individual instances at least by 1640, conclude that immediate antipathy toward the Negro served to bring on his decline. In truth, the argument focuses on a comparatively brief period—twenty years at the most—during which evidence of the legal recognition of slavery and of racial feeling appear more or less simultaneously. There seems to be little reason not to believe that the two factors, rather than presenting a distinct order of causality, might not have reacted upon each other, "dynamically joining hands to hustle the Negro down the road to complete degradation."

In some part, then, slavery may have emerged not because of a desire to discriminate against the Negro but as the incidental result of increasing pressure to define length and conditions of service for white settlers. In the first years of the colony formal indentures were not the rule, and many persons spent long, indefinite periods as servants. Eventually, in order to assure a continuing flow of indentured labor, it became necessary to write into law strict limitations on servitude that held out the hope of life as a freeman and landowner. The initial statute in Virginia was one of 1642/43 fixing the limits of service for persons arriving without indentures at four years for those over the age of 20, five years for those from 12 to 20, and seven years for children under 12. This law applied specifically to English servants, but subsequent modifications guaranteed a fixed term for all white Christians, no matter from where they came.

The Negro servant, however, was another case. His coming was involuntary, and his bargaining power nonexistent. It became clearer and clearer to white masters that there was no reason for releasing a Negro servant in a few years and every advantage in claiming his labor indefinitely. Thus, in the same decades of the 1640s and 1650s in which the term of indenture for whites was becoming fixed and short, the Negro was coming to be regarded as a "servant for life."

The life-time service of many Negroes was at first a matter of custom rather than law, but court decisions recognizing the principle were becoming more frequent. The earliest known case involved three runaway servants, one a Negro, who were recovered in Maryland and brought to trial in 1640. The two white men had their time of service extended by a year plus three years of labor on public works, but the Negro was ordered to serve for the balance of his life. The fate of Manuel, a mulatto who had been bought "as a Slave for Ever" in September, 1644, and then was adjudged not to be a slave and freed in 1665, was an exception; but it indicates the prevailing trend. Another example concerns the same Anthony Johnson who had established on the Eastern Shore a colony of Negroes indentured to him. In 1653 Johnson was involved in a suit brought by one of his men, John Casor, over the length of time for which Casor was obligated. Johnson succeeded in making good his claim to the man's service for life.

The first recognition in statutory law of this state of affairs occurred in March, 1660/61. At that, this law was no more than an oblique recognition that life servitude was now a *possibility* for some Negroes; for it was enacted to deal with English servants who might "run away in company with any negroes who are incapable of making satisfaction by addition of time."

Besides the widening gap in the length of service demanded of white and Negro servants, a few other distinctions began to appear in these years to the disadvantage of the black man. These restrictions bear some of the marks of racial prejudice. Negroes were excluded, for instance, by a statute of January, 1639/40 from the requirement of possessing arms and ammunition. Three years later Negro women servants, but not white women servants, were counted as tithables for purposes of taxation. And in 1641 the outcome of a suit brought by a Negro servant to confirm his ownership of some hogs suggested that Negroes, even when indentured for a fixed time, were more closely restricted than whites in their right to possess personal property.

Once the law of 1660/61 had admitted the possibility of life servitude, there followed a period lasting down to about 1675 or 1680 during which a number of laws confirmed or defined further the Negro's lower status. More and more, these differentiations cut the Negro "apart from all other servants and gave a new depth to his bondage." By 1670, for instance, the laws of the colony clearly sought to make service for life the *normal* condition under which Negroes would in the future be introduced into Virginia.

One step in this progressive decline of the Negro's position was the elimination of Christianity as a factor which might ameliorate his servitude. The seventeenth century was inclined to take seriously the proposition that conversion entitled heathen servants to liberty. The fact was not lost on Virginians, however, that a literal application of this principle could undermine the whole structure of perpetual servitude which had so recently evolved. The General Assembly as early as 1667 eased the concern of owners of Negroes already in the colony by decreeing that baptism "doth not alter the condition of the person as to his bondage or ffreedome."

Sealing off Christianity as a means of freedom for Negroes yet to be imported could not be altered so directly, however. There was still a reluctance to legislate frankly along color lines, and the first attempt to insure life service for new Negroes drew the simple religious test of heathen and Christian on the assumption that most of the Negroes would certainly be unconverted. This occurred in the law of 1670 already cited in connection with life servitude. It stated that "all servants not being christians imported into this colony by shipping" were to be "slaves for their lives." A certain number of Christianized Negroes escaped with short indentures under this enactment; but a 1682 law partially closed the loophole by denying eventual freedom to servants whose parentage and native country were not Christian and who were not themselves Christian at the time of their first purchase. This was a test few of the new arrivals could meet. The 1705 act which codified much of the existing law on slaves and servants restated this formula a little more directly by declaring all servants imported into Virginia, except Turks and Moors, who were not Christian in their native country or who were not free in a Christian country should be held as slaves, regardless of any later conversion to Christianity. In effect, then, Christianity ceased to shield the newly imported Negro from slavery, just as it had not after 1667 offered any hope of freedom to those who were already here.

Another direct result of perpetual servitude was an alteration in the methods of determining status for Negro children. There had always been a problem about the illegitimate offspring of all bound servants. Now, however, the former legislation which depended principally on additional terms of service—by the mother to compensate her master for time lost during pregnancy and by the father to compensate the parish for care of the child—could no longer apply to most Negro parents. Where both parents were Negroes serving for life, the necessity for punishment, as a matter of fact, ceased to exist. By custom children born of such a union assumed the status of the parents and became permanent and, in time, welcome additions to their owner's labor force. If only one parent were a Negro, however, determination of the child's status became more complicated. Here Virginia early arrived at the solution that children born in the colony should "be held bond or free only according to the condition of the mother." An illegitimate offspring of a mulatto mother, on the other hand, served as an indentured laborer and eventually became free.

Whatever may have been the custom of the day, the law continued during these years to regard the Negro's personal rights as substantially those of any other servant. Statutory law sometimes employed the word slave, but nearly always so that it read clearly in the context of servant for life. It is arguable that the distinction between being a servant for life and a chattel slave was of no practical advantage; yet there was a difference. For one thing, there was less difficulty about the possibility of gaining freedom. Also, the courts were more inclined to deal with a servant, even one bound perpetually, as a man rather than as a species of property.

During the last quarter of the century, however, the status of the Negro in the eyes of the law began to change once more. His personal rights were reduced to a minimum and he was left as a true chattel slave. Thus, it was comparatively late in the seventeenth century before slavery became fixed in the form in which we know it in the eighteenth and nineteenth centuries.

Now there appeared rudimentary "black codes," the first of the laws controlling the conduct, freedom of movement, and personal rights of Negroes that were to become so common a feature of slavery. A 1680 statute, ostensibly enacted to prevent insurrection but in actual practice designed to curb freedom of movement and resistance to a white man, marked the effective beginning of these regulations. Subsequent laws soon established trial procedures which differed from those for white servants.

Color now became the determining factor of slavery. Though there had undoubtedly been some racial antipathy toward Negroes almost from the beginning, the Virginians seemed in no hurry to write it into law. The first law in which "Negro" was clearly used to show racial feeling rather than to distinguish two types of bound labor was perhaps the 1670 enactment forbidding free Negroes and Indians to own white servants. The first act on Negro insurrections in 1680 carried the feeling a step further by punishing the black man who should "presume to lift up his hand in opposition against any christian," and the perpetual banishment after 1691 of any white who married a Negro or mulatto more or less completed the circle. Yet, as late as 1705, in defining slave status the law still clung to the elaborate fiction of heathen birth rather than color. But by this time everyone must have known color was the real badge of slavery.

The last door of escape from a life-time of slavery was closed against the Negro in 1691, when owners were forbidden to free a slave except by transporting him from the colony within six months. Except for a handful of slaves freed by special acts of the General Assembly the practical possibility of manumission had virtually ceased to exist.

From a legal point of view perhaps the final step in reducing a human to the level of slavery is to say point-blank that he has ceased to be a man and has become a species of property. In Virginia this was foreshadowed as early as 1669. In 1705 the Assembly stated explicitly that "all negro, mulatto, and Indian slaves, in all courts of judicature, and other places, within this dominion, shall be held, taken, and adjudged to be real estate. . . ." There was an attempt in 1748 to make slaves personal rather than real property, but it was part of a law which received the royal disallowance. It was difficult to apply the principle that the slave was mere property in every case, however; and in practice both law and custom were forced from time to time to recognize the slave as a person. But the fact remains that in becoming a slave the Negro had become a piece of property first and a man only secondarily.

If the development of slavery was such a slow process, requiring almost until the end of the seventeenth century to reach its final stage, then the assumption that the colonial planters immediately saw the Negro as an ideal answer to such problems as the chronic labor shortage and the rigorous heat of the Southern climate becomes untenable. In fact, the colonists continued for some time to prefer white labor, even with the disadvantage of short indentures. Much of the degradation in status of the Negro may have come about because the planters wanted white labor and set out to make the terms of indentured service more attractive. Lacking similar bargaining power, the Negro was more or less caught in the backwash. Not even the extension of the headright system to Negroes in 1635 had any immediate effect on the number of Negroes imported, for only in the last ten years of the century did the patent books record any significant numbers of African headrights.

It is also absolutely fundamental to any understanding of this formative period to remember how small the Negro population of Virginia actually was before 1680 or 1690. It may be more than coincidence that the appearance of true slavery and the beginning of a sizeable influx of Negroes into Virginia coincide so closely. From the first arrival to the beginning of the last quarter of the century there was never more than an occasional importation of Negroes. The census of 1624–1625 counted only 23. In 1648 an estimate listed 300 "Negro servants" as compared with 15,000 white settlers, the

Negroes being no more than 2% of the colony's total population. By Governor Berkeley's estimate in 1671, Negroes comprised about 4% of the total, or 2000 out of a population of 48,000.

Over the decade of the 1670s the black population rose another thousand to 3000. By 1700 there were about 16,390 Negro inhabitants of Virginia. Thus, the closing thirty years of the seventeenth century saw a small, but significant, step-up in the arrival of Negroes; but the mass importations belong to the eighteenth century.

As the new century opened, there was no doubt that slavery had become a fixed, legally defined institution in the colony of Virginia. The use of Negro labor was moreover finding wider acceptance, and larger importations of slaves were beginning to occur. The way stood open for the enormous extension of slavery which occurred in the first half of the eighteenth century.

part II

The Foreign Slave Trade

Capturing slaves in Africa. Most slaves were sold to traders by African middlemen, but on occasion Europeans actually kidnapped blacks for slavery.
Source: Library of Congress

Middle passage—The deck of a slave ship.
Source: Library of Congress

2
Middle Passage

Daniel Mannix and Malcolm Cowley

From: *Black Cargoes* (New York: The Viking Press, 1962), pp. 104–130. Copyright 1962 by Daniel P. Mannix. All rights reserved. Reprinted by permission of The Viking Press, Inc., and Harold Matson Company, Inc.

Most colonial slaves, especially at the beginning, were necessarily transplanted Africans. These men, women, and children were ripped from their homes, tribes, and families to feed the insatiable needs of the commercial agriculture of the New World. All told, according to one estimate, some fourteen million innocent black men were captured and forcibly abducted in the course of the 350 years that the international slave trade flourished. Some estimates are even higher.

The trade in black slaves began in the fifteenth century with the early Portuguese expeditions along the West African coast. At first the cruel enterprise was modest in size. But then, with the discovery of America and the rise of plantation agriculture in the New World, the trade burgeoned.

Unfortunately, it was highly profitable. A few slaves were captured or kidnapped by Europeans, but the vast majority were bought by European or American merchants from African middlemen for rum, iron, gunpowder, cloth, or assorted European and American artifacts. When sold in Latin America, the Caribbean sugar islands, or the mainland tobacco and rice colonies, they brought large profits in the shape of coin, produce, or commercial credits. The trade, moreover, enabled the northern mainland colonies to buy what they needed from England. Britain, itself a temperate land, would not or could not take the surplus products of the northern colonies, and these communities were always searching for a means to pay British

17

creditors. Slaves sold in Jamaica for sugar and molasses or bills of exchange, or in Virginia for tobacco, could provide funds to buy British manufactures and luxuries, and the foreign slave trade became an important element in the commercial prosperity of towns like Newport, Salem, New London, New York, and Boston.

As conducted until well into the nineteenth century the trade consisted of three "legs." The first was the outward voyage from America or Europe to the West African coast. At the coast ships anchored and their captains bargained with local chieftains for a cargo of slaves, usually unfortunates captured in the interior and brought overland in long "coffles." The third leg was, of course, the voyage to the home port with the proceeds of sales to the planters. In between was the incredibly brutal and dangerous "middle passage" so vividly described in this selection. There have been many grim chapters in the long record of man's inhumanity to man, but few have been so cruel and callous as the carrying of "black cargoes" from Africa to the New World.

As soon as an assortment of naked slaves was taken aboard a Guinea-man, the men were shackled two by two, the right wrist and ankle of one to the left wrist and ankle of another. Then they were sent to the hold or, at the end of the eighteenth century, to the "house" that the sailors had built on deck. The women—usually regarded as fair prey for the sailors—and the children were allowed to wander by day almost anywhere on the vessel, though they spent the night between decks in other rooms than the men. All the slaves were forced to sleep without covering on bare wooden floors, which were often constructed of unplaned boards. In a stormy passage the skin over their elbows might be worn away to the bare bones.

William Bosman says, writing in 1701, "You would really wonder to see how these slaves live on board; for though their number sometimes amounts to six or seven hundred, yet by careful management of our masters of ships"—the Dutch masters, that is—"they are so regulated that it seems incredible: And in this particular our nation exceeds all other Europeans; for as the French, Portuguese and English slave-ships are always foul and stinking; on the contrary ours are for the most part clean and neat." Slavers of every nation insisted that their own vessels were the best in the trade. Thus, James Barbot, Jr., who sailed on an English ship to the Congo in 1700, was highly critical of the Portuguese. He admits that they made a great point of baptizing the slaves before taking them aboard, but then, "It is pitiful," he says, "to see how they crowd those poor wretches, six hundred and fifty or seven hundred in a ship, the men standing in the hold ty'd to stakes, the women between decks and those that are with child in the great cabin and the children in the steeridge which in that hot climate occasions an intolerable stench." This youngest Barbot adds, however, that the Portuguese provided the slaves with coarse thick mats, which were "softer for the poor wretches to lie upon than the bare decks . . . and it would be prudent to imitate the Portuguese in this point." The English never displayed that sort of prudence, and neither did they imitate the Dutch, who had special ships built for the trade, Barbot says, "very wide, lofty and airy betwixt decks, with gratings and scuttles . . . to let in more air. Some also have small ports . . . and that very much contributes to the preservation of those poor wretches who are so thick crowded together."

There were two schools of thoughts among the Guinea captains, called the "loose-packers" and the "tight-packers." The former argued that by giving the slaves a little more room, with better food and a certain amount of liberty, they reduced the mortality among them and received a better price for each slave in the West Indies. The tight-packers answered that although the loss of life might be greater on each of their voyages, so too were the net receipts from a larger cargo. If many of the survivors were weak and emaciated, as was often the case, they could be fattened up in a West Indian slave yard before being offered for sale. The argument between the two schools continued as long as the trade itself, but for many years after 1750 the tight-packers were in the ascendant. So great was the profit on each slave landed alive in the West Indies that hardly a captain refrained from loading his vessel to her utmost capacity. The hold of a slaving vessel was usually about five feet high. That seemed like waste space to the Guinea merchants, so they built a shelf or plat-form in the middle of it, extending six feet from each side of the vessel. When the bottom of the hold was completely covered with flesh, another row of slaves was packed on the platform. If there was as much as six feet of vertical space in the hold, a second plat-form might be installed above the first, sometimes leaving only twenty inches of headroom for the slaves; they could not sit upright during the whole voyage. The Reverend John Newton writes from personal observation:

> The cargo of a vessel of a hundred tons or a little more is cal-culated to purchase from 220 to 250 slaves. Their lodging rooms below the deck which are three (for the men, the boys and the women) besides a place for the sick, are sometimes more than five feet high and sometimes less; and this height is divided toward

the middle for the slaves lie in two rows, one above the other, on each side of the ship, close to each other like books upon a shelf. I have known them so close that the shelf would not easily contain one more.

The poor creatures, thus cramped, are likewise in irons for the most part which makes it difficult for them to turn or move or attempt to rise or to lie down without hurting themselves or each other. Every morning, perhaps, more instances than one are found of the living and the dead fastened together.

Dr. Falconbridge stated in his Parliamentary testimony that "he made the most of the room," in stowing the slaves, "and wedged them in. They had not so much room as a man in his coffin either in length or breadth. When he had to enter the slave deck, he took off his shoes to avoid crushing the slaves as he was forced to crawl over them." Taking off shoes on entering the hold seems to have been a widespread custom among surgeons. Falconbridge "had the marks on his feet where [the slaves] bit and pinched him."

In 1788 Captain Parrey of the Royal Navy was sent to measure such of the slave vessels as were then lying at Liverpool and to make a report to the House of Commons. He discovered that the captains of many slavers possessed a chart showing the dimensions of the ship's half deck, lower deck, hold, platforms, gunroom, orlop, and great cabin, in fact of every crevice into which slaves might be wedged. Miniature black figures were drawn on some of the charts to illustrate the most effective method of packing in the cargo.

On the *Brookes,* which Captain Parrey considered to be typical, every man was allowed a space six feet long by sixteen inches wide (and usually about two feet, seven inches high); every women, a space five feet, ten inches long by sixteen inches wide; every boy, five feet by fourteen inches; every girl, four feet, six inches by twelve inches. The *Brookes* was a vessel of 320 tons. By the law of 1788 it was permitted to carry 454 slaves, and the chart, which later became famous, showed how and where 451 of them could be stowed away. Captain Parrey failed to see how the captain could find room for three more. Nevertheless, Parliament was told by reliable witnesses, including Dr. Thomas Trotter, formerly surgeon of the *Brookes,* that before the new law was passed she had carried 600 slaves on one voyage and 609 on another.

Taking on slaves was a process that might be completed in a month or two at Bonny or Luanda. On the Gold Coast, where slaves were less plentiful, it might last from six months to a year or more. Meanwhile the captain was buying Negroes, sometimes one or two a day, sometimes a hundred or more in a single lot, while haggling over each purchase.

Those months when a slaver lay at anchor off the Guinea Coast, taking on her cargo, were the most dangerous stage of her triangular voyage. Not only was her crew exposed to African fevers and the revenge of angry natives; not only was there the chance of her being taken by pirates or by a hostile man-of-war; but also there was the constant threat of a slave mutiny. Captain Thomas Phillips says, in his account of a voyage made in 1693–1694:

> When our slaves are aboard we shackle the men two and two, while we lie in port, and in sight of their own country, for 'tis then they attempt to make their escape, and mutiny; to prevent which we always keep centinels upon the hatchways, and have a chest full of small arms, ready loaden and prim'd, constantly lying at hand upon the quarter-deck, together with some granada shells; and two of our quarter-deck guns, pointing on the deck thence, and two more out of the steerage, the door of which is always kept shut, and well barr'd; they are fed twice a day, at 10 in the morning, and 4 in the evening, which is the time they are aptest to mutiny, being all upon deck; therefore all that time, what of our men are not employ'd in distributing their victuals to them, and settling them, stand to their arms; and some with lighted matches at the great guns that yaun upon them, loaden with partridge, till they have done and gone down to their kennels between decks.

The danger of mutiny was greatest when all the slaves on board belonged to a single tribe, especially if it was one of the warlike tribes from the Gold Coast. On the other land, the Gold Coast slaves despised other Negroes, and this fault of theirs proved useful to the white men. Phillips says, "We have some 30 or 40 gold coast negroes, which we buy . . . to make guardians and overseers of the Whidaw negroes, and sleep among them to keep them from quarreling; and in order, as well as to give us notice, if they can discover any caballing or plotting among them, which trust they will discharge with great diligence; . . . when we constitute a guardian, we give him a cat of nine tails as a badge of his office, which he is not a little proud of, and will exercise with great authority."

In spite of such precautions, mutinies were frequent on the coast, and some of them were successful. Even a failed mutiny might lead to heavy losses among the slaves and the sailors. James Barbot, Sr., of the *Albion-Frigate*, made the mistake of providing his slaves with knives so they could cut their meat. The slaves tore pieces of iron from the forecastle door, broke off their shackles, and killed the guard at the entrance to the hatchway. Before the mutiny was quelled, twenty-eight slaves either had been shot dead or had thrown themselves overboard. Bosman went through two mutinies. In the second of these the slaves would have mastered the ship had it not been aided by a French and an English vessel. About twenty slaves were killed. William Snelgrave survived more perils on the coast than any other Guinea captain of the early eighteenth century. Among the perils were three mutinies, one at Old Calabar, when there were four hundred slaves on his father's ship and only ten sailors not disabled by fever, and the other two on the Gold Coast. Both the Gold Coast mutinies were led by Coromantees, against hopeless odds. About the first of these he says:

> This Mutiny began at Midnight. . . . Two Men that stood Centry at the Forehatch way . . . permitted four [slaves] to go to that Place, but neglected to lay the Gratings again, as they should have done; whereupon four more Negroes came on Deck . . . and all eight fell on the two Centries who immediately called out for help. The Negroes endeavoured to get their Cutlaces from them, but the Lineyards (that is the Lines by which the Handles of the Cutlaces were fastened to the Men's Wrists) were so twisted in the Scuffle, that they could not get them off before we came to their Assistance. The Negroes perceiving several white Men coming towards them, with Arms in their Hands, quitted the Centries and jumped over the Ship's Side into the Sea. . . .
>
> After we had secured these people, I called the Linguists, and ordered them to bid the Men-Negroes between Decks be quiet; (for there was a great noise amongst them.) On their being silent, I asked, "What had induced them to mutiny?" They answered, "I was a great Rogue to buy them, in order to carry them away from their own Country, and that they were resolved to regain their Liberty if possible." I replied, "That they had forfeited their Freedom before I bought them, either by Crimes or by being taken in War." . . . Then I observed to them, "That if they should gain their Point and escape to the Shore, it would be of no Advantage to them, because their Countrymen would catch them, and sell them to other Ships." This served my purpose, and they seemed to be convinced of their Fault.

Mutinies were frequent during the years from 1750 to 1788, when Liverpool merchants were trying to save money by reducing the size of their crews. A small crew weakened by fever was no match for the slaves, especially if it had to withstand a simultaneous attack from the shore. On January 11, 1769, the *Nancy* out of Liverpool, Captain Williams, was lying at anchor off New Calabar. She had 132 slaves on board, who managed to break their shackles and assail the crew. The slaves were unarmed, but "it was with great difficulty, though [the crew] attacked them sword in hand, to make them submit." Meanwhile the natives on shore heard the fighting and swarmed aboard the *Nancy* from their canoes. They seized the slaves (whom they later resold to other ships, as Captain Snelgrave had prophesied) and looted the cargo. There was a wild scene of plunder, with black men running through the vessel, breaching rum casks, throwing ships' biscuit and salt beef into the canoes, and robbing the sailors of everything they possessed. Afterward they cut the cables and set the *Nancy* adrift. Another slaver lying in the river sent a boat to rescue Captain Williams and the surviving seamen. The vessel, however, was wrecked.

William Richardson, a young sailor who shipped on a Guineaman in 1790, tells of going to the help of a French vessel on which the slaves had risen while it was at anchor in a bay. The English seamen jumped into their boats and pulled hard for the Frenchman, but by the time they reached it there were "a hundred slaves in possession of the deck and others tumbling up from below." The French vessel had its netting rigged—a customary precaution for slavers lying at anchor—and the nets prevented the Englishmen from boarding. Even after they had broken through the nets, the slaves put up a desperate resistance. "I could not but admire," Richardson says, "the courage of a fine young black who, though his partner in irons lay dead at his feet, would not surrender but fought with his billet of wood until a ball finished his existence. The others fought as well as they could but what could they do against fire-arms?"

There are fairly detailed accounts of fifty-five mutinies on slavers from 1699 to 1845, not to mention passing references to more than a hundred others. The list of ships "cut off" by the natives—often in revenge for the kidnaping of freemen—is almost as long. On the record it does not seem that Africans submitted tamely to being carried across the Atlantic like chained beasts. Edward Long, the Jamaica planter and historian, justified the cruel punishments inflicted on slaves by saying, "The many acts of violence they have committed by murdering whole crews and destroying ships when they had it in their power to do so have made these rigors wholly chargeable on their own bloody and malicious disposition which calls for the same confinement as if they were wolves or wild boars." For "wolves or wild boars" a modern reader might substitute "men who would rather die than be enslaved."

As long as a vessel lay at anchor, the slaves could dream of seizing it. If they managed to kill the crew, as they did in perhaps one mutiny out of ten, they could cut the anchor cable and let the vessel drift ashore. That opportunity was lost as soon as the vessel put to sea. Ignorant of navigation, which they regarded as white man's magic, the slaves were at the mercy of the captain. They could still die, but not with any hope of regaining their freedom.

The captain, for his part, had finished the most dangerous leg of his triangular voyage. Now he had to face only the ordinary perils of the sea, most of which were covered by his owners' insurance against fire, shipwreck, pirates and rovers, letters of mart and counter-mart, barratry, jettison, and foreign men-of-war. Among the risks not covered by insurance, the greatest was that the cargo might be swept away by disease. The underwriters refused to issue such policies, arguing that they would expose the captain to an unholy temptation. If insured against disease among his slaves, he might take no precautions against it and might try to make his profit out of the insurance.

The more days at sea, the more deaths among his cargo, and so the captain tried to cut short the next leg of his voyage. If he had shipped his slaves at Bonny or Old Calabar or any port to the southward, he might call at one of the Portuguese islands in the Gulf of Guinea for an additional supply of food and fresh water, usually enough, with what he had already, to last for three months. If he had traded on the Windward Coast, he made straight for the West Indies. Usually he had from four to five thousand nautical miles to sail—or even more, if the passage was from Angola to Virginia. The shortest passage—that from the Gambia River to Barbados—might be made in as little as three weeks, with favoring winds. If the course was much longer, and if the ship was becalmed in the doldrums or driven back by storms, it might take more than three months to cross the Atlantic, and slaves and sailors would be put on short rations long before the end of the Middle Passage.

On a canvas of heroic size, Thomas Stothard, Esq., of the Royal Academy, depicted "The Voyage of the Sable Venus from Angola to the West Indies." His painting is handsomely reproduced in the second volume of Bryan Edwards' *History of the West Indies*, where it appears beside a poem on the same allegorical subject by an unnamed Jamaican author, perhaps Edwards himself. In the painting the ship that carries the Sable Venus is an immense scallop shell, in which she sits upright on a velvet throne. Except for bracelets, anklets, and a collar of pearls, she wears nothing but a narrow embroidered girdle. Her look is soft and sensuous, and in grace she yields nothing—so the poem insists—to Botticelli's white Venus,

> In FLORENCE, where she's seen;
> Both just alike, except the white,
> No difference, no—none at night
> The beauteous dames between.

The joint message of the poem and the painting is simple to the point of coarseness: that slave women are preferable to English girls at night, being passionate and accessible; but the message is embellished with a wealth of classical details, to show the painter's learning. Two legendary dolphins draw the bark of Venus toward the West. Triton leads one of them, while blowing his wreathèd horn. Two mischievous loves gambol about the other dolphin. There are cherubs above the woolly head of Venus, fanning her with ostrich plumes. In the calm distance a grampus discharges his column of spray. Cupid, from above, is shooting an arrow at Neptune, who strides ahead bearing the Union Jack. As the poet (who calls the dolphins "winged fish") describes the idyllic scene:

> The winged fish, in purple trace
> The chariot drew; with easy grace
>   Their azure rein she guides:
> And now they fly, and now they swim;
> Now o'er the wave they lightly skim,
>   Or dart beneath the tides.

Meanwhile the Sable Venus, if she was a living woman borne from Angola to the West Indies, was roaming the deck of a ship that stank of excrement, so that, as with any slaver, "You could smell it five miles down wind." She had been torn from her husband and her children, she had been branded on the left buttock, and she had been carried to the ship bound hand and foot, lying in the bilge at the bottom of a dugout canoe. Now she was the prey of the ship's officers, in danger of being flogged to death if she resisted them. Her reward if she yielded was a handful of beads or a sailor's kerchief to tie around her waist.

Here is how she and her shipmates spent the day.

If the weather was clear, they were brought on deck at eight o'clock in the morning. The men were attached by their leg irons to the great chain that ran along the bulwarks on both sides of the ship; the women and half-grown boys were allowed to wander at will. About nine o'clock the slaves were served their first meal of the day. If they were from the Windward Coast, the fare consisted of boiled rice, millet, or cornmeal, which might be cooked with a few lumps of salt beef abstracted from the sailors' rations. If they were from the Bight of Biafra, they were fed stewed yams, but the Congos and the Angolans preferred manioc or plantains. With the food they were all given half a pint of water, served out in a panni-kin.

After the morning meal came a joyless ceremony called "danc-ing the slaves." "Those who were in irons," says Dr. Thomas Trotter, surgeon of the *Brookes* in 1783, "were ordered to stand up and make what motions they could, leaving a passage for such as were out of irons to dance around the deck." Dancing was prescribed as a therapeutic measure, a specific against suicidal melancholy, and also against scurvy—although in the latter case it was a useless torture for men with swollen limbs. While sailors paraded the deck, each with a cat-o'-nine-tails in his right hand, the men slaves "jumped in their irons" until their ankles were bleeding flesh. One sailor told Parliament, "I was employed to dance the men, while another person danced the women." Music was provided by a slave thumping on a broken drum or an upturned kettle, or by an African banjo, if there was one aboard, or perhaps by a sailor with a bagpipe or a fiddle. Slaving captains sometimes advertised for "A person that can play on the Bagpipes, for a Guinea ship." The slaves were also told to sing. Said Dr. Claxton after his voyage in the *Young Hero,* "They sing, but not for their amusement. The captain ordered them to sing, and they sang songs of sorrow. Their sickness, fear of being beaten, their hunger, and the memory of their country, &c, are the usual subjects."

While some of the sailors were dancing the slaves, others were sent below to scrape and swab out the sleeping rooms. It was a sickening task, and it was not well performed unless the captain imposed an iron discipline. James Barbot, Sr., was proud of the disci-pline maintained on the *Albion-Frigate.* "We were very nice," he says, "in keeping the places where the slaves lay clean and neat, appointing some of the ship's crew to do that office constantly and thrice a week we perfumed betwixt decks with a quantity of good vinegar in pails, and red-hot iron bullets in them, to expel the bad air, after the place had been well washed and scrubbed with brooms." Captain Hugh Crow, the last legal English slaver, was famous for his housekeeping. "I always took great pains," he says, "to promote the health and comfort of all on board, by proper diet, regularity, exercise, and cleanliness, for I considered that on keeping the ship clean and orderly, which was always my hobby, the success of our voyage mainly depended." Consistently he lost fewer slaves in the Middle Passage than the other captains, some of whom had the filth in the hold cleaned out only once a week. A few left their slaves to wallow in excrement during the whole Atlantic passage.

At three or four in the afternoon the slaves were fed their second meal, often a repetition of the first. Sometimes, instead of African food, they were given horse beans, the cheapest provender from Europe. The beans were boiled to a pulp, then covered with a mixture of palm oil, flour, water, and red pepper, which the sailors called "slabber sauce." Most of the slaves detested horse beans, especially if they were used to eating yams or manioc. Instead of eating the pulp, they would, unless carefully watched, pick it up by handfuls and throw it in each other's faces. That second meal was the end of their day. As soon as it was finished they were sent below, under the guard of sailors charged with stowing them away on their bare floors and platforms. The tallest men were placed amidships, where the vessel was widest; the shorter ones were tumbled into the stern. Usually there was only room for them to sleep on their sides, "spoon fashion." Captain William Littleton told Parliament that slaves in the ships on which he sailed might lie on their backs if they wished—"though perhaps," he conceded, "it might be difficult all at the same time."

After stowing their cargo, the sailors climbed out of the hatchway, each clutching his cat-o'-nine-tails: then the hatchway gratings were closed and barred. Sometimes in the night, as the sailors lay on deck and tried to sleep, they heard from below "an howling melancholy noise, expressive of extreme anguish." When Dr. Trotter told his interpreter, a slave woman, to inquire about the cause of the noise, "she discovered it to be owing to their having dreamt they were in their own country, and finding themselves when awake, in the hold of a slave ship."

More often the noise heard by the sailors was that of quarreling among the slaves. The usual occasion for quarrels was their problem of reaching the latrines. These were inadequate and hard to find in the darkness of the crowded hold, especially by men who were ironed together in pairs.

> In each of the apartments [says Dr. Falconbridge] are placed three or four large buckets, of a conical form, nearly two feet in diameter at the bottom and only one foot at the top and in depth about twenty-eight inches, to which, when necessary, the negroes have recourse. It often happens that those who are placed at a distance from the buckets, in endeavoring to get to them, tumble over their companions, in consequence of their being shackled. These accidents, although unavoidable, are productive of continual quarrels in which

some of them are always bruised. In this situation, unable to proceed and prevented from going to the tubs, they desist from the attempt; and as the necessities of nature are not to be resisted, they ease themselves as they lie.

In squalls or rainy weather, the slaves were never brought on deck. They were served their two meals in the hold, where the air became too thick and poisonous to breathe. Says Dr. Falconbridge, "For the purpose of admitting fresh air, most of the ships in the slave-trade are provided, between the decks, with five or six airports on each side of the ship, of about six inches in length and four in breadth; in addition to which, some few ships, but not one in twenty, have what they denominate wind-sails." These were funnels made of canvas and so placed as to direct a current of air into the hold. "But whenever the sea is rough and the rain heavy," Falconbridge continues, "it becomes necessary to shut these and every other conveyance by which the air is admitted. . . . The negroes' rooms very soon become intolerably hot. The confined air, rendered noxious by the effluvia exhaled from their bodies and by being repeatedly breathed, soon produces fevers and fluxes which generally carry off great numbers of them."

Dr. Trotter says that when tarpaulins were thrown over the gratings, the slaves would cry, "Kickeraboo, kickeraboo, we are dying, we are dying." "I have known," says Henry Ellison, a sailor before the mast, "in the Middle Passage, in rains, slaves confined below for some time. I have frequently seen them faint through heat, the steam coming through the gratings, like a furnace." Falconbridge gives one instance of their sufferings.

> Some wet and blowing weather [he says] having occasioned the port-holes to be shut and the grating to be covered, fluxes and fevers among the negroes ensued. While they were in this situation, I frequently went down among them till at length their rooms became so extremely hot as to be only bearable for a very short time. But the excessive heat was not the only thing that rendered their situation intolerable. The deck, that is, the floor of their rooms, was so covered with the blood and mucus which had proceeded from them in consequence of the flux, that it resembled a slaughter-house. . . . Numbers of the slaves having fainted they were carried upon deck where several of them died and the rest with great difficulty were restored. It had nearly proved fatal to me also. The climate was too warm to admit the wearing of any clothing but a shirt and that I had pulled off before I went down; notwithstanding which, by only continuing among them for about a quarter of an hour, I was so overcome with the heat, stench and foul air

that I nearly fainted; and it was only with assistance that I could get on deck. The consequence was that I soon after fell sick of the same disorder from which I did not recover for several months.

Not surprisingly, the slaves often went mad. Falconbridge mentions a woman on the *Emilia* who had to be chained to the deck. She had lucid intervals, however, and during one of these she was sold to a planter in Jamaica. Men who went insane might be flogged to death, to make sure that they were not malingering. Some were simply clubbed on the head and thrown overboard.

While the slaves were on deck they had to be watched at all times to keep them from committing suicide. Says Captain Phillips of the *Hannibal*, "We had about 12 negroes did wilfully drown themselves, and others starv'd themselves to death; for," he explained, " 'tis their belief that when they die they return home to their own country and friends again." This belief was reported from various regions, at various periods of the trade, but it seems to have been especially prevalent among the Ibo of eastern Nigeria. In 1788, nearly a hundred years after the *Hannibal*'s voyage, Ecroide Claxton was the surgeon who attended a shipload of Ibo. "Some of the slaves," he testified, "wished to die on an idea that they should then get back to their own country. The captain in order to obviate this idea, thought of an expedient, viz., to cut off the heads of those who died intimating to them that if determined to go, they must return without heads. The slaves were accordingly brought up to witness the operation. One of them by a violent exertion got loose and flying to the place where the nettings had been unloosed in order to empty the tubs, he darted overboard. The ship brought to, a man was placed in the main chains to catch him which he perceiving, made signs which words cannot express expressive of his happiness in escaping. He then went down and was seen no more."

Dr. Isaac Wilson, a surgeon in the Royal Navy, made a Guinea voyage on the *Elizabeth*, Captain John Smith, who was said to be very humane. Nevertheless, Wilson was assigned the duty of whipping the slaves. "Even in the act of chastisement," Wilson says, "I have seen them look up at me with a smile, and, in their own language, say, 'presently we shall be no more.' " One woman on the *Elizabeth* found some rope yarn, which she tied to the armorer's vise; she fastened the other end round her neck and was found dead in the morning. On the *Brookes* when Thomas Trotter was her surgeon, there was a man who, after being accused of witchcraft, had been sold into slavery with his whole family. During his first night on shipboard he tried to cut his throat. Dr. Trotter sewed up the wound, but on the following night the man not only tore out the sutures but tried to cut his throat on the other side. From the ragged edges of the wound and the blood on his fingers, he seemed to have used his nails as the only available instrument. His hand were tied together after the second wound, but he then refused all food, and he died of hunger in eight or ten days.

"Upon the negroes refusing to take food," says Falconbridge, "I have seen coals of fire, glowing hot, put on a shovel and placed so near their lips as to scorch and burn them. And this has been accompanied with threats of forcing them to swallow the coals if they persisted in refusing to eat. This generally had the required effect"; but if the Negroes still refused, they were flogged day after day. Lest flogging prove ineffective, every Guineaman was provided with a special instrument called the "speculum oris," or mouth opener. It looked like a pair of dividers with notched legs and with a thumb-screw at the blunt end. The legs were closed and the notches were hammered between the slave's teeth. When the thumbscrew was tightened, the legs of the instrument separated, forcing open the slave's mouth; then food was poured into it through a funnel.

Even the speculum oris sometimes failed with a slave determined to die. Dr. Wilson reports another incident of his voyage on the *Elizabeth,* this one concerning a young man who had refused to eat for several days. Mild means were used to divert him from his resolution, "as well as promises," Wilson says, "that he should have anything he wished for; but still he refused to eat. He was then whipped with the cat but this also was ineffectual. He always kept his teeth so fast that it was impossible to get anything down. We then endeavored to introduce a Speculum Oris between his teeth but the points were too obtuse to enter and next tried a bolus knife but with the same effect. In this state he was for four or five days when he was brought up as dead to be thrown overboard. . . . I finding life still existing, repeated my endeavours though in vain and two days afterwards he was brought up again in the same state as before. . . . In his own tongue he asked for water which was given him. Upon this we began to have hopes of dissuading him from his design but he again shut his teeth as fast as ever and resolved to die and on the ninth day from his first refusal he died."

One deadly scourge of the Guinea cargoes was a phenomenon called "fixed melancholy." Even slaves who were well fed, treated with kindness, and kept under relatively sanitary conditions would often die one after another for no apparent reason; they simply had no wish to live. Fixed melancholy seems to have been especially rife among the Ibo and among the food-gathering tribes of the Gaboon, but no Negro nation was immune to it. Although the disease was noted from the earliest days of the trade, perhaps the best description of it was written by George Howe, an American medical student who shipped on an illegal slaver in 1859:

> Notwithstanding their apparent good health [Howe says] each morning three or four dead would be found, brought upon deck, taken by the arms and heels, and tossed overboard as unceremoniously as an empty bottle. Of what did they die? And [why] always at night? In the barracoons it was known that if a Negro was not amused and kept in motion, he would mope, squat down with his chin on his knees and arms clasped about his legs and in a very short time die. Among civilized races it is thought almost impossible to hold one's breath until death follows. It is thought the African can do so. They had no means of concealing anything and certainly did not kill each other. One of the duties of the slave-captains was when they found a slave sitting with knees up and head drooping, to start them up, run them about the deck, give them a small ration of rum, and divert them until in a normal condition.

It is impossible for a human being to hold his breath until he dies. Once he loses consciousness, his lungs fill with air and he recovers. The simplest explanation for the slaves' ability to "will themselves dead" is that they were in a state of shock as a result of their being carried through the terrifying surf into the totally unfamiliar surroundings of the ship. In certain conditions shock can be as fatal as physical injury. There may, however, be another explanation. The communal life of many tribes was so highly organized by a system of customs, relationships, taboos, and religious ceremonies that there was practically nothing a man or a woman could do that was not prescribed by tribal law. To separate an individual from this complex system of interrelationships and suddenly place him, naked and friendless, in a completely hostile environment was in some respects a greater shock than any amount of physical brutality.

Dr. Wilson believed that fixed melancholy was responsible for the loss of two-thirds of the slaves who died on the *Elizabeth*. "No one who had it was ever cured," he says, "whereas those who had it not and yet were ill, recovered. The symptoms are a lowness of spirits and despondency. Hence they refuse food. This only increases the symptoms. The stomach afterwards got weak. Hence the belly ached, fluxes ensued, and they were carried off." But flux, or dysentery, is an infectious disease spread chiefly by food prepared in unsanitary conditions. The slaves, after being forced to wallow in filth, were also forced to eat with their fingers. In spite of the real losses from fixed melancholy, the high death rate on Guinea ships was due to somatic more than to psychic afflictions.

Along with their human cargoes, crowded, filthy, undernourished, and terrified out of the wish to live, the ships also carried an invisible cargo of microbes, bacilli, spirochetes, viruses, and intestinal worms from one continent to another; the Middle Passage was a crossroads and marketplace of diseases. From Europe came smallpox, measles (less deadly to Africans than to American Indians), gonorrhea, and syphilis (which last Columbus's sailors had carried from America to Europe). The African diseases were yellow fever (to which the natives were more resistant than white men), dengue, blackwater fever, and malaria (which was not specifically African, but which most of the slaves carried in their bloodstreams). If anopheles mosquitoes were present, malaria spread from the slaves through any new territories to which they were carried. Other African diseases were amoebic and various forms of bacillary dysentery (all known as "the bloody flux"), Guinea worms, hookworm (possibly African in origin, but soon endemic in the warmer parts of the New World), yaws, elephantiasis, and leprosy.

The particular affliction of the white sailors after escaping from the fevers of the Guinea Coast was scurvy, a deficiency disease to which they were exposed by their monotonous rations of salt beef and sea biscuits. The daily tot of lime juice (originally lemon juice) that prevented scurvy was almost never served on merchantmen during the days of the legal slave trade, and in fact was not prescribed in the Royal Navy until 1795. Although the slaves were also subject to scurvy, they fared better in this respect than the sailors, partly because they made only one leg of the triangular voyage and partly because their rough diet was sometimes richer in vitamins. But sailors and slaves alike were swept away by smallpox and "the bloody flux," and sometimes they went blind from various forms of ophthalmia, the worst of which seems to have been a gonorrheal infection of the eyes.

Smallpox was feared more than other diseases, since the surgeons had no means of combating it until the end of the eighteenth century. One man with smallpox infected a whole vessel, unless— as sometimes happened—he was tossed overboard when the first scabs appeared. Captain Wilson of the *Briton* lost more than half his cargo of 375 slaves by not listening to his surgeon. It was the last slave brought on board who had the disease, says Henry Ellison, who made the voyage. "The doctor told Mr. Wilson it was the smallpox," Ellison continues. "He would not believe it, but said he would keep him, as he was a fine man. It soon broke out amongst the slaves. I have seen the platform one continued scab. We hauled up eight or ten slaves dead of a morning. The flesh and skin peeled off their wrists when taken hold of, being entirely mortified." But dysentery, though not so much feared, could cause as many deaths. Ellison testifies that he made two voyages on the *Nightingale,* Captain Carter. On the first voyage the slaves were so crowded that thirty boys "messed and slept in the long boat all through the Middle Passage, there being no room below"; and still the vessel lost only five or six slaves in all, out of a cargo of 270. On the second voyage, however, the *Nightingale* buried "about 150, chiefly of fevers and flux. We had 250 when we left the coast."

Dr. Claxton sailed from Bonny on the *Young Hero,* Captain Molyneux. "We had 250 slaves," he says, "of whom 132 died, chiefly of the flux. . . . The steerage and the boys' room were insufficient to receive the sick, so greatly did the disorder prevail. We were therefore obliged to place together those that were and those that were not diseased, and in consequence the disease and mortality spread more and more." The hold was swimming with blood and mucus. Toward the end of her voyage the *Young Hero* met another vessel with almost the same name—the *Hero,* Captain Wilson—and learned that she had lost 360 slaves, more than half her cargo. Most of them had died of smallpox. When moved from one place to another, they left marks of their skin and blood upon the deck, and the other surgeon told Claxton that it was "the most horrid sight he had ever seen."

The average mortality in the Middle Passage is impossible to state accurately from the surviving records. Some famous voyages were made without the loss of a single slave, as notably by Captains John Newton, William Macintosh, and Hugh Crow. On one group of nine voyages between 1766 and 1780, selected at random, the vessels carried 2362 slaves and there were no epidemics of disease. The total loss of slaves was 154, or about 6½ percent. On another list of twenty voyages compiled by Thomas Clarkson the abolitionist, the vessels carried 7904 slaves and lost 2053, or 26 percent. Balancing high and low figures together, the English Privy Council in 1789 arrived at an estimate of 12½ percent for the average mortality in the Middle Passage. That comes close to the percentage reckoned long afterward from the manifests of French vessels sailing from Nantes. Between 1748 and 1782 the Nantes slavers bought 146,799 slaves and sold 127,133 on the other side of the Atlantic. The difference of 19,666 would indicate a loss of 13 percent in the voyage.

Of course there were further losses. To the mortality in the Middle Passage, the Privy Council added 4¹/₂ percent for the deaths of slaves in harbors before they were sold, and 33 percent for deaths during the seasoning process, making a total of 50 percent. If those figures are correct (U. B. Phillips, the author of *American Negro Slavery*, thinks they are somewhat high), then only one slave was added to the New World labor force for every two purchased on the Guinea Coast.

To keep the figures in perspective, it might be added that the mortality among slaves in the Middle Passage was possibly no greater than that of white indentured servants or even of free Irish, Scottish, and German immigrants in the North Atlantic crossing. On the better commanded Guineamen it was probably much less, and for a simple economic reason. There was no profit in a slaving voyage until the Negroes were landed alive and sold; therefore the better captains took care of their cargoes. If the Negroes died in spite of good care, the captains regarded their deaths as a personal affront. "No gold-finders," lamented Captain Phillips of the *Hannibal,* who lost nearly half of his cargo from the bloody flux, "can endure so much noisome slavery as they do who carry negroes; for those have some respite and satisfaction, but we endure twice the misery; and yet by their mortality our voyages are ruin'd, and we pine and fret our selves to death, to think that we should undergo so much misery, and take so much pains to so little purpose." It was different on the North Atlantic crossing, where even the hold and steerage passengers paid their fares before coming aboard, and where it was of little concern to the captain whether they lived or died.

After leaving the Portuguese island of São Thomé—if he had watered there—a slaving captain bore westward along the equator for a thousand miles, and then northwestward toward the Cape Verde Islands. This was the tedious part of the Middle Passage. Along the equator the vessel might be delayed for weeks by calms or storms; sometimes it had to return to the African coast for fresh provisions. Then, "on leaving the Gulf of Guinea," says the author of a *Universal Geography* published in the early nineteenth century, ". . . that part of the ocean must be traversed, so fatal to navigators, where long calms detain the ships under a sky charged with electric clouds, pouring down by turns torrents of rain and of fire. This *sea of thunder,* being a focus of mortal diseases, is avoided as much as possible, both in approaching the coasts of Africa and those of America." It was not until reaching the latitude of the

Cape Verde Islands that the vessel fell in with the Northeast Trades and was able to make a swift passage to the West Indies.

Ecroide Claxton's ship, the *Young Hero,* was one of those delayed for weeks before reaching the trade winds. "We were so streightened for provisions," he testified, "that if we had been ten more days at sea, we must either have eaten the slaves that died, or have made the living slaves *walk the plank,*" a term, he explained, that was widely used by Guinea captains. There are no authenticated records of cannibalism in the Middle Passage, but there are many accounts of slaves killed for various reasons. English captains believed that French vessels carried poison in their medicine chests, "with which they can destroy their negroes in a calm, contagious sickness, or short provisions." They told the story of a Frenchman from Brest who had a long passage and had to poison his slaves; only twenty of them reached Haiti out of five hundred. Even the cruelest English captains regarded this practice as Latin, depraved, and uncovered by their insurance policies. In an emergency they simply jettisoned part of their cargo.

The most famous case involving jettisoned slaves was that of the *Zong* out of Liverpool, Luke Collingwood master. The *Zong* had left São Thomé on September 6, 1781, with a cargo of four hundred and forty slaves and a white crew of seventeen. There was sickness aboard during a slow passage; more than sixty Negroes died, with seven of the seamen, and many of the remaining slaves were so weakened by dysentery that it was a question whether they could be sold in Jamaica. On November 29, after they had already sighted land in the West Indies, Captain Collingwood called his officers together. He announced that there were only two hundred gallons of fresh water left in the casks, not enough for the remainder of the voyage. If the slaves died of thirst or illness, he explained, the loss would fall on the owners of the vessel; but if they were thrown into the sea it would be a legal jettison, covered by insurance. "It would not be so cruel to throw the poor sick wretches into the sea," he argued, "as to suffer them to linger out a few days under the disorders to which they were afflicted."

The mate, James Kelsal, demurred at first, saying there was "no present want of water to justify such a measure," but the captain outtalked him. To quote from a legal document, "The said Luke Collingwood picked, or caused to be picked out, from the cargo of the same ship, one hundred and thirty-three slaves, all or most of whom were sick or weak, and not likely to live; and ordered the crew by turns to throw them into the sea; which most inhuman order was cruelly complied with." A first "parcel," as the sailors called them, of fifty-four slaves went overboard that same day, November 29. A second parcel, this time of forty-two, followed them on December 1, still leaving thirty-six slaves out of those condemned to be jettisoned. (One man seems to have died from natural causes.) Also on December 1 there was a heavy rain and the sailors collected six casks of water, enough to carry the vessel into port. But Collingwood stuck to his plan, and the last parcel of condemned slaves was brought on deck a few days later. Twenty-six of them were handcuffed, then swung into the sea. The last ten refused to let the sailors come near them; instead they vaulted over the bulwarks and were drowned like the others.

On December 22 the *Zong* dropped anchor in Kingston harbor after a passage of three months and sixteen days. Collingwood sold the remainder of his slaves, then sailed his vessel to England, where his owners claimed thirty pounds of insurance money for each of the one hundred and thirty-two jettisoned slaves. The underwriters refused to pay, and the case was taken to court. At a first trial the jury found for the owners, since "they had no doubt . . . that the case of slaves was the same as if horses had been thrown overboard." The underwriters appealed to the Court of Exchequer, and Lord Mansfield presided. After admitting that the law supported the owners of the *Zong,* he went on to say that "a higher law [applies to] this very shocking case." He found for the underwriters. It was the first case in which an English court ruled that a cargo of slaves could not be treated simply as merchandise.

Often a slave ship came to grief in the last few days of the Middle Passage. It might be taken by a French privateer out of Martinique, or it might disappear in a tropical hurricane, or it might be wrecked on a shoal almost in sight of its harbor. There was a famous wreck on Morant Keys off the eastern end of Jamaica; the sailors took refuge on a sandpit with a scanty store of provisions but plenty of rum, then massacred the slaves who tried to follow them. Only thirty-three Negroes survived (and were later exposed for sale in Kingston) out of about four hundred. On a few ships there was an epidemic of suicide at the last moment. Thus, when the *Prince of Orange* anchored at St. Kitts in 1737, more than a hundred Negro men jumped overboard. "Out of the whole," Captain Japhet Bird reported, "we lost 33 of as good Men Slaves as we had on board, who would not endeavour to save themselves, but resolv'd to die, and sunk directly down. Many more of them were taken up almost drown'd, some of them died since, but not the Owners Loss, they being sold before any Discovery was made of the Injury the Salt

Water had done them. . . . This Misfortune was owing to one of their Countrymen, who came on board and in a joking manner told the Slaves that they were first to have their Eyes put out, and then to be eaten, with a great many other nonsensical Falsities."

These, however, were exceptional misfortunes, recounted as horror stories in the newspapers of the time. Usually the last two or three days of the Middle Passage were a comparatively happy period. All the slaves, or all but a few, might be released from their irons. When there was a remaining stock of provisions, the slaves were given bigger meals—to fatten them for market—and as much water as they could drink. Sometimes on the last day—if the ship was commanded by an easy-going captain—there was a sort of costume party on deck, with the women slaves dancing in the sailors' cast-off clothing. Then the captain was rowed ashore to arrange for the disposition of his cargo.

There were several fashions of selling the slaves. In a few instances the whole cargo was consigned to a single rich planter, or to a group of planters. More often a West Indian factor took charge of retail sales, for a commission of 15 percent on the gross amount and 5 percent more on the net proceeds. When the captain himself had to sell his slaves, he ferried them ashore, had them drawn up in ragged line of march, and paraded them through town with bagpipes playing, before exposing them to buyers in the public square. J. G. Stedman, a young officer in the Scots Brigade employed as a mercenary by the Dutch in their obstinate efforts to suppress the slave revolts in Surinam, witnessed such a parade. "The whole party was," he says, ". . . . a resurrection of skin and bones . . . risen from the grave or escaped from Surgeon's Hall." The slaves exposed for sale were "walking skeletons covered over with a piece of tanned leather."

But the commonest method of selling a cargo was a combination of the "scramble"—to be described presently—and the vendue or public auction "by inch of candle." First the captain, probably with the West Indian factor at his side, went over the cargo and picked out the slaves who were maimed or diseased. These were carried to a tavern and auctioned off, with a lighted candle beside the auctioneer; bids were received until an inch of candle had burned. The price of these "refuse" slaves sold at auction was usually less than half of that paid for a healthy Negro; sometimes it was as little as five or six dollars a head. "I was informed by a mulatto woman," Falconbridge says, "that she purchased a sick slave at Grenada, upon speculation, for the small sum of one dollar, as the poor wretch was apparently dying of the flux." There were some slaves who could not be sold for even a dollar, and they were often left to die on the wharfs without food or water.

There were horse traders' methods of hiding the presence of disease. Yaws, for example, could be concealed by a mixture of iron rust and gunpowder, a practice which Edward Long, the Jamaica historian, denounces as a "wicked fraud." Falconbridge tells of a Liverpool captain who "boasted of his having cheated some Jews by the following stratagem: A lot of slaves, afflicted with the flux, being about to be landed for sale, he directed the surgeon to stop the anus of each of them with oakum. . . . The Jews, when they examine them, oblige them to stand up, in order to see if there be any discharge; and when they do not perceive this appearance, they consider it as a symptom of recovery. In the present instance, such an appearance being prevented, the bargain was struck, and they were accordingly sold. But it was not long before a discovery ensued. The excruciating pain which the prevention of a discharge of such an acrimonious nature occasioned, not being to be borne by the poor wretches, the temporary obstruction was removed, and the deluded purchasers were speedily convinced of the imposition."

The healthy slaves remaining after an auction were sold by "scramble," that is, at standard prices for each man, each woman, each boy, and each girl in the cargo. The prices were agreed upon with the purchasers, who then scrambled for their pick of the slaves. During his four voyages Falconbridge was present at a number of scrambles. "In the *Emilia,*" he says, "at Jamaica, the ship was darkened with sails, and covered round. The men slaves were placed on the main deck, and the women on the quarter deck. The purchasers on shore were informed a gun would be fired when they were ready to open the sale. A great number of people came on board with tallies or cards in their hands, with their own names upon them, and rushed through the barricado door with the ferocity of brutes. Some had three or four handkerchiefs tied together, to encircle as many as they thought fit for their purpose." For the slaves, many of whom thought they were about to be eaten, it was the terrifying climax of a terrifying voyage. Another of Falconbridge's ships, the *Alexander,* sold its cargo by scramble in a slave yard at Grenada. The women, he says, were frightened out of their wits. Several of them climbed over the fence and ran about Saint George's town as if they were mad. In his second voyage, while lying in Kingston harbor, he saw a sale by scramble on board the *Tyral,* Captain Macdonald. Forty or fifty of the slaves jumped overboard—"all of which, however," Falconbridge told the House of Commons, "he believes were taken up again."

part III

Colonial Slavery

3

Negro Slavery in the North and Negro Labor

Arthur Zilversmit

From: *The First Emancipation* (Chicago: University of Chicago Press, 1967), pp. 7–24, 33–40. Footnotes deleted. Reprinted by permission.

Although slavery was mainly a southern institution, Northerners had connections to the slave trade, and all the mainland colonies had some slaves. Most northern slaves were in the middle colonies: on the eve of the Revolution, New Jersey had about 11,000 slaves, and throughout the colonial period slaves in New York amounted to about 14 percent of the population. Arthur Zilversmit discusses the condition of the slaves in the North, the types of labor they performed, and the growth of the slave codes. Although slaves were found in nearly all occupations in the northern colonies, slavery was not so vital to the northern economy as it was to the southern plantation system; consequently, northern slavery was not so well entrenched as in the South.

The American Revolution brought a new climate of opinion regarding slavery. The mid-eighteenth-century ideological and religious critics of slavery were greatly strengthened by the Revolution. In the North the foes of slavery formed antislavery societies and agitated for the end of the slave trade and the abolition of slavery. Some slaves won their freedom in the courts and others obtained freedom for service in the Revolutionary cause. Some masters simply

41

freed their slaves. Finally, the northern states passed laws providing for the gradual abolition of slavery.

In the South abolition was defeated. The southern states did pass laws making manumission easier and improving the slave codes, but the institution itself was not fundamentally changed. By the early decades of the nineteenth century antislavery sentiment died in the South, and laws and attitudes hardened toward black Americans. The rise of the Cotton Kingdom in the Southwest, the slave insurrection in Haiti, and fear of rebellion and racial conflict all served to end antislavery agitation and make the peculiar institution the cornerstone of southern society.

TREATMENT OF NEGROES

Although most northern slaves probably escaped the barbarous treatment endured by the Negroes who worked the West Indian plantations, their lives were undeniably harsh. Life as a slave often began with kidnapping in Africa and with the terror of the crowded hold of a slave ship. The newly imported slave found himself in an inhospitable climate, without friends and unable to understand what the white man wanted. As runaway slave advertisements testify, many of them escaped their new masters before they had learned to speak English. Other slaves were brought to the North after they had been enslaved elsewhere, either in the island colonies or on the southern plantations. These Negroes were again parted from friends and family.

In the early years of the eighteenth century, many masters thought of their slaves as little better than beasts of burden. According to an early antislavery writer, New Jersey masters dressed their slaves in rags and forced them to go barefoot in the cold of winter. They showed their contempt for their Negroes by naming them Toby, Mando, Mingo—names ordinarily reserved for dogs and horses.

Since they regarded Negroes as subhuman, many masters strenuously resisted the attempts of the Society for the Propagation of the Gospel in Foreign Parts (SPG) to convert the slaves. Elias Neau, who served as catechist to the Negroes of New York, complained in 1708 that despite the passage of a law that denied that Negroes became free when they were baptized, some masters still refused to send their slaves to school to be prepared for baptism. Those Negroes who asked for permission to attend his school were "either threatened to be sold to Virginia or else to be sent into the

Country." A Rye, New York, clergyman reported that some of his parishioners were "so profane as to say that they do not think that baptism will be of any service" to the Negroes and some Long Island masters maintained that "a Negro hath no soul." Elias Neau was one of the few white men who would "condescend familiarly to discourse with the poor slaves," who, since they were "put to the vilest drudgeries," were "esteemed the scum and offscourings of men." Neau himself was despised because of his work with the slaves. He could often be observed "creeping into Garrets, Cellars and other nauseous places, to exhort and pray by the poor slaves when they are sick." The Reverend John Sharpe reported in 1713 that New York masters paid little attention to their slaves' religion and that most of the Negroes were married outside of the church and were buried by other slaves with "Heathenish rites . . . performed at the grave."

Delaware and Pennsylvania masters were also reluctant to have their slaves instructed and baptized. The Reverend George Ross confirmed reports of the neglect of Negro education, which he attributed "to the conduct of those slaves who after their initiation grew turbulent and boisterous aiming at a freedom which though no part of their Christian privilege, it appeared they had most at heart." This made the whites suspicious of the sincerity of the Negroes "who had no other benefit in view . . . but an exemption from a yoke, which is not in the least inconsistent with true Christian liberty." As late as 1755, residents of Dover, Pennsylvania, threatened to tie and whip their slaves if they went to church or answered to their Christian names.

The British were disturbed by the refusal of the colonists to allow their slaves to be baptized and repeatedly urged colonial governors to secure laws to facilitate the conversion of Negroes and Indians. The governor of New York reported in 1699 that such a bill "would not go downe with the Assembly"; they have a notion, he explained, "that the Negroes being converted . . . would emancipate them . . . [and] they have no other servants in this country but Negroes." It was not until 1706 that the New York Assembly complied with the crown's wishes and passed a law denying the "Groundless opinion" that baptism emancipated Negroes. New Jersey provided for slave baptism in 1704, but the law also permitted the branding of any Negro convicted of theft and the castration of a slave who by force or "perswasion" had sexual intercourse with a white woman. The crown disallowed the law since it provided punishments that were "never . . . allowed by or known" in the laws of England. The slave baptism sections of the law were never reenacted, and New York remained the only northern colony to comply with this royal request.

Even when the law encouraged slave baptism, however, bringing religion to the slaves could lead to practical problems. As a Westchester County, New York, minister ruefully noted, Negroes would not or could not "live up to the Christian covenant in one notorious instance at least, viz., matrimony." They married according to heathen rites and were casual in breaking marital ties. But if the church tried to provide religious marriages for slaves, then the masters would "object and say it is not lawful to part man and wife, and how can we sell one of them?" Another minister agreed that slave marriages would lead to "difficulties and inconveniences"; whether the husband and wife were in the same or different families. If they were both held by the same master, then he was obliged "either to keep or sell both, let his necessities be ever so pressing." If the slaves had different masters, as was "most usual," then when one master left the neighborhood, the families were separated (as happened in the case of the minister's own Negro woman) and it was "almost impossible, to keep them faithful" under these circumstances.

The slave family, then, was a precarious institution subject to the needs and wishes of the master. Contemporary advertisements show that in some instances masters sold husbands, wives, and children separately, and groups of slaves were frequently offered for sale with no mention of family ties. Some masters were explicit. In 1732 a New England master offered to sell his nineteen-year-old Negro woman and her six-month-old child either "together or apart." A New Jersey master showed more consideration. He proposed to sell a Negro man, woman, and child: "They being man and wife would make it most agreeable to sell them together; however, a few miles separation will not prevent the sale." The anomalous position of the family in a slave society was painfully apparent in an advertisement of a New Jersey master who offered a reward for the return of his nine-year-old Negro girl who "Was Stolen by Her Mother."

The enforced separation of Negro families was often tragic. On a visit to Perth Amboy, New Jersey, in 1797 William Dunlap observed a slave woman whose master had separated her from her beloved child: "the Mother by her cries has made the town re-echo & has continued her exclamations for 2 hours incessantly & still continues them. I am sick, at oppression." The separation of slave families was not always the result of callous indifference. A New

Jersey man sent his son the "boy" he had requested although he was

> Sorry . . . to part with Him, but so much more so that you are necessitated to Sel him. I presume you know not what other Shift to make or you wo[ul]d not do it . . . the boy is much afected at leaving the House and being Sold out of the famely; indeed all the famely Seem more affected than usual on Such ocasions.

Some masters, when forced to sell their Negroes, did concern themselves with the happiness of their slaves. A New Jersey inn-keeper who wanted to sell seven Negroes made it clear that "The man and wife and three children must not be parted, nor the mother and son; as they have lived long in one family together, it would be most agreeable if they could be fixed near each other."

Although individual masters tried to preserve family ties, the slave family was unprotected by law, weakened by insecurity, and easily destroyed. The weakness of the family encouraged casual sexual relationships rather than permanent bonds. Masters did not necessarily disapprove of their slaves' attitude toward sex; Samuel Sewall accused masters of conniving at the fornication of their slaves to save themselves the expense of finding wives for them. Slave-owners might even encourage promiscuity. A traveler in New England in 1639 heard a Negro woman weeping outside his house and discovered that her master wanted to breed Negroes but that she refused to go to bed with a young Negro man; when her master ordered her to do so, she kicked her partner out of bed. "This she took in high disdain beyond her slavery, and this was the cause of her grief." A great deal of miscegenation occurred under slavery. A New Jersey master was said to have had children by each of three Negro women he owned. "Whenever he could dispose of these his own offspring, he sold them, in the same manner as he would have disposed of his hogs."

The crown was not only concerned with slave baptism but was disturbed by tales of mistreatment, and it repeatedly urged royal governors to obtain laws to restrain masters from "Inhuman Severitys" and to provide the death penalty for the willful murder of a slave as well as "a fit penalty . . . for the maiming of them." The colonists, however, devoted their attention to working out a system for the control of their slaves—the black codes. All the colonies were anxious to pass laws to restrain slaves from running away. A Massachusetts law of 1680 forbade shipowners taking on board any Negro without the governor's consent. The Connecticut

Assembly found in 1690 that "many persons of this Colony doe for their necessary use purchase negroe servants" who often "run away to the great wronge, damage and disapoyntment of their masters." To prevent this, any Negro found outside of the town limits was to be apprehended and returned to his owner. A Rhode Island law of 1703 prohibited Negroes and Indians (slave or free) from being on the streets at night. Violators were to be punished by whipping "not exceeding fifteen stripes upon their naked backs, except their incorrigible behaviour require more."

The New York Assembly observed in 1702 that the number of slaves in the colony was steadily increasing and that these slaves were often "guilty of Confederating together in running away, or other ill-practices." Therefore, it prohibited unauthorized meetings of more than three slaves, the offending Negroes to be punished by up to forty lashes on the bare back. In 1705, during a war with France, New York enacted a more drastic fugitive slave law. Designed to prevent intelligence from reaching the enemy and to discourage slaves from taking advantage of the war to seek refuge in Canada, the law called for the execution of any slave found more than forty miles north of Albany. Various East Jersey statutes were designed to prevent freemen from concealing fugitive slaves, and New Jersey's comprehensive slave code of 1714 required anyone finding a slave more than five miles from home without a pass to whip the offender.

In a move to protect the community from petty thievery, most colonies enacted laws to prevent freemen from trading with slaves. An East Jersey law of 1683 took note of the fact "that Negro and Indian Slaves, . . . under pretence of Trade, . . . do frequently Steal from their Masters and others." Since it was "a known Truth, that without a receiver, the Theif would soon desert his practice," the law prohibited freemen from selling liquor or other goods to slaves, and slaves who attempted to sell goods were whipped. Thirteen years later, East Jersey set up special courts to try slaves for theft. Convicted slaves were to suffer corporal punishment "not exceeding forty stripes." A Pennsylvania law of 1706 provided that slaves who stole less than five pounds were to be whipped, but those who were convicted by special courts of greater thefts should be whipped, branded, and banished from the colony (which usually meant being sold to the plantation colonies). A Connecticut law of 1708 punished slaves who stole with up to thirty lashes; and a Rhode Island law of 1718 set up special courts for the trial of Negroes accused of purloining. This was the only instance in which New England law established special trial procedures for Negroes.

New York and New Jersey had the most severe black codes of the northern colonies. New York provided a firm legal basis for slavery by making slaves of all children born of slave mothers (no other northern colony gave slavery this specific legal sanction). The New York law of 1702 specifically permitted masters "to punish their slaves for their Crimes and offences att Discretion, not extending to life or Member." The law further provided that a slave found guilty of striking a Christian freeman was to be jailed up to fourteen days and to suffer corporal punishment not extending to life and limb. Since slaves were property and could not "without great loss . . . be subjected in all Cases criminal, to the strict Rules of the Laws of England," special procedures were set up for the punishment of petty theft—the master was to make restitution and the slave to suffer corporal punishment. Slave testimony was only allowed to be used in cases of slave conspiracies. Following an "Execrable and Barberous" crime committed by an Indian and a Negro slave, who murdered their master, mistress, and five children, the assembly extended special trial procedures to capital crimes. Clearly designed to terrorize the slaves, the new law provided that a slave convicted of murder or of conspiracy to murder a free person was to "Suffer the paines of Death in such manner and with such Circumstances as the aggravation and Enormity of their Crime . . . shall merritt." What the assembly meant by "the paines of Death" was clear: the Negro woman implicated in the crimes that provoked the act was burned to death and the Indian slave was hung, after being "put to all the torment possible for a terror to others."

The horror of a slave revolt soon convinced New Yorkers that the laws were still inadequate to control their barbarous slaves. In the spring of 1712 a group of slaves who conspired to revenge themselves by murdering their masters succeeded in killing nine people, wounding five or six more, and thoroughly alarming the residents of New York City. When they were caught, six slaves immediately committed suicide (a wise move, in view of what followed) and twenty-one were executed: "some were burnt others hanged, one broke on the wheele, and one hung live in chains." As the governor observed, "there has been the most exemplary punishment inflicted that could possibly be thought of." Many slaveowners immediately blamed Elias Neau's catechism school for encouraging the Negroes to revolt and seek their freedom, but it was soon established that only two of the accused slaves had ever attended the school. One of them, who had been baptized, "dyed protesting his innocence and was (but too late for him) pityed and declared guiltless even by the prosecutors." Another Negro, who had wanted to be baptized but was refused this by his master, was hung alive in chains. The Reverend John Sharpe went to visit him five days after his punishment began.

> He declared to me he was innocent of . . . [his master's] murder with a seeming concern for his master's misfortune. He was often delirious by long continuance in that posture, thro hunger, thirst and pain but he then answered directly to what I enquired and called me by my name so that I might conclude he had some intervals of the exercise of his reason.

New York reacted to the Negro plot with a new, even more severe, law that added a whole list of crimes to those to be tried in special slave courts. If convicted, the slave was to suffer the death penalty, administered in a manner consistent with the enormity of the crime. A master could choose to have his slave tried by a regular jury (the choice was the master's and not the slave's and was merely a recognition of the master's property rights). The law severely limited the rights of free Negroes under the assumption that free Negroes could aid rebellious slaves. Severe as it was, this act was "much mitigated in its severities by the Council's amendments." Governor Robert Hunter realized that the Lords of Trade might consider the act too harsh but, he explained, "after the late barbarous attempt of some of their slaves nothing less would please the people."

New Jersey's slave code, enacted in 1714, was also a product of the fear engendered by the New York Negro plot. The section dealing with murder and related crimes was almost identical with the provisions of the New York law, and it established special courts for the trial of slaves. To discourage masters from helping their slaves avoid punishment (to save themselves the loss involved in the destruction of their property), masters were to be compensated for executed Negroes.

In 1700 Pennsylvania established special courts to try Negroes for high crimes, but since the statute creating these courts allowed the castration of Negroes convicted of the attempted rape of white women, it met the same fate as the New Jersey law of 1704—the crown was unwilling to countenance such cruelty. Six years later, the assembly enacted a slightly altered version of the same law, changing the punishment for attempted rape to whipping, branding, and deportation. Since the execution of a slave was "so great a hardship," masters might send Negroes accused of a capital crime out of the colony "to escape justice, to the ill example of others."

Pennsylvania therefore followed the example of New York and New Jersey, compensating masters of executed Negroes. Pennsylvania's slave code, like those of the other middle colonies, prohibited Negroes from meeting in groups or carrying arms.

Special slave courts established in New York and Pennsylvania lasted until after the Revolution. In New Jersey, however, slave trials were held in the regular courts of the colony after 1768, when the trial procedures established in the 1714 code were found to be "inconvenient."

After the slave conspiracy of 1712, New Yorkers were increasingly alarmed by the dangers of a growing free Negro population. Most colonists thought the combination of the words "free" and "Negro" was anomalous and that by their mere presence, freed Negroes would incite slaves to seek liberty. The slave code of 1712 severely penalized free Negroes who concealed fugitive slaves: they could be fined ten pounds for every night they hid a fugitive—a penalty that probably meant reenslavement, since few freed Negroes had much money. In addition, the act barred any Negro freed thereafter from owning any lands or houses. Furthermore, the New York Assembly claimed that "the free Negroes of this Colony are an Idle slothfull people and prove very often a charge on the place they are." Therefore, masters who wished to emancipate their slaves would have to post two bonds of at least £200 each to guarantee that they would pay their ex-slaves twenty pounds per year for the rest of their lives. Across the Hudson, New Jerseyites came to similar conclusions about free Negroes, and the 1714 slave code contained the same language and provisions on manumission as the New York law, prohibiting free Negro landholding and requiring masters to pay twenty pounds per year to every Negro they freed.

These laws made manumission virtually impossible. It would be difficult to imagine that even the most charitable slaveowner could afford to place such a heavy burden on his estate for an indeterminate period. The shortsightedness of the policy soon became obvious. Governor Robert Hunter of New York, after hearing of a case in which a Negro, freed by his master's will, had been forced to remain in bondage because the executors refused to post the required bond, recommended changes in the law. The limitations on manumissions, he charged, cut off "all hopes from those slave[s] who by a faithful and dilligent discharge of their duty, may at last look for the reward of a manumission by their masters will." This would not only tend to make slaves careless of their master's interests but would "excite 'em to insurrections more bloody than any they have yet attempted, seeing that . . . death is made more eligible than life, for the longer they live, the longer they are slaves." The assembly was forced to agree that the regulations governing manumissions had proved to be "very Inconvenient, prejudicial" and would "very much Discourage and Dishearten" the slaves from serving their masters truly and faithfully. Accordingly, in 1717 the legislators eliminated the requirement for annual payments to freedmen, although benevolent masters would still have to post bonds to reimburse the community in case the emancipated Negroes became incapable of supporting themselves and had to rely on public charity. And to correct an obvious injustice, the new law allowed another person to post the required bonds if the executors of an estate refused to do so. New Jersey's restrictions on manumission remained unchanged until 1769, when the legislature eliminated the requirement for annual payments and adopted a procedure similar to New York's.

As early as 1702 Connecticut passed a law regulating manumissions, but its object was merely to prevent masters from escaping the responsibility for maintaining old or sick slaves by freeing them "after they have spent the principall part of their time and strength in their masters service." The law held masters responsible for the support of their slaves even after their manumission. Massachusetts enacted a similar statute a year later but made manumissions more difficult by requiring masters to post a £50 bond to secure the community in case their former slaves became public charges. Rhode Island required a £100 bond. Pennsylvania's manumission law, similar in language to those of New York and New Jersey, declared that "free Negroes are an idle and slothful people . . . [who] often prove burdensome to the neighborhood and afford ill examples to other Negroes." In effect, however, the law was more liberal and closer in spirit to those of the New England colonies. Masters who wished to manumit their Negroes were required to post only a £30 bond, but any Negro freed before he was twenty-one could be bound out to service (making him, in effect, an indentured servant or apprentice). Even the mildest regulations discouraged manumissions, however. A Connecticut master could manumit his slaves without posting any bonds or paying an annual sum; still, he knew that he and his heirs could be held responsible for an indeterminate sum to provide for a Negro who might suffer an incapacitating illness or accident.

New York and New Jersey were the only northern colonies to bar Negroes from owning property. A New London Town Meeting asked the Connecticut Assembly for such a law, and although the lower house complied, it was never enacted into law. When New York revised its slave code in 1730, it eliminated the ban on free Negro landowning, but this ban remained in effect in New Jersey until after independence. Pennsylvania's slave code imposed other restrictions on free Negroes. They could be sold into slavery if they lived in marriage with whites. Freedmen trading with other Negroes without a license or concealing fugitive slaves were to be fined and if unable to pay the fine were to be reenslaved.

In colonial New England Negroes occupied a unique legal position. The Puritans' aim of establishing a bible commonwealth led them to grant Negro slaves rights based on the Mosaic laws of bondage, which regarded slavery as a mark of personal misfortune and not as evidence of inherent inferiority. Consequently, New England slaves enjoyed rights that were regarded as incompatible with slavery in other colonies. Slaves could own property and serve as witnesses even against white men. The wife of a slave could not be compelled to testify against her husband. Slaves could sue in the regular courts. The right to institute civil suits proved to be an entering wedge for abolition—Negroes could sue their masters for their freedom if there was any doubt about the validity of the master's title. Furthermore, slaves had the same procedural rights in courts as freemen; they were indicted by grand juries and tried by ordinary juries, they were allowed to appeal the decisions of lower courts, and they could challenge jurors in the same manner as free defendants.

The harsh slave codes of the middle colonies were the product of fear—a fear that was often reinforced by the discovery of Negro plots or rumors of Negro risings. In 1741 New Yorkers fled the city in the wake of rumors of another slave revolt. Carts to transport goods out of the city were at a premium and hysteria gripped the community. Several fires, mysterious in origin, had led to the plot rumors, and investigators, by forcing Negroes to "confess" and implicate others to save themselves, established a long but tenuous chain of evidence. Two Negroes, whose masters testified that they had both been home at the time of the fires, were nonetheless sentenced to be burned to death. A last minute reprieve failed to save them for, at the insistence of the crowd, they were burned anyway. A total of eleven Negroes were burned at the stake, eighteen were hung, and fifty deported to the West Indies. There is no evidence that there was any slave plot nor, for that matter, any connection between the fires and the hapless Negroes. Despite the fury with which the slaves were punished, at least one contemporary realized that he was witnessing an outbreak of mass hysteria. A New Englander compared events in New York to the Salem witchcraft trials. He predicted that "Negro & Spectre evidence will turn out alike," maintaining that the Salem tragedy had proved that extorted confessions were worthless, and he begged New Yorkers "not to go on to Massacre & destroy your own Estates by making Bonfires of the Negros."

Although many rumored slave risings proved to be as groundless as those that precipitated the 1741 panic, white men had to investigate any suspicious movements among the slaves to avoid a repetition of the 1712 disaster. An alert white man was able to prevent a revolt of Somerset County, New Jersey, Negroes who supposedly planned to murder slaveowners, ravish their women, and burn their property. The plan was uncovered before any damage was done when a drunken plotter challenged a white man, telling him that "English-men were generally a pack of Villains, and kept the Negroes as Slaves, contrary to a positive Order from King George." When the white man called the Negro a rascal, the slave pointedly asserted that he was "as good a Man as himself, and that in a little Time he should be convinced of it." This threat, veiled as it was, led to a thorough examination. One slave escaped, one was hung, and one had his ears cut off. Numerous other Negroes were soundly whipped. One commentator wryly noted that the reason the slaveowners had executed only one slave was probably because "they could not well spare any more." There were other plots and many more ominous rumors, leaving slaveowners with the uneasy feeling that they might wake up one night with knives at their throats. During war time, many suspected that the slaves would rise and join the enemy, and a great rash of slave-plot rumors broke out in the first few years of the Revolution. Some men feared that their departure for military service would leave their wives and children at the mercy of the slaves. Even when there was no danger of a slave rebellion, individual Negroes could revenge themselves on their masters by burning their property or poisoning the master and his family. Slave plots, both real and imagined, as well as individual acts of vengeance, contributed to the widespread fear of the Negro population and resulted in the severe laws enacted for their control.

The courts, which administered these laws, decreed harsh punishments. Before the penal reforms of the late eighteenth century, courts often inflicted cruel punishments, but slaves probably suffered more severe penalties than white men. A New York City court ordered a slave who had escaped from prison and stolen a boat to be tied to a cart and given ten lashes at every corner as he was dragged around the city. He was also branded on the forehead with the letter *R*, so that he could more easily be identified if he were to run away again. A New Jersey Negro sentenced to death in 1694 first had his right hand cut off and then was hung; later his body was burned. In the wake of the New York "Negro plot" of 1741, two New Jersey Negroes, convicted of barn-burning, were burned alive, and in 1750 two New Jersey Negroes, convicted of murder, were burned alive in front of all the other Negroes in the area. A Negro who had been forced to witness a similar execution near Poughkeepsie, New York, shortly before the Revolution, remembered it to the end of his days. A young slave had fired his master's barn, confessed, and was condemned to be burned to death: "He was fastened to the stake, and when the pile was fired, the dense crowd excluded the air, so that the flames kindled but slowly, and the dreadful screams of the victim were heard at a distance of three miles." It was a horrible sight and his master "who had been fond of him, wept aloud." He asked the sheriff to put the Negro out of his misery. The sheriff complied by drawing his sword, "but the master, still crying like a child, exclaimed 'Oh, don't run him through!' " The sheriff then parted the crowd, the flames shot up and he commanded the Negro to "swallow the blaze," which finally put him out of his misery.

Northern masters did not usually punish their slaves as severely as slaveowners in the plantation colonies. Cadwallader Colden was forced to send a sullen and abusive Negro woman to the West Indies because "the Custome of the Country . . . will not allow us to use our Negroes as you doe in Barbados." He was convinced that the woman would "make as good a slave as any in the Island after a little of your Discipline." In their master's advertisements northern runaways were rarely identified by whip marks, but chronic runaways were sometimes punished by having to wear a heavy iron collar around their necks. As late as 1806 a visitor to Pennsylvania saw a twelve-year-old Negro boy wearing such a device, with an iron bow attached to each side of the iron collar, crossing the boy's head. A New Jersey runaway had "an iron Collar with two Hooks" around his neck and a pair of hand cuffs with a six-foot chain. Another New Jersey slave had been forced to wear an iron collar because he had plotted with another Negro "to rob his master and attempt for New-York." Runaway Joe was in very bad shape. He had "one leg a little shorter than the other, part of one of his great toes cut off, lost some foreteeth, and his back is much scarrified and in lumps by whipping."

Horrible as the punishments meted out to Negroes convicted

of crimes may have been, they were exceeded by instances of cruelty committed by sadistic masters. In 1804 Carl A. Hoffmann of New York was convicted of seriously mistreating his slave. His twelve-year-old Negro had committed some fault; to punish him, Hoffmann tied his hands and legs, forced him to eat two teaspoonfuls of salt, and then hung him from the ceiling in a closed room where he was suspended for two days without food or water. After the boy was taken down, Hoffmann administered 139 lashes. He was not through. He finished off by rubbing salt and brandy into the boy's cut back.

Another sadistic master was Amos Broad. He kicked a Negro child when it did not walk well. He stripped his female slave, whipped her, threw her into the snow, and then threw water on her. He forced her to take an unneeded purgative. His wife participated in horsewhipping the slave, and when his "wench" brought in a teapot with too much water in it, he poured some of the scalding liquid on her hands. The case was brought to trial by the New York Manumission Society, which persuaded Broad to free his slaves. In addition, Broad and his wife were fined $1250. At an earlier time, similar instances of unrefined cruelty may have taken place, but then there was no one to come to the defense of the abused slaves.

The conduct of these perverted masters was certainly exceptional and aroused widespread horror and indignation. Yet by allowing one man virtually unlimited control over another, the slave laws of the middle colonies provided ample opportunities for aberrant behavior and unrestrained cruelty.

The harsh slave codes of the middle colonies, devised at the beginning of the eighteenth century, were designed to control an alien population, regarded as heathen in origin and barbarous by nature. The laws denied the slave equal protection by refusing to accept his testimony against whites, by providing special courts, and by inflicting different punishments. In the case of slaves, the laws assumed guilt, not innocence—any Negro found away from home without a pass was presumed to be a runaway, any slave engaged in trade was presumed to be a thief, and any slave having sexual intercourse with a white woman was presumed to be a rapist. The laws discouraged manumissions and severely limited the rights of free Negroes. Especially in New York and New Jersey, the object of the slave codes was to keep the Negroes terrified and to prevent them from inflicting their revenge upon the whites. Although the colonists' views of the Negro underwent a gradual transformation and the Negroes became more assimilated into the European-American culture, the laws took little notice of this change until after the nation's independence was established. . . .

NEGRO LABOR

Although Negro slavery as defined in the colonial black codes was a system of race relations, it was first and foremost an economic system. Negroes were first imported and later commanded high prices because they were needed as a labor force in a land that for white men meant opportunity, a chance for economic independence. As Cadwallader Colden told a Londen merchant, despite "the great numbers which every year come into the Country," great difficulties resulted from a chronic labor shortage. Freemen emigrated because they wanted their own land; they were not content to remain as laborers. In 1647 the Dutch West India Company was advised to send slaves to America because the new colony could be more extensively cultivated by slave labor. White agricultural laborers, "conveyed thither at great expense," sooner or later became tradesmen and neglected agriculture. Slaves, on the other hand, "being brought and maintained ... at a cheap rate," could raise abundant produce. By the end of the seventeenth century the labor market in New York had not improved. The Earl of Bellomont noted that there were not over a hundred laboring men to be had in the colony for the high wage of three shillings per day and that most of the work was done by Negroes. White men preferred earning more money in trade or keeping sloops.

New England also suffered from a labor shortage. Emanuel Downing told Governor John Winthrop that he could not see "how wee can thrive vntill wee gett into a stock of slaves suffitient to doe all our buisines." White servants did not want to work for other men and would do so only for "verie great wages." Slaves, on the other hand, would also be cheaper since "wee maynteyne 20 Moores cheaper than one Englishe servant." Philadelphia merchants repeatedly opposed attempts to levy a high duty on imported Negroes on the grounds that this would aggravate the shortage of labor. And at times slaves were also in short supply. A Philadelphian told Cadwallader Colden in 1725 that despite continued efforts she had been unable to procure "a Negroe man that would Suit thy business." Henry Lloyd, prosperous lord of the manor of Lloyd's Neck, had the same problem in 1746, although he had "taken a great deal of pains to buy a good Slave."

Some historians have questioned the value of slave labor within the diversified northern economy. Taking the southern plantations as the norm, these writers assume that Negro labor could only be employed advantageously on large tracts, worked by the gang system. They believe that because Negroes were ignorant, unskilled, and irresponsible, they could work only at simple tasks under close supervision. Although it is true that Negroes had to be more highly skilled and better trained to work in the diversified economy of the North, it is also true that northern Negroes received this training and became skilled in virtually all aspects of northern agriculture, manufacturing, and crafts.

The colonial economy was predominantly agricultural, and most slaves in the North as well as in the South were farm laborers. Many Negroes advertised for sale were "fit for country business"— farming and related skills. A New Jersey farmer offered to rent his 470-acre property with "three very good Negroes, who understand all the Branches of Farming." Other farms were leased "with Negroes and Stock." Although most New England farmers who relied on slave labor employed only one or two Negroes on their small plots, the Narragansett planters of Rhode Island, some of whose farms extended over 1000 acres, used slave labor extensively in the cultivation of food and forage crops and in raising the pacing horses for which the area was famous. Robert Hazard of South Kingstown converted part of his 12,000 acres into a dairy farm and employed twenty-four Negro women in the creamery alone.

Slaves were trained to do many of the tasks essential to maintaining the near self-sufficiency of large colonial farms. The owner of a 2000-acre plantation in Morris County, New Jersey, leased his property with twenty Negroes "bred to farming and Country Work." This group included "a good Blacksmith, a Mason, and a Shoemaker." Another New Jersey farm was advertised for sale with "sundry valuable men, women, and children slaves, one of them an excellent miller, and another a cooper." The rest were "house and farm slaves." On a third New Jersey plantation the slaves could perform a variety of tasks. One Negro was a miller, a carter, and a farmer.

A younger woman was "an excellent house-servant, and besides washing and ironing," she could "spin wool and flax, knit," and manage the dairy, making butter and cheese. In some instances, the slaves were capable of running the entire farm by themselves; a group of New Jersey slaves were "brought up from their Infancy to the farming Business" and had "managed the Farm for some Years, without an Overseer." On a large farm north of Albany, New York, Negroes served as cooks, domestics, woodcutters, threshers, seamstresses, and laundresses. Besides the slaves engaged in household work and in "cultivating to the highest advantage a most extensive farm," there was a slave who was "a thoroughbred carpenter and shoemaker." Another slave was "an universal genius who made canoes, nets, and paddles; shod horses," and mended farm tools. He also "managed the fishing . . . reared hemp and tobacco, and spun both; made cider, and tended wild horses . . . which it was his province to manage and break." On this well-run estate, there were slaves trained "For every branch of domestic economy."

Wheat was an important crop in the middle colonies, and slaves not only helped to raise the grain but also processed it into flour. In 1745 a New Jersey man offered to sell his 300-acre plantation with "Things necessary for carrying on grinding, bolting and baking," including three Negroes, "one of them a good Miller" and two who could do the baking, bolting, and "Country Work."

As the colonial economy became more diversified Negro labor early assumed an important role in the beginning of American manufacturing enterprises. Many iron forges in New Jersey and Pennsylvania relied heavily on the labor of Negro slaves. When the owners of Andover Furnace in Sussex County, New Jersey, offered to lease the works, they included six slaves "who are good Forgemen, and understand the making and drawing of Iron well." Charles Read, another New Jersey ironmaster, had two slaves for sale—one "a good finer, and the other a good hammer-man." Negroes were capable of filling responsible positions in the industry, and one manufacturer sought to buy or hire a Negro who "fully understands managing a Bloomery." Slaves were also used to extract the ore; a New York newspaper carried notice of the sale of two Negro men who "understands Mining."

Other manufacturing enterprises found Negro slaves equally useful. "A Very convenient and commodious Tan-Yard" in Gloucester, New Jersey, used three Negro men "who understand the Business well." A Bostonian's slave had been "brought up in a ship Carpenters Yard as a Sawyer & boarers of holes" and had also been "employ'd at the Smith's business." Another Boston Negro was "for many years used to the distilling business," and a Pennsylvania slave could produce a less potent beverage—he was skilled at "brewing and bottling spruce-beer." Colonial entrepreneurs could buy a business complete with a skilled labor force to run it. A tobacco-pipe manufacturer of Flushing, New York, offered to sell twenty acres of clay land, suitable for pipe making, "with two Negro slaves . . . and other conveniencies to carry on that business."

Negro slaves also entered the ranks of colonial craftsmen. New York Negroes worked as carpenters, cabinetmakers, plasterers, locksmiths, and butchers. Some slaves were very highly skilled; a baker and a cooper were described as "Masters of their Trades." A

Negro was even employed in the prestigious "goldsmith's business." Some valuable pieces of colonial furniture may have been produced by slave artisans; a Pennsylvanian employed two Negroes in the "Joiner's and Windsor Chair businesses." Runaway slaves advertised in the Pennsylvania press included a brick layer and plasterer, a barber, and a slave who could "bleed and draw Teeth, Pretending to be a great Doctor." A "good house carpenter and joyner" could be purchased in Boston in 1718. Another Boston Negro was a rope-maker, and a Negro slave served as pressman for the first newspaper published in New Hampshire. New Jersey masters were frequently forced to advertise for runaway craftsmen. Since labor was in short supply an employer did not often question the status of a skilled Negro who offered his services. "A Mulatto Fellow named Jack" was "a good taylor"; his master suspected that he was "probably . . . sulking in some part of the country, working at that trade." Another runaway could "handle a File, and understands the Brass Founder's Business."

In the New England colonies, many vessels were manned in part by Negro slaves. The Massachusetts fishing and whaling fleets included Negro crew members, and runaway slaves were sometimes taken on board by the masters of undermanned ships. A Pennsylvania Negro, "fit for town or country," was used for "the management of Shallops and other small craft." Several New Jersey slaves were employed as ferry boat operators, and a mulatto runaway was "bred to . . . loading and unloading boats." Negro slaves even served at the difficult task of piloting ships through New York harbor.

Negro women performed many chores on the farm and in the home. A New Yorker offered to sell his twenty-year-old slave woman who did "all sorts of House work"; she could "Brew, Bake, Boyle soaft Soap, Wash, Iron & Starch" and she was "a good Darey Woman." She could also "Card and Spin at the Great Wheel." An "excellent cook" was advertised for sale in 1781. She was "honest, industrious, neat, and a very good oeconomist, spins very well, and is fond of children." Her master suggested that she would "particularly suit a genteel tavern or a family that entertains much." Another Negro woman was not only skilled in "country work," but she could also be used as a city servant, "being a good house servant and a good seamstress." Not all women were suitable for farm work; a Pennsylvania master offered to sell a strong and healthy Negro girl because she was not "capable of country work." She was, however, experienced in taking care of children.

Many Negro women were children's maids. In 1721 Cadwallader Colden tried to buy a young thirteen-year-old Negro girl for his wife who wanted her "Cheifly to keep the children & to sow & theirfore would have her Likely & one that appears to be good natured." Shortly before the Revolution, a New York newspaper noted the sale of an unusually talented children's governess. She had been born in the West Indies, spoke French well, and was "very well calculated to wait upon young ladies and children . . . Amongst children, where the French language is desired to be used, she is as proper a Person . . . as can be procured."

Housework was also done by male slaves. One of these, "a likely Black Man," was "of a good size for a house servant, short and stout." He was a good cook and could wash, bake, scrub, and clean furniture. He could also do "all kinds of farming work." His master informed the public that "He is sold for no other fault, but that he does not know when he is well treated, and is dissatisfied with good living." Another Negro man was only "a tolerable cook," but he could "shave and dress a wig very well." He had been employed as a house servant for some time, and was sold for no fault "likely to affect a purchaser who needs not intrust a servant with liquor or the laying out of money." Young boys served as waiters and older men were valets. A New Jersey master advertised two slaves for sale in 1776, "one of them a valuable and compleat farmer in all its branches . . . The other a genteel footman and waiter who understands the care of horses well, the management of a carriage, drives either on the box or as postillion." He was "in every respect suitable for a genteel family, or a single Gentleman, and is fond of farming." "A Likely negro boy" could do housework, shave and dress, and was also "a very good gardener" and could do "farming work." Many household servants participated in home manufacturing—making soap, spinning, and making candles—and even some "gentlemen's servants" were also farmers and gardeners.

Although some of the richest colonists could afford the luxury of a full staff of Negro attendants—butlers, waiters, maids, and footmen—most northern slaveowners employed their Negroes as laborers. Considerable time was needed to train new Negroes for the labor of the area, which required "skill & dexterity as well as strenth," but the Negroes received the requisite training and became valuable servants who could be sold for high prices.

part IV

The Life of a Slave

Driving slaves to market in the South.
Source: New York Historical Society

A slave auction in a southern city.
Source: Library of Congress

RAFFLE

Mr. Joseph Jennings respectfully informs his friends and the public that, at the request of many acquaintances, he has been induced to purchase from Mr. Osborne, of Missouri, the celebrated

DARK BAY HORSE, "STAR,"

Aged five years, square trotter and warranted sound; with a new light Trotting Buggy and Harness; also, the dark, stout

MULATTO GIRL, "SARAH,"

Aged about twenty years, general house servant, valued at *nine hundred dollars*, and guaranteed, and

Will be Raffled for

At 4 o'clock P. M., February first, at the selection hotel of the subscribers. The above is as represented, and those persons who may wish to engage in the usual practice of raffling, will, I assure them, be perfectly satisfied with their destiny in this affair.

The whole is valued at its just worth, fifteen hundred dollars; fifteen hundred

CHANCES AT ONE DOLLAR EACH.

The Raffle will be conducted by gentlemen selected by the interested subscribers present. Five nights will be allowed to complete the Raffle. BOTH OF THE ABOVE DESCRIBED CAN BE SEEN AT MY STORE, No. 78 Common St., second door from Camp, at from 9 o'clock A. M. to 2 P. M.

Highest throw to take the first choice; the lowest throw the remaining prize, and the fortunate winners will pay twenty dollars each for the refreshments furnished on the occasion.

N. B. No chances recognized unless paid for previous to the commencement.

JOSEPH JENNINGS.

As this suggests, slaves, as property, could even be raffled.
Source: New York Historical Society

4

New Orleans
The Mistress of the Trade

Frederic Bancroft

From: *Slave Trading in the Old South* (New York: Frederick Ungar Publishing Co., 1959), pp. 312–328. Footnotes deleted. Reprinted by permission.

Nothing illustrated more dramatically the fact that slaves were property than the notorious slave markets of the Old South. Being chattels, slaves were bought and sold, raffled, gambled, and inherited. As part of the Compromise of 1850, Congress banned the slave trade in the nation's capital, but did not regulate the interstate slave trade, which was a flourishing business in the Old South. The southwestern states were eager for fresh labor, and the natural growth of their slave population fell short of the demand. Hence they bought from the older slave states of the Upper South and the Atlantic Coast. The older states became breeding grounds for the markets of the newer areas, and the funds they obtained from the sale of slaves became an important source of revenue for them. Frederic Bancroft estimated that approximately 700,000 slaves were sold in the interregional trade between 1830 and 1860, and that about the same number were sold within the individual states themselves. Under the circumstances, it was likely that during his lifetime, a given slave would change masters at least once; the frequency of being sold was greater for the urban slave. Many slaves also belonged to one man but were periodically hired out to work for another master.

The need for slave labor and the sanction of the slave trade by southern whites led to the growth of markets described in this selection. Although the New Orleans market was the most striking one, other cities reported similar scenes. To be hustled into a slave pen, separated from one's family and friends, and inspected like an animal during the actual selling were among the most brutal experiences that an American slave could undergo. On the block the slave had no enforceable rights and children were sometimes separated from their mothers. Most slaves were sold for their potential labor, with young, healthy males bringing the highest prices. But, as Bancroft notes, women on occasion were sold as "fancy girls" in the New Orleans market for concubinage.

By far the most busy and picturesque slave-emporium was New Orleans—the modern Delos of the trade for the lower Southwest. It was the most populous and foreign city either south or west of Baltimore, having 116,000 inhabitants in 1850 and 168,000 in 1860. Nowhere else, except next to the Exchange in Charleston and in the market-place in Montgomery, was slave-trading on a large scale so conspicuous. In New Orleans it sought public attention: slave-auctions were regularly held in its two grand hotels besides other public places; and in much frequented streets there were slave-depots, show-rooms, show-windows, broad verandas and even neighborhoods where gayly dressed slaves were prominently exhibited. In New Orleans, markets and buyers were most numerous, money was most plentiful, profits were largest. Slave-trading there had a peculiar dash: it rejoiced in its display and prosperity; it felt unashamed, almost proud.

One could buy there so-called negroes of every shade of color and kind of occupation:—native Africans, black as ebony, some of them imported half a century previously, others recently smuggled in and knowing only a few words of any language of civilization; Creole octoroon young women as light as southern Europeans, with straight hair, beautiful figures, regular features, and so bright and intelligent that outside of the South they might have passed as ladies from some French colony or from Central or South America; calkers, masons, butlers, coopers, coachmen, lady's-maids, nurses either wet or dry, waiters, waitresses, accomplished seamstresses, highly expert engineers; preachers, who would work in the field six days a week and on Sunday expound the Bible as they fancied they understood it; even a slater that had "served his time at the trade"; "a first-rate wheelwright and whitesmith," and "a No. 1 confectioner and candy-maker"; bakers either French or American; "a sugar kettle setter"; "a likely negro boy" that would "be exchanged for dry goods, boots and shoes"; a horse-doctor, a spinner, a tiger-man, an ox-driver; a valet that spoke English, French, Spanish and German and "would suit any gentleman for traveling"; highly skilful gardeners, some long accustomed to beautifying the yards of American planters, others those of Creoles; Maryland cooks who thought that they could not be equaled in the preparation of terrapin or the frying of chicken; better still, Creole cooks, such masters of the French *cuisine* with Louisiana variations as to make every repast a delight; little children from jet black to blond, with or without mothers, for "orphans" were numerous; butchers, carpenters, blacksmiths, plasterers and whitewashers, barbers and hairdressers in great numbers, and now and then a foreman capable of managing a rice, a sugar or a cotton plantation; and even an old mammy from Virginia or South Carolina, demure and purring like a cat with kittens, still boasting of the "quality" of "my ol' massa." Indeed, it would not have been difficult to find there slaves from every Southern State, from Cuba or from even several different parts of Africa. There were always in this market many kidnaped free negroes, stolen slaves, unclaimed runaways, vagrants, drunkards and general good-for-nothings, recently sold for jail-dues—all gathered, one or a few at a time, by speculators, thieves or cheats and brought here where they could best be disposed of and where even the riffraff, infancy and decrepitude had a price. All these and still other varieties, besides, of course, fieldhands, stevedores, washers and ironers by the hundred, were to be found in this gay semi-French metropolis of the Southwest. They were here as if by the law of gravitation as well as by that of trade. Many were here as the result of the death, the spendthrift habits or the misfortunes of masters that lived in or near Louisiana, but many more because interstate traders had purchased them in remote States for this market.

How appropriately might this modern mistress of the trade have emblazoned along her great crescent levee the welcome that Delos gave the slave-trader: "Merchant, come into port, discharge your freight—everything is sold!" New Orleans was the trader's paradise. It promised him success, riches, notoriety, as well as every luxury and indulgence that his coarse nature could appreciate. And all large and many small traders throughout the South were in touch with it.

Until late in the 'forties the aversion to being called a trader was hardly felt in New Orleans. Pitts & Clarke's *Directory for 1842* indicated the occupation of at least 185 men—including the well-known slave-traders B. M. Campbell, Thomas Boudar, Theophilus Freeman and John Hagan—by following each name by the concise term "trader"; and it also designated at least 49 persons as "brokers" and 25 as "auctioneers," most of whom sold slaves. Others may have been overlooked in this search, and, as in other cities, undoubtedly many traders escaped the notice of the enumerators. Thus more than 200, probably not less than 300, residents were engaged in slave-trading, although the volume of this business was presumably not half what it became by the end of the 'fifties. But before this time the word *trader* had come to be shunned, and accordingly it is impossible even approximately to enumerate the traders. A search through the *Directory for 1856*—the latest of the slavery period at hand—finds only 17 names followed by the words "slave-depot," "slaves," "slave trader" or "slave dealer," 16 followed by "trader" and 38 by "auctioneer." Undoubtedly most of these auctioneers sold slaves, and several of them, as we shall see, like some in Richmond and Charleston, disposed of more than any regular trader. Then, too, the brokers, the general agents, the commission merchants and factors welcomed opportunities to participate in some phase of slave-trading. Furthermore, sporting and gambling tendencies in the Crescent City were especially favorable to inconspicuous speculating in slaves by residents. And very numerous were the non-resident traders that came to sell here or to buy for western Louisiana or for Texas. Accordingly it seems safe to believe that the volume of the New Orleans trade, counted in transactions and dollars, was larger than that of Richmond and Charleston combined.

Sometimes ten or more of the advertisements of the largest interstate traders were placed in a row, each having a little black figure or figures representing a man or a woman running and carrying a parcel. They could not escape notice; they also gave brief details of the business and of the source and frequency of the importations. These conclusively show that Virginia slaves were preferred: if a trader specialized in negroes from any State except Louisiana, it was from Virginia; if from two, Virginia was one and South Carolina was likely to be the other. The many slaves brought from Missouri and Kentucky were rarely advertised as such because less desirable.

It was much to prosper and to be generally known in one's county and State; it was vastly more to be known to sellers as far away as the Eastern Shore of Maryland and to buyers in Texas, and to deal with "famous" planters and to fancy oneself their friend. Such, at different times, were Franklin and Armfield, the Woolfolks, Bolton, Dickins & Co., the Forrests and divers others. Such, too, were the Campbells, B. M. and Walter L., whose possession and goodwill of perhaps the best old stand in Baltimore soon enabled them to develop a large business and establish a reputation for paying the highest cash prices. Then small-town buyers were glad to advertise as their agents. Originally they purchased only in Maryland and Virginia, but in 1860 they had "a large supply of all classes of negroes . . . imported from Virginia, Maryland and Georgia," and during the whole season were receiving "large lots of the choicest negroes" to be had in those States. The senior partner made the purchases and the junior partner managed the sales. Some interstate traders, without becoming residents, went to the same city year after year, renting the same quarters or boarding their negroes at some jail or depot until all were disposed of. Others flourished most where they were least known, and after advertising or displaying their stock for a season, departed to return no more. Not so the Campbells. Each was steadily resident and active in his special place. Whenever practicable, they avoided the risks to health from penning up negroes in depressing idleness. They had a physician regularly visit those kept in Baltimore, and he worked some of the "trusties" on his farm, pending shipment to New Orleans. Most of the New Orleans traders believed in quick sales, large profits and leaving the risks to others; and negroes not sold by late spring were commonly disposed of at reduced prices, to avoid the jeopardy of close confinement and illness during the depressing heat of a New Orleans summer. The Campbells made a virtue and a profit out of a very different practice; they established a farm in a healthy and accessible region about eighty miles north of New Orleans, where the slaves that were not sold by June could cheaply and profitably be kept and trained while becoming acclimated. There, too, the little children, the "breeding women" and the ailing of all kinds could be cared for until most salable. During the long and hot season, when the southern metropolis was avoided, persons needing slaves were invited to come to the farm. Thus Walter L. Campbell, as he advised the public in five New Orleans newspapers, had "negroes for sale all the time." Still better, he was able to reopen his yard in October with a supply of more than 100 that were able-bodied, trained, fully acclimated and very valuable.

Of the traders . . . Thomas Foster and C. M. Rutherford belonged to a class that, theoretically at least, preferred the usual two and one-half percent commission for buying or selling for others. They sought slaves of all kinds, and each had a jail and a yard. One of them laconically explained his business thus:

C. M. RUTHERFORD, COMMISSION AGENT FOR THE SALE OF SLAVES, OFFICE AND YARD, No. 68 Baronne street, New Orleans.

Foster was one of the best known of his class. Finally he was not able to resist the temptation to speculate, and selling on commission became a secondary consideration.

C. F. Hatcher illustrated how an enterprising trader could quickly rise, perhaps without speculation or considerable risk. In 1856 he was superintendent of a slave-depot at 195 Gravier street belonging to J. L. Carman & Co., "auctioneers." By 1860 he was advertising throughout the South to inform "merchants, planters, traders and owner of slaves" that he had made extensive alterations in his stand and was prepared to receive from 200 to 300 slaves to sell on commission; that he could furnish slaveowners with good meals and comfortable rooms at reasonable rates, and that he should constantly keep a good stock of all kinds of slaves for sale, including nurses, hairdressers, etc. As was common, he offered liberal advances on all property placed in his hands; but he must be first choice or none: he would not receive slaves that had been in other yards or depots. His pride was his new and "very commodious show-room." He also dealt in real estate, especially land in Texas, Mississippi and Louisiana, and advertised his slave-trading business in leading marts for New Orleans supplies. To his establishment all might come with their slaves, get board and lodging and find buyers —exactly as drovers and ranchmen bring their carloads of steers or sheep to the stockyards and live at the drover-hotels. Not to be out-done by Campbell, he kept his office open summer and winter and also had a farm or large slave-yard in the piny woods, nearer and more accessible than Campbell's. Prospective buyers needed only to call at 195 Gravier street, examine the descriptive list of his stock and then take a short ride on train or boat.

"Orders from commission merchants respectfully solicited," said Thomas Foster's advertisement. That refers to a phase of slave-trading then little noticed by the public and now almost forgotten. The agent that disposed of a planter's crop and bought for him supplies not easily obtained near home was called his commission merchant or factor. The accounts were expected to be settled annually. The sugar planters were within easy reach of New Orleans and usually went there at least once a year for business and pleasure. It was quite different with the cotton planters in northern and west-ern Louisiana, eastern Texas, Arkansas and Mississippi. If they sent their produce and orders to New Orleans, their commission mer-chant or factor also bought or sold slaves for them according to whether they had a surplus or a marked deficit with him. And he dealt with a regular trader, a commission merchant or an auctioneer.

To inspect some of the depots, pens, yards, booths or sales-rooms and to attend a large public sale of slaves was one of the first aims of visitors from afar. In 1856–1860 there were at least 25 such places within a few squares of the St. Charles Hotel, and nearly all were on Gravier (where there were not less than 11 or 12), Baronne (where there were 6 or more), Magazine or Common streets. In the French quarter there were about half as many, mostly on Esplanade street near the corner of Chartres or in the neighborhood of Exchange Place and St. Louis street.

On a Mississippi River steamboat a youth from Ohio met a clerk from New Orleans and accepted his invitation to call at 71 and 73 Baronne street. The Ohioan was surprised to find there a large building bearing the sign,

> ## VIRGINIA SLAVES FOR SALE HERE.

Subsequently the resident showed the visitor through several other principal marts. The first question asked strangers was, "Do you want to buy some niggers?" At one place the keeper rang a little bell such as schoolteachers use. Promptly "from their stables at the rear of the building, the stock came marching [in], in two files, the one of men and boys, the other of women and girls." There were also three or four babes in arms. "The tallest in each line headed the column, then the next in height, and so on down to the toddlekins at the foot of the class. The files stood ranged along opposite walls, as if drawn up for a spelling match. They were dressed in coarse stuff, an appropriate, simple uniform being provided for each sex." Just then appeared three sugar-planters to purchase some fieldhands. "They walked up and down the rows, making many inquiries, and examining closely the human chattels they expected to buy. We learned that a good Knight of Labor was worth about $1500. One of the planters picked out a number of slaves, male and female, who, one by one, stepped from the ranks, and stood huddled together in a group. There was much chaffering as to the price of certain children who, being regarded as incumbrances, mere colts or calves, were thrown in for good measure. . . ."

When Charles Mackay entered one of the show-rooms he was greeted with: "*Achetez-moi. Je suis bonne cuisinière et couturière. Achetez-moi!*" From the other side of the room some of the men also entreated him to buy them. One, apparently white, and supposed to be an Irishman, of the quality of county Cork—got up from his seat as the visitor passed, and, with an unmistakable brogue, said: "I am a good gardener, your honour. I am also a bit of a carpenter, and can look after the horses, and do any sort of odd job about the house."—"But you are joking; you are an Irishman?"—"My father was an Irishman," he answered.—"Is there not a mistake here?" the visitor inquired of the owner of the slave-depot. "This is a white man."—"His mother was a nigger." That was conclusive, no matter how light one might be. "We have sometimes much whiter men for sale than he is. Look at his hair and lips. There is no mistake about him."

Another English traveler, when in New Orleans in 1855, went to a trader's booth with a planter who wished to buy three slave women. About 60 slaves were in what reminded him of a country school-room. "The most of them were from Virginia and seemed anxious to get masters." At the head of one line was a woman with a child in her arms and who was pregnant and had been separated from her husband in Alabama. "Buy me, master, I am a good field-hand and can work at anything," or a similar appeal came from everyone on whom the visitor looked. He erroneously inferred that this eagerness to be sold was because "they must find the confinement irksome."

Why those files according to six and in a descending line? For the convenience of purchasers and to eliminate family ties. One negro was selected here, one there, and then urgent appeals to take another on account of kinship or marriage might be considered. A cheerful, pleading humility in slaves was often influential. But the urgency of their efforts to sell themselves was prompted by prospects of rewards or punishments. An ex-slave, a blacksmith's apprentice, speaking of his experience in a New Orleans yard, told the author that when a buyer came to the office, all of the kind asked for were put in line, and, he added: "Ef yo' talked up bright an' smaht an' was sol', p'r'aps de niggah-tradah'd give yo' a dollah." Another Virginia slave, bought in an Esplanade street pen by an owner of a brickyard, made this explanation: "Pussuns had ter be on dere p's an' q's an' showin' off so as to sell well when some one come ter buy 'em, an' ef yo' didn't put on dat pleasin' look, yo' 'd pay fer it when de pussuns went out o' de ya'd. An' ef dey sol' yo' on trial an' yo' was brought back, yo' 'd be 'mos' killed."

Miss Bremer saw "nothing especially repulsive in these places excepting the whole thing"! The "groups of colored men and women, of all shades between black and light yellow," standing or sitting unemployed at the doors, indicated the nature of the business within. She believed that they were well fed and clothed. She noticed that the slightest kind or jocose word called forth a sunny smile, full of good humor. She also went to see "some of the rooms in which the slaves were lodged for the night, and which were great garrets without beds, chairs or tables." As a rule, in all such places the floor was the only bed, a dirty blanket the only covering, a miscellaneous bundle the only pillow.

C. E. Girardey & Co. advertised in far-away Charleston that they "WANTED, FOR A LOUISIANA SUGAR PLANTATION, several gangs, varying from 50 to 150, of good PLANTATION NEGROES, accustomed either to the culture of Cotton or Rice. Planters having such, and withing to secure them a good home, will forward full descriptive lists—lowest possible cash price—when deliverable, at once or after the crops, and most accessible route from Charleston of their whereabouts." That was a cleverly worded means of obtaining supplies wholesale; for, as we know, masters preferred a planter and cash, if no considerable reduction in price was required. A few months later Girardey & Co. were offering a Georgia-coast gang of 67, to be sold in one or two lots. Of course they did not restrict themselves to gangs or families. Their office was at 37 Magazine street, but most of their large vendues were at the City Hotel, on the northeast corner of Common and Camp streets. There at noon, February 21, 1860, one could have found them selling at auction, "singly and in families," "84 choice plantation slaves, 33 being from one plantation near Georgetown, South Carolina." On many other days they likewise sold large numbers, such as "40 choice slaves, young and very likely," "54 prime slaves," "57 choice plantation slaves," and 12 "choice family slaves." This last meant not that they were to be kept in families, but only that they were domestic servants. The eldest was but 23 and the youngest two were Louisa, a "very smart house-servant," aged 11, and Jim, "very handy and intelligent," aged 12. Except a hairdresser and her babe of 22 months, all were· sold separately. On another day they sold at auction "Gracieuse, aged about 32, a creole speaking French and English, one of the best creole cooks in the city," with her two boys, 5 and 3 years of age. As if to illustrate what slaveselling might come to, they offered this speculation to the highest bidder:—

> The slave girl CATHERINE, a dark griffe, aged 13 years, very likely; is subject to fits, and supposed to be occasioned from tape worm. Not guaranteed except in title.—Terms—Cash.

Perhaps the largest slave-seller in New Orleans during the 'forties and the 'fifties—for auctioneers often outtraded the regular traders—was Joseph A. Beard. In appearance he was of the butcher or saloon-keeper type—"a short, thick man, with a red face." He became known as "Major Beard, the great slave-auctioneer of New Orleans." Like other traders, he often changed partners. Late in the 'fifties his office was at 38 Magazine street and most of his vendues were at Bank's Arcade, hard by, which was one of the five or six most popular marts; but he willingly went wherever profit invited. By 1859 his auctions were conducted by Gardner Smith, at first a silent partner. In January, 1859, Gardner Smith sold for Beard & Co., at Bank's Arcade, 13 "valuable Creole slaves," which usually meant that they were mulattoes, spoke French and had French names. Early in 1860 the firm was Beard, Pitts and Gardner Smith. A few months later Gardner Smith & Co., at 81 Common street, combined the businesses of slave-auctioneer, regular trader and keeper of a slave-yard and boarding-house for masters and traders—for "gentlemen who wish to stay in the house with their slaves"! Beard's successful understudy was planning to rival Hatcher—but the Civil War was only a few months off.

Julian Neville was another great auctioneer; and another great auction-mart, "The American Exchange" was in the St. Charles Hotel. Neville had apparently outstripped all competitors by 1860. His advertisements of sales of real estate and negroes sometimes covered nearly an entire page of the *Picayune*—more space than those of all other auctioneers together. Because good sugar plantations required expensive machinery as well as trained laborers, it was often advantageous to sell all together; to divide them was like dividing a factory. At the St. Charles it was least difficult to attract men with experience and capital sufficient for such enterprises. The sale of "Belle Chasse" was an example. This plantation was about a nine-mile drive from New Orleans. Judah P. Benjamin, distinguished as lawyer, planter and United States Senator, had been half-owner of it, and on it had built what was called one of the best plantation houses in Louisiana. By purchases in 1853 and 1854, amounting to nearly $168,000, Samuel Packwood acquired the whole. About five years later, he died. As usual, the heirs could not afford to operate such an estate. "Belle Chasse" must be sold at auction. Fortunately for the 161 negroes,—as the number was by the day of the sale—the entire property was disposed of *en bloc*, March 10, 1860. That it brought $250,000 warrants the belief that the best mart and the best auctioneer had been chosen. For such success and distinction the title of captain or major would have been deemed inadequate. Therefore, if never before, Neville was "Colonel"—a title usually reserved for men owning many slaves or supposed to have marked social, political or military standing.

McCerren, Landry & Co. were so prosperous that they fitted up Masonic Hall, at the corner of St. Charles and Perdido streets, as an "auction mart" with "a large, commodious and attractive salesroom, with spacious accommodations for slaves." Local editorial items called attention to their Tuesday and Saturday sales of real estate, slaves and various other kinds of property. Here is a sample:

> McCerren, Landry & Co., auctioneers, sell at their auction mart, at 11 o'clock a neat two-story brick dwelling, in the First District, on Triton Walk. Also several slaves, a splendid sorrel trotter and two mares.

This selling of negroes, beasts and many other kinds of property at the same time was common everywhere, almost necessary, and gave slavery a very inhuman aspect. And the slaves were scattered much more widely than the beasts. Paid advertisements in Charleston, Montgomery, Jackson (Mississippi), Nashville and Memphis newspapers announced that 136 slaves, "selected by Mr. Nich. Lewis [their deceased master]; out of many thousand," would be sold near Huntsville, Alabama, in January, 1860, to the highest bidders, along with "47 head of mules and horses, 54 head of cattle, the oxen, stock hogs, killing hogs and 90 head of sheep." In front of Ferguson & Wilkinson's auction store, Norfolk, were sold 3 horses, 2 carts, 1 fine buggy, 20 cases of boots, 6 or 8 casks of hams, 5000 cigars, etc. and "a likely negro girl 19 years old with a likely boy child of 18 months." Some combinations were still more grotesque. At the courthouse door in Covington, Georgia, on the first Tuesday in April, 1852, the sheriff delivered to the highest bidders two negroes, Nelson, about 32 years of age, Rachel, about 45, "also, a roan mule, about eight years old, and one sorrel mule, about seven or eight years old, and one two-horse wagon; levied on . . . to satisfy two mortgage fi fas" etc. At Montezuma, Macon county, Georgia, January 9, 1860, there was a public sale of about 100 "young and likely" negroes: "amongst the number [were] four good carpenters, two plantation blacksmiths, a superior pressman—having had several years experience in printing offices in Macon—and a first rate ostler. . . . Also, a fine lot of mules and horses, together with 'Morgan Comet,' a superior young stallion, from Vermont."

Two English ladies, the Misses Turnbull, were much shocked in New Orleans by a handbill announcing a raffle for several things, including a mulatto seamstress and lady's-maid, 18 years of age, together with a horse, wagon and other things. It was something to attract "sports." Success prompts repetition and imitation. "The enterprising and go-ahead Colonel Jennings has got a raffle under way now, which eclipses all his previous undertakings in that line," said the New Orleans *True Delta*. It was for "the celebrated trotting horse 'Star,' buggy and harness" and a "stout mulatto girl 'Sarah,' aged about twenty years, general house servant."

The yellow slave girls gave special interest to such raffles. Inter-race sexual immorality was one of the worst features of slavery. A southern judge and ex-Confederate soldier wrote to the author that "the moral results of slavery, in its most favorable aspects, are unprintable." We are here concerned with only the printed evidence of the trade in slave girls and young women for sexual purposes, in addition to work as servants. In small numbers and of varying complexions they were to be seen in nearly all southern markets. Traders gladly exhibited them and were proud of the high prices they commanded; visitors were curious to see them and sure to tell about them later. Miss Bremer wrote of some in Richmond: "In another 'jail' were kept the so-called 'fancy girls' for fancy purchasers. They were handsome fair mulattoes, some of them almost white girls." Her comment on those seen in Augusta, Georgia, was: "Many of these children [from 12 to 20 years of age] were fair mulattoes, and some of them very pretty. One girl of twelve was so white, that I should have supposed her to belong to the white race; her features, too, were those of the whites. The slave-keeper told us that the day before, another girl, still fairer and handsomer, had been sold for $1500. These white children of slavery become, for the most part, victims of crime, and sink to the deepest degradation." This item appeared in an editorial article in the Memphis *Eagle and Enquirer*, June 26, 1857:

> A slave woman is advertised to be sold in St. Louis who is so surpassingly beautiful that $5000 has been already offered for her, at private sale, and refused.

To gamblers, traders, saloonkeepers, turfmen and debauchees, owning a "fancy girl" was a luxurious ideal. And Longfellow's lines described what was supposed to be no rarity among traders taking a considerable number of purchases to the New Orleans market:

> The Slaver led her from the door,
> He led her by the hand,
> To be his slave and paramour
> In a strange and distant land!

New Orleans—where thousands of sporting men and voluptuaries lived and other thousands came for the racing season, the Carnival and dissipation—was fully tenfold the largest market for "fancy girls." The prospect of great profit induced their conspicuous display. At the mart where the planter came to buy when the Ohio youth was inspecting it, a handsome quadroon girl, gaily dressed and adorned with ribbons and jewels, sat in a show-window to attract attention. "She, too, was for sale, as a choice house-servant, at a high price on account of her beauty. As our friend the planter was about to leave the premises he glanced at this girl, and asked what the trader would take for her. Being told, he shook his head, leered at the slave, and said, with an oath, 'Too expensive.' " Charles Casey, an English traveler, saw "a beautiful quadroon girl, neatly dressed and very intelligent," sell for $2000 in Evans's Arcade, in New Orleans, at a time when fieldhands brought from $600 to $800. And "Ole Charley" Logan bought a bright mulatto girl, Violetta, for $600, in Columbia, South Carolina, took her to New Orleans in one of his coffles and sold her for $1500.

In April 1848, between 70 and 80 slaves attempted to escape to the North from Washington on a schooner called the "Pearl." It was overtaken near the mouth of the Potomac, the would-be runaways were lodged in a Washington jail and most of them met the usual fate in such cases—they were "sold South." Among them were six intelligent and superior mulatto children of Milly and Paul Edmondson—Mary and Emily (16 and 14 years of age) and four of their brothers. The father had been freed many years previously. The slave mother and her 14 children were the inheritance of a feeble-minded maiden lady whose property was cared for by her guardian. The six Edmondson children and many other unfortunates of the "Pearl" were sold to the firm of Bruin & Hill. Since 1834 Joseph Bruin had been an interstate trader in New Orleans, getting his supplies in Maryland and Virginia, just like George Kephart; and since 1836 he had covetously watched the growing Edmondson children, for he had been promised an opportunity to buy them if they should be for sale. Now the time that they feared and he hoped for had come. He paid $4500 for these six and put them in his jail in Alexandria, Virginia. The lady for whom Mary Edmondson had been working offered Bruin $1000 for her, which was much more than she cost. He answered that he could get twice that much for her in New Orleans. In a few weeks the six Edmondson children and about 40 other slaves were shipped from Baltimore to New Orleans, where the girls were required to stand on an open porch fronting the street so as to attract the attention of possible purchasers. One of the girls in the yard, who had been sold conditionally for the worst of purposes and was soon returned as unsatisfactory, was mercilessly flogged. Owing to the effect of yellow fever on the trade, Bruin soon concluded to send those unsold back to Baltimore. Before the end of the summer Mary and Emily were again in Bruin's Alexandria jail.

Meantime philanthropic efforts had been made to buy some of the Edmondsons out of slavery, and one of the boys was soon purchased for $900. Finally the old father, Paul Edmondson, resolved to go to New York and try to collect enough money to pay for Emily and Mary. Bruin & Hill gave him a general letter of introduction, September 5, 1848, offering to sell the two girls for $2250. If $1200 should be paid, or satisfactory assurances received, within 15 days, then the girls would be kept in Alexandria 25 days longer before being sent to the South Carolina market, along with others. The time elapsed and the coffle was made ready. At the last moment, Emily and Mary, who had become favorites with Bruin's family, were allowed to remain until later. As the others marched off—the men handcuffed together and the women and children following—they were compelled to sing, aided by fiddles and banjoes, so as to prevent an expression of their actual feelings and to deceive on-lookers. Paul Edmondson soon returned, accompanied by a representative of the Abolitionists in New York that had been aroused by the eloquence of Henry Ward Beecher and had contributed the required $2250. Bruin signed the papers and gave Mary and Emily each a five dollar gold piece. Instead of being sold as "fancy girls," they were taken to New York to be educated.

Quite different was the fate of another Emily—Emily Russell, also a pretty mulatto girl and one of the unfortunates of the "Pearl." She had hoped to reach her mother, a washwoman who had saved enough to buy her own freedom and go to New York. Emily and several others seem to have been taken first to a Baltimore slavepen and not placed in Bruin's in Alexandria until early in January, 1850. Learning that they were presently to be sent to New Orleans, Emily appealed to her mother, who besought the financial aid of Abolitionists. They agreed to contribute to the purchase of Emily and perhaps others, if obtainable for a reasonable price. The traders answered thus:—

Alexandria, Jan. 31, 1850.

. . . All I have to say about the matter is, that we paid very high for the negroes and cannot afford to sell girl Emily for less than $1800. This may seem a high price to you, but, cotton being very high, consequently slaves are high. We have two or three offers for Emily from gentlemen from the South. She is said to be the finest-looking woman in this country. As for Hagar and her seven children, we will take $2500 for them. Sally and her four children, we will take for them $2800. You may seem a little surprised at the difference in prices, but the difference in the negroes makes the difference in price. We expect to start South with the negroes on the 8th February, and if you intend to do anything, you had better do it soon.—Yours, respectfully,

Bruin & Hill

Not cotton, but being "the finest-looking woman in this country" and having "two or three offers for Emily from gentlemen from the South," made her so valuable, as was shown by asking only $2500 for Hagar and her seven children. It was impossible for the philanthropists to collect any one of these sums in the few days before the starting of the coffle overland afoot. Emily had to accompany the others. What stupid recklessness to begin such a march in February! About midway on it, Emily died. When her mother, knowing why the girl was so prized, heard of her death, she exclaimed: "The Lord be thanked! He has heard my prayers at last!"

It was at the French Exchange, in the rotunda of the St. Louis Hotel, that superior-looking girls, varying from mulatto to octoroon, were most often to be seen on the auction-block. French was generally spoken, the whole setting was Creole and all the more strange and fascinating to northern visitors. This hotel stood near the center of the old city and covered almost the entire square bounded by St. Louis, Chartres, Toulouse and Royal streets. Less costly and impressive than the St. Charles, it was so superior in *cuisine,* in the size and the attractiveness of its ballrooms, that the gayest social functions were held there. An arcade 127 by 40 feet extended from St. Louis street to a grand rotunda, 80 feet in diameter, with galleries around it and crowned by a lofty dome, letting in a blaze of light and having a very ornamental ceiling. On the sides were pillars 50 feet in height and on the walls were "works in *chiaroscuro,* representing various successful actions gained during the struggle for independence." The floor was of variegated marble. Extending nearly half-way around the rotunda was a marble bar, which, with its decorations and equipments, was said to be the finest and largest then known. The number and the vivacity of its patrons betokened the superlative quality of the drinks served there.

Opposite the bar were half a dozen small platforms with marble desks for auctioneers. About them, on busy days, were casks of wine, bales, kegs, boxes, crates, furniture, bric-a-brac, books, groceries, drygoods and nearly everything that comes into an auction-mart. The sales of general merchandise began at ten o'clock. Soon the auctioneers were shouting, gesticulating, turning quickly from side to side, sometimes speaking merrily, sometimes almost eloquently. The Creoles called them *encanteurs,* the old French word, instead of *crieurs à l'enchère,* the modern term. Like the announcements of sales by order of any Louisiana court, these *encanteurs* twice said everything that was important—once in each language. Some of them did so with such speed and facility that there seemed to be a simultaneous flow of two distinct streams of words.

What most persons came to see was the slave-auctions. Looking down from the circular galleries on the moving scenes, it was very noticeable that a large proportion of the slaves were of a light color and seemed more intelligent than those in marts outside of New Orleans. At about eleven o'clock, different groups had been brought in from the yards on Esplanade, Moreau, Baronne, Gravier and Common streets and lined up ready for inspection. At one side of the rotunda there were rooms where slaves might be locked up for any temporary purpose and where the scrutiny of men or women might be as close as anyone wished. In no other market was inspection more important than in New Orleans, where the worst in health and character, as well as the best, were gathered.

Auctioneers never felt more important than when selling slaves, and for the *encanteur* there was no place like *la Bourse de l'Hotel St. Louis à midi*—the French Exchange at noon. He assumed his most impressive mien, puffed himself up and his wooden mallet made his marble desk ring out a warning that the important hour to begin the slave-sales had arrived. *"Et maintenant, messieurs, commençons l'encan de ces esclaves de valeur."* The chatter of voices lessened and many persons drew near him as he ordered a slave to mount the nearest appropriately sized box or crate. Here is an apparently realistic account of an auction of a young mother and her two year old boy. She was "very sprucely dressed in a dark bombasine gown, which set off her waist and shoulders to great advantage," and a white cap with lace knots and gay ribbons gave her a coquettish air. The *encanteur* was profuse in praise of mother and child, "and shadowed forth the perfections, both of her mind and body"; she was, moreover, "a good Christian and an accomplished cook!" . . . *"Deux cents gourdes!* Why bless me! . . . *Elle en vaut au moins mille.* And then look at that boy! *Dans quelques ans il sera fort comme un lion ce gamin là!"* . . .—"Four hundred dollars!"—. . . "You show your good sense, sir: *on voit que vous vous y connoisez.* . . . Amanda Mix, step forward a little more: there, set the child down, and let the gentlemen see how firm you stand on your cornstalks! There is a beautiful picture! You need not blush, Amanda" (shouts of laughter, in which the ebony beauty heartily joined); "you deserve the compliment. Why, gentlemen, there has not been so splendid a lot in this market within my recollection." Soon the bidding reached $550.

"I say, here is a woman of most excellent parts—young, well pro-
portioned and strong; as tractable as a lamb; extremely honest and
industrious; with a child that, in a very few years, will be a mine of
wealth to its proprietor; and yet for these inestimable articles the
paltry sum of five hundred and fifty dollars only has been offered!
. . . —"Six hundred dollars!"—Doubtless by pre-arrangement, the
auctioneer called on her to draw out from her bosom a neatly
folded recommendation. "This is to certify that Amanda Mix is a
most excellent servant, always obedient, never grumbles, is seldom
sick, and is exceedingly fond of children." Phrenology, then in
vogue, was the facile plaything of small wits. The auctioneer felt
the heads of the mother and the child and declared that each bore
strong evidence of philoprogenitiveness and divers other qualities
valuable in slaves. Then a fresh gushing of praise.—"Six hundred
and seventy-five dollars!"—"Gentlemen, the matter is creeping to
a close: *allons, courage, encore une fois!*" Yet notwithstanding so
many merits, mother and child were sold for $700. That was because
the year was about 1840. Had it been near the end of the 'fifties they
might have brought thrice as much but the older features would
have been about the same.

Forty years after the last slave was sold in this once notorious
St. Louis Hotel, the building was standing—standing battered like
a haunted house with ten thousand curses on it. Window panes
were out, locks were broken and doors were nailed up with rough
boards or fastened in some crude way. The many "For Rent" signs
had so long in vain appealed to the public that they were tattered
and yellow from despair. Of the rooms once occupied by flourishing
shopkeepers, all save one were empty, except of dirt and rubbish,
and that one contained several piles of rusty and forgotten junk.
Finally a caretaker was found—a pale Creole, dressed in black and
looking both sad and famished. First, one should see the grand
halls for receptions and balls, where even the wealthiest guests of
the St. Charles gave their most ambitious entertainments. The dome
was indeed large, but when it so impressed travelers, that of the
National Capitol had not been constructed and that of the Library
of Congress had not been thought of. After the days of slavery the
floors of the second and upper stories were extended under the
dome. This made the old rotunda dark. In 1902 it was damp and
mouldy; the wood was in decay, and the marble pavement—once
clicking to the step of innumerable idlers, visitors, speculators and
planters, as well as to the heavy tramp of slaves in their new shoes
—was loose, broken, and, in places, destroyed. There stood the
formerly grand and gorgeous bar—almost black with humid dirt.

Here was an auctioneer's stand from which, it was believed, hundreds of slaves had been sold. In that side-room with barred windows many had been locked up before and after sale. It was almost as damp and gloomy as a dungeon cell. In moving about in it one aroused swarms of strange flying insects. Yes, undoubtedly, from this room——but then it may have been light and dry. The once gay and busy arcade was only less dismal than the rotunda.

Across Chartres street an aged Creole was complacently sitting in front of his secondhand furniture-store. It was all an old, old story and true. He himself had seen "tousan' an' tousan' o' nagr'" sold right there in the rotunda in the days when the light streamed down from dome to pavement. The law in Louisiana did not allow young children to be parted from their mothers, but he had often seen families auctioned off, no two of whose members went to the same buyer. Mulatto girls would sometimes bring from $2200 to $2500; the best hairdressers might sell for as much as $3500, for they could each earn many hundreds a year for their owners by going to regular patrons. (The New Orleans ladies prided themselves on an artistic *coiffure,* daily.) He also spoke of several of the double-tongued *encanteurs,* especially Vignie.

To have forgotten Vignie would have discredited his recollections, for Vignie was better known in the French quarter than Beard, and only less well known in the American quarter. At one time, he was perhaps the most prosperous auctioneer in New Orleans and alone did nearly three-fifths as much business as the whole firm of Beard & May. His total commissions in the best years probably exceeded $10,000 or $15,000—more than thrice what those sums would mean today. Certainly a large part came from the sale of slaves. Before 1860 he was selling less often in the French than in the American quarter, where the trade was rapidly increasing. But he and other *encanteurs* continued frequently to chant the praises of *esclaves de valeur* at the French Exchange until stopped by the Civil War.

5

The Negro
Slave Family

E. Franklin Frazier

From: *Journal of Negro History*, XV, No. 2 (April 1930), pp.
218–234, 236–237, 240–248, 250–259. Footnotes deleted.
Copyright © by The Association for the Study of Negro
Life and History, Inc.

*E. Franklin Frazier's discussion of the slave family illuminates several
important aspects of slave life. Because slaves were defined as
property, they could not contract legal marriages. Children born to
a slave woman belonged to her master; neither the mother nor the
father had any claims on such offspring. In all things the master
was the ultimate authority. He even granted permission to marry.
If he decided that the mother had to work in the fields he could
usually enforce his will, thus often leaving the raising of slave children to older women. The parents had a limited role in raising their
children; indeed, some slaves did not even know their fathers.*

*Many slaves did establish stable marriages and families though
these were not sanctioned by law. The history of slavery is full of
heroic stories of the intense family ties of slaves. We know, for
example, that one of the main factors prompting slaves to run away
was the selling of a spouse. Yet the stability of the family depended
upon the will of the master and ingenuity of the individual slaves.
An indifferent master or one crushed by financial difficulties could
break up families if he found it profitable to do so. Moreover, an
increase in the number of slaves was an increase in the master's
investment, and some masters accordingly encouraged promiscuous
behavior. Family stability also depended upon the occupation and*

status of the slave. Slave artisans in the cities had greater opportunities to develop stable family relationships than did those on the plantations.

Overall, uncertainty stalked the slave family. The selling of children and separating of husband and wife occurred too often. The position of the father was weakened by the very nature of slavery, which demanded submission. Finally, masters exploited female slaves sexually, a practice that further undermined the husband's position and the family.

INFLUENCE OF MASTERS ON FAMILY RELATIONS

Undoubtedly the masters had an interest not only in the propagation of their slave property; but they were concerned about the connection which the sexual union of slaves on the plantations established. Usually, it appears, slaves secured permission to marry. An overseer in a letter to his employer said, "I have given Chesley Permission to marry Molly, Sarah's daughter. I would like to Noe if you object to it. I have put up a New house for Chesley." Referring to another such instance, he said, "Esaw and biner has asked permission to Marry. I think it a good Match. What say you to it?"

...The master's control over the mating of his slaves went further than merely giving permission to the slave to marry the person of his choice. It was often, it appears, a command to marry according to the wishes of the master. A slave who had been purchased and compelled to leave his wife and family, according to one narrative, was "compelled to take a young woman named Hannah, as a wife, and to abandon his former one. By Hannah he had a good many children but after he had been with her about eight years he was sold away from her and their children to one Robert Ware, of Decatur Town, in DeKalb County, Georgia, about ten miles from Stevens' place." A young mulatto girl, whose fiancée had escaped to the North through Harriet Tubman, also fled to the North "in fear and desperation" when she learned that her master had determined to give her to one of his Negro slaves as a wife. With the instructions to the slaves as to the amount of tobacco they were expected to cultivate, according to a slave, "was the order for us to 'get married,' according to Slavery, or in other words, to enrich his plantation by a family of young slaves."

...Aside from the economic motive that might prompt slave holders to have their slaves marry, it appears in the following excerpt that mistresses sought this means of controlling the master's sex relations with the female slaves:

> Mistress told sister that she had best get married, and that if she would, she would give her a wedding. Soon after a very respectable young man, belonging to Mr. Bowman, a wealthy planter, and reputed to be a good master, began to court my sister. This very much pleased Mistress, who wished to hasten the marriage. She determined that her maid should be married, not as slaves usually are, but that with the usual matrimonial ceremonies should be tied the knot to be broken only by death. The Sabbath was appointed for the marriage, which was to take place at the Episcopal Church. I must here state that no slave can be married lawfully, without a fine from his or her owner. Mistress and all the family, except the old man, went to church, to witness the marriage ceremony, which was to be performed by their minister, Parson Reynolds. The master of Josiah, my sister's destined husband, was also at the wedding, for he thought a great deal of his man. Mistress returned delighted from the wedding, for she thought she had accomplished a great piece of work. But the whole affair only enraged her unfeeling husband, who, to be revenged upon the maid, proposed to sell her. To this his wife refused consent. Although Mrs. T. had never told him her suspicions or what my sister had said, yet he suspected the truth, and determined to be revenged. Accordingly, during another absence of Mistress, he again cruelly whipped my sister. A continued repetition of these things finally killed our Mistress, who the doctor said, died of a broken heart. After the death of this friend, sister ran away leaving her husband and one child and finally found her way to the North. None of our family ever heard from her afterwards, until I accidentally met her in the streets in Philadelphia. My readers can imagine what a meeting ours must have been. She is again married and in prosperity.

To the same extent that the slave in forming a conjugal relation was subject to the wishes of his master he was under the will of the latter in continuing that relationship. Beyond the will of the master were the contingencies of family fortunes such as changes in the economic status and deaths which affected the stability of the slave family. Washington Irving, who recognized as a peculiar evil of slavery the fact that slaves are "parted from their children" reflected philosophically in his journals, "but are not white people so, by schooling, marriage, business, etc." Bruce who writes with detachment concerning slavery tells how the division of the property upon the death of his master broke up his family. "My parents belonged," he said, "to Lemuel Bruce, who died about the year 1836, leaving two children, William Bruce and Rebecca Bruce, who went to live with their aunt, Mrs. Prudence Perkinson; he also left two families of slaves, and they were divided between his two children; my mother's family fell to Miss Rebecca, and the other family, the head of which was known as Bristo was left to William H. Bruce. Then it was that family ties were broken, the slaves were all hired out, my mother to one man and my father to another. I was too young then to know anything about it, and have to rely entirely on what I have heard my mother and others older than myself say."

. . . It appears, however, that consideration for the family ties of the slaves prevented the breaking of families at times when the estate had to be divided. In one instance in dividing up an estate among the mother and her four children, the slaves "were placed in five lots, and these were so arranged as to keep the families together." Since these lots were of unequal value the difference in the distribution was made up from other property. John Thompson, who writes in his autobiography that the first act of slavery recorded in his memory was the sale of his sister, says in referring to the division of the estate upon the death of his mistress that his "father's family" went to the same master.

There is, however, plenty of testimony to show that the family bonds of the slaves were ignored when economic considerations were involved. The demand for slaves on the plantations of the lower South always increased their economic value. One slave says that he was sold for three hundred and ten dollars when ten years of age because of the rise in the price of cotton. Harriet Tubman tells how the dilapidated state of things about the "Great House" was the occasion for the disappearance of slaves—either sold or hired out. It was in the slave trade where men were dealing with slaves as commodities that the least sentiment was shown towards the family ties of the slaves. The *Alexandria Gazette* commenting on the slave trade in the national capital, said, "Here you may behold fathers and mothers leaving behind them the dearest objects of affection, and moving slowly along in the mute agony of despair; there, the young mother, sobbing over the infant whose innocent smile seems but to increase her misery. From some you will hear the burst of bitter lamentation, while from others the loud hysteric laugh breaks forth, denoting still deeper agony. Such is but a faint picture of the American slave-trade."

In an autobiography of a slave we are furnished with a transaction in St. Louis where the marital relations between a slave, who lost his wife, was decided by the bidding of the speculators in slaves.

A man and his wife, both slaves, were brought from the country to the city, for sale. They were taken to the room of Austin & Salvage, auctioneers. Several slave-speculators, who are always to be found at auctions where slaves are to be sold, were present. The man was first put up and sold to the highest bidder. The wife was next ordered to ascend the platform. I was present. She slowly obeyed the order. The auctioneer commenced, and soon several hundred dollars were bid. My eyes were intensely fixed on the face of the woman, whose cheeks were wet with tears. But a conversation between the slave and his new master attracted my attention. I drew near them to listen. The slave was begging his new master to purchase his wife. Said he, 'Master, if you will only buy Fanny, I know you will get the worth of your money. She is a good cook, a good washer, and her last mistress liked her very much. If you will only buy her now how happy I shall be.' The new master replied that he did not want her, but if she sold cheap he would purchase her. I watched the countenance of the man while the different persons were bidding on his wife. When his new master bid on his wife you could see the smile upon his countenance, and the tears stop; but as soon as another would bid, you could see the countenance change and the tears start afresh.

. . . Among the restraining influences upon the selling of slaves without regard for their family ties should be mentioned the blood relationships to the masters. Loguen speaks of being the pet of his white father who sought to save his mother from being sold. A mulatto who relates how his white grandfather objected to the breaking up of a family, tells how his grandfather's wishes were disregarded in the case of his own family when it came to dividing up the estate.

When I was about six years of age, the estate of Samuel Campbell, my grandfather, was sold at auction. His sons and daughters were all present at the sale, except Mrs. Banton. Among the articles and animals put upon the catalogue, and placed in the hands of the auctioneer, were a large number of slaves. When everything else had been disposed of, the question arose among the heirs, "What shall be done with Letty (my mother) and her children?" John and William Campbell, came to mother, and told her they would divide her family among the heirs, but none of them should go out of the family. One of the daughters—to her everlasting honor be it spoken—remonstrated against any such proceeding. Judith, the wife of Joseph Logan, told her brothers and sisters, "Letty is our own half sister, and you know it; father never intended they should be sold." Her protest was disregarded, and the auctioneer was ordered to proceed. My mother, and her infant son, Cyrus, about one year old, were put up together and sold for $500. Sisters and brothers selling their own sister and her children.

THE FAMILY GROUP

We have considered so far the influence of the masters in general on the integrity of the slave family. We now propose to inquire into the nature of the slave family as a group of persons having social relations. It is our purpose to determine to what extent there was developed in slavery a family consciousness and a family organization in which the rôles of the different members of the family were defined and recognized. Moreover, we are especially interested in determining the extent of control, the building up of a family tradition, and how the personality of the Negro was formed in the matrix of the family. Of course, in such an investigation we must take into the account the relation to the masters who figured more or less in the world of the Negro slave.

Let us consider first the extent to which the slave was acquainted with his ancestry. From the biographies and autobiographies of slaves it appears that the knowledge which slaves had of their ancestry varied considerably. Bishop Lane, who was born in 1834 in Madison County, Tennessee, says that he was "reared almost motherless and fatherless, having no parental care and guidance given" him. Another slave who remained with his parents until nine years of age knew his parents and the names of his five brothers and sisters. Booker Washington, who was born in slavery about 1858 or 1859, knew nothing of his ancestry except his mother and the reports that his father was a white man living on a nearby plantation. Although Frederick Douglass possessed no knowledge of his father and knew his mother only through "little glimpses" of her at night when she came to see him, he was well acquainted with his mother's parents who had some standing in the neighborhood. Josiah Henson, who was born June 15, 1789, in Charles County, Maryland, says that his knowledge of his father was restricted to his appearance "one day with his head bloody and his back lacerated. He was in a state of great excitement, and though it was all a mystery to me at the age of three or four years, it was explained at a later period, and I understood that he had been suffering the cruel penalty of the Maryland law for beating a white man. His right ear had been cut off close to his head, and he had received a hundred lashes on his back. He had beaten the overseer for a brutal assault on my mother, and this was his punishment. Furious at such treatment, my father became a different man, and was so morose, disobedient, and intractable that Mr. N—— determined to sell him. He accordingly parted with him, not long after, to his son, who lived in Alabama; and neither my mother nor I ever heard of him again."

... In a large number of stories of the lives af slaves we find a knowledge not only of the mother but also the name of the father as well. In some cases the slaves as set forth in the excerpt below were able to trace their descent to an ancestor who was brought to America from Africa.

> My name is John Brown. How I came to take it, I will explain in due time. When in slavery I was called Fed. Why I was so named, I cannot tell. I never knew myself to have any other name, nor always by that; for it is common for slaves to answer to any name as it suits the humour of the master. I do not know how old I am, but think I may be any age between thirty-five and forty. I fancy I must be about thirty-seven or eight as nearly as I can guess. I was raised on Betty Moore's estate, in Southampton County, Virginia, about three miles from Jerusalem Court House and the little Nottoway river. My mother belonged to Betty Moore. Her name was Nancy; but she was called Nanny. My father's name was Joe. He was owned by a planter named Benford, who lived at Northampton, in the same state. I believe my father and his family were bred on Benford's plantation. His father had been stolen from Africa. He was of the Eboe tribe. I remember seeing him once, when he came to visit my mother. He was very black. I never saw him but that one time, and though I was quite small, I have a distinct recollection of him. He and my mother were separated, in consequence of his master going further off, and then my mother was forced to take another husband. She had three children by my father; myself, and my brother and sister, twins. My brother's name was Silas, and my sister's Lucy. My mother's second husband's name was Lamb. He was the property of a neighboring planter and miller named Collier. By him she had three children; two boys, Curtis and Cain, and a girl between them called Irene.

... In the biographies and autobiographies of Negroes we find frequent references to white ancestry. Bishop L. H. Holsey writes, "I was born in Georgia, near Columbus, in 1842, and at that time was the slave of James Holsey, who was also my father. He was a gentleman of classical education, dignified in appearance and manner of life, and represented that old antebellum class of Southern aristocracy who did not know enough of manual labor to black their own shoes or saddle their own horses. Like many others of his day and time he never married, but mingled to some extent, with those families of the African race that were his slaves—his personal property."

... The white ancestry of Negroes, including the well-known cases of Douglass and Washington, who played a prominent part in the history of the Negro, has frequently been emphasized by those who have made a study of Negro life. At the same time this fact has been regarded as a cause of demoralization of the sex life of the Negroes. White ancestry is significant in the study of Negro family not only because it became the basis of social distinctions among the slaves and formed the group which was most often emancipated, but because the numerous instances of white fathers enhanced the dominating rôle of the Negro mother in the slave family. Douglass, whose father was reputed to be white, says succinctly: "Of my father I know nothing." Washington did not even know the name of the white man who was said to have been his father. In many cases, of course, the white father was not only known but his paternal interest in the family was such as to create fond attachment between his slave children and himself.

. . . In some slave families we find a high degree of organization and a deep sense of family solidarity. When [J. W. C.] Pennington's father was given a whipping, says he, "This act created an open rupture with our family—each member felt the deep insult that had been inflicted upon our head; the spirit of the whole family was roused; we talked of it in our nightly gatherings, and showed it in our daily melancholy aspect."

Moreover, in his family there was such solidarity that the offence against the family affected his conception of himself which he found in his rôle as a skilled mechanic. "I had always aimed to be trustworthy," said he, "and feeling a high degree of mechanical pride, I had aimed to do my work with dispatch and skill; my blacksmith's pride and taste was one thing that had reconciled me so long to remain a slave. I sought to distinguish myself in the finer branches of the business by invention and finish; I frequently tried my hand at making guns and pistols, putting blades in pen knives, making fancy hammers, hatchets, sword-canes, &c., &c. Besides I used to assist my father at night in making straw hats and willow-baskets, by which means we supplied our family with little articles of food, clothing and luxury, which slaves in the mildest form of the system never get from the master; but after this, I found that my mechanic's pleasure and pride were gone. I thought of nothing but the family disgrace under which we were smarting, and how to get out of it."

The organization and the solidarity of the slave family, too, was based upon the economy of the slave household and the organization of the family group within the cabin. Although some writers have laid great stress upon the indiscriminate mixing of the sexes and kindred in the slave huts, there is much evidence to show that it was equally true that the family groups were often treated as units and rationed as such. Moreover, it should not be forgotten that there was greater regard for the integrity of the slave family in Maryland, Virginia, and North Carolina, where slavery was disintegrating, than on the large plantations of the lower South. Because of the dependence of the children upon the mothers it appears that the mother and smaller children were sold together. . . .

It was the mother who ultimately provided the child's needs and at the cost often of great suffering defied the masters. "I remember well my mother often hid us all in the woods, to prevent master selling us," said a former slave. "When we wanted water, she sought for it in any hole or puddle, formed by falling trees or otherwise: it was often full of tadpoles and insects: she strained it, and gave it round to each of us in the hollow of her hand. For food, she gathered berries in the woods, got potatoes, raw corn, &c. After a time the master would send word to her to come in, promising he would not sell us. But, at length, persons came, who agreed to give the prices he set on us. His wife, with much to be done, prevailed on him not to sell me; but he sold my brother, who was a little boy. My mother, frantic with grief, resisted their taking her child away; she was beaten and held down: she fainted, and when she came to herself, her boy was gone. She made much outcry, for which the master tied her up to a peach tree in the yard, and flogged her." . . .

CARE OF CHILDREN

The control of the children by parents on the plantation was not of long duration. On some plantations the care of the children was assigned to an old woman. When there was no woman to serve in this capacity the children were left alone. Booker T. Washington says, "The early years of my life, which were spent in the little cabin, were not very different from those of thousands of other slaves. My mother, of course, had little time in which to give attention to the training of her children during the day. She snatched a few moments for our care in the early morning before her work began, and at night after the day's work was done. One of my earliest recollections is that of my mother cooking a chicken late at night, and awakening her children for the purpose of feeding them."

If the cabins were far from the field, it seemed that the mothers took their children to the field to suckle. Generally the mothers were permitted to return to the cabins to nurse their children during the day. Bibb says that his wife's "business was to labor out in the field the greater part of her time, and there was no one to take care of poor little Frances, while her mother was toiling in the field. She was left at the house, to creep under the feet of an unmerciful old mistress, whom I have known to slap with her hand the face of little Frances, for crying after her mother, until her little face was left black and blue."

... At a certain age the children were assigned to labor on the plantation. Steward says, "When eight years of age, I was taken to the 'great house' or the family mansion of my sister, to serve as an errand boy, where I had to stand in the presence of my master's family all the day, and a part of the night, ready to do anything which they commanded me to perform."

... A slave born in Maryland described his childhood saying, "Accordingly, when between five or six years of age, I was assigned to the duties of housework, to wait on my mistress and to run errands. When she went out driving I had to accompany her in the capacity of a page, to open the gates and to take down guard fences for her to drive through. That I might be found at night as well as by day my sleeping apartment was in her chamber on a truckbed, which was during the day time snugly concealed under her bedstead and drawn out at night for the reposing place of Isaac's weary body while he dreamed of days yet to come. I remained in this distinguished position until I was about fifteen years old, when a change in common with all slave life had to be made either for the better or for the worse."

In other cases the children were given work in the fields with the other slaves. Josiah Henson referred to his earliest employments as to carry buckets of water to the men at work, and to hold a horse-plough, used for weeding between the rows of corn, and as he grew older and taller to take care of master's saddle-horse. "Then," said he, "a hoe was put into my hands, and I was soon required to do the day's work of a man; and it was not long before I could do it, at least as well as my associates in misery."

Often the slave child's early years were spent with the white children on the plantation. Lunsford Lane spent his early boyhood in playing with the other boys and girls, colored and white, in the yard, and occasionally doing such little matters of labor as one of so young years could. "I knew no difference between myself and the white children," said he, "nor did they seem to know any in turn. Sometimes my master would come out and give a biscuit to me, and another to one of his own white boys; but I did not perceive the difference between us. I had no brothers or sisters, but there were other colored families living in the same kitchen, and the children playing in the same yard, with me and my mother."

The older brothers and sisters were often charged with the care and discipline of the young children. "At this period," said a slave, "my principal occupation was to nurse my little brother whilst my mother worked in the field. Almost all slave children have to do the nursing, the big taking care of the small, who often came poorly off in consequence. I know this was my little brother's case. I used to lay him in the shade, under a tree, sometimes, and go to play, or curl myself up under a hedge, and take a sleep."

. . . Douglass received his religious training under one of the slaves who had acquired status as a religious teacher. Douglass said, "I was early sent to Doctor Isaac Copper, with twenty or thirty other children, to learn the Lord's prayer. The old man was seated on a huge three-legged oaken stool, armed with several large hickory switches, and from the point where he sat, lame as he was, he could reach every boy in the room. After standing a while to learn what was expected of us, he commanded us to kneel down. This done, he told us to say everything he said. "Our Father"—this we repeated after him with promptness and uniformity—"who art in Heaven" was less promptly and uniformly repeated, and the old gentleman paused in the prayer to give us a short lecture, and to use his switches on our backs."

Davis says that both his mother and father "were pious members of the Baptist church." He adds that "because of their godly example, I formed a determination, before I had reached my 12th year, that if I was spared to become a man, I would try to be as good as my parents. My father could read a little, and make figures, but could scarcely write at all. His custom, on those Sabbaths when we remained at home, was to spend his time in instructing his children or the neighboring servants out of a New Testament, sent him from Fredericksburg by one of his older sons. I fancy I can see him now, sitting under his bush arbor, reading that precious book to many attentive hearers around him. Such was the esteem I had for my pious father, that I have kept that blessed book ever since his death, for his sake; and it was the first New Testament I read, after I felt the pardoning love of God in my soul."

It was in regard to the religious life that we find most of tradition regarding the ancestors in the slave families. "My grandmother was an exceedingly pious woman," says Frederick. [H. L.] Holsey describes his mother as "an intensely religious woman." Another slave, whose autobiography is bombastic and full of episodes designed to show that the author possessed occult powers, says he was like his mother who "had a presentiment that she was not designed by Providence to rear me."

The religious instruction of the slaves was intended as a means of control and teaching morality. It affected considerably the strength of the marital bond between slaves as well as the relations with the children.

> . . . The benefits may be seen by the most superficial observer. They have so improved that they seem to be almost another set of beings. Their improvement has been in proportion to their instruction. They are orderly, well-behaved and seem to strive to fulfil the relative duties of life. They are faithful in their marriage relations. Immorality is discountenanced. They generally attend the house of God on the Sabbath. . . .
>
> . . . Parents love their children, and in most cases, the children obey their parents. The duties of husband and wife are faithfully performed. I have heard of few instances of want of chastity amongst them, and but one case, in several years, has occurred of an unmarried woman having a child, on a plantation comprising, perhaps, 10 or 15 such. . . .

MARRIAGE

Consistent with the slave code, the slave, as a rule, could not enter into a marriage contract. "A slave cannot even contract matrimony, the association which takes place among slaves, and is called marriage, being properly designated by the word *contubernium*, a relation which has no sanctity, and to which no civil rights are attached."

An opinion handed down by Judge Matthews in Louisiana in 1819 held that while slaves with the consent of their master may marry and had the *moral* power to agree to marry, such an act did not produce any civil effects. Moreover, it was also stated in the judicial opinion that the contractual and legal character of such unions were dormant during slavery but became actual from the moment of freedom.

Although slaves were not legally married the act of marrying is mentioned repeatedly in the slave narratives. One slave writes, "I was married to Lucilla Smith, the slave of Mrs. Moore. We called it and we considered it a true marriage, although we knew well that marriage was not permitted to the slaves, as a sacred right of the loving heart. Lucilla was seventeen years old when we were married. I loved her with all my heart and she gave me a return for my affections, with which I was contented."

Lunsford Lane tells of his marriage in slavery. "Perceiving that I was getting along so well, I began, slave as I was, to thing about taking a wife. So I fixed my mind upon Miss Lucy Williams, a slave of Thomas Devereau, Esq., an eminent lawyer in the place; but failed in my undertaking. Then I thought I never would marry; but at the end of two or three years my resolution began to slide away, till finding I could not keep it longer I set out once more in pursuit of a wife. So I fell in with her to whom I am now united, Miss Martha Curtis, and the bargain between us was completed. I next went to her master, Mr. Boylan, and asked him, according to custom, if I might 'marry this woman?' His reply, was 'Yes, if you will behave yourself?' I told him I would. 'And make her behave herself?' To this I also assented; and then proceeded to ask the approbation of my master, which was granted. So in May 1828, I was bound as fast in wedlock as a slave can be."

It has been shown above that the slave was compelled to obtain permission from his master in order to enter into marital relations with other slaves. The reality and influence of the family in the life of the slaves is evidenced by the fact that in the act of marrying the authority of the parents is also often recognized. . . .

In the case of the house servants especially there was some sort of ceremony connected with the marriage. One slave remembers attending a marriage in Richmond in the house of the master. Another ex-slave telling the story of her life, says her

> Mother was sixteen when she was married and her father eighteen, and both belonged to the same people. She said her father used to come up from the quarters to see her mother. They married in the white folks dining-room, and everything was fixed up lovely for them. . . .

A ceremony connected with the marriage of slaves which appears frequently in the documents is "jumping over the broom." The grandson of a slave whose family had acquired considerable stability which persisted into freedom describes his grandparents' marriage as follows:

> According to the customs of slavery Miles got the consent of Doctor Ridley to marry Charlotte. His acquiescence was equivalent to license and ceremony. True enough, such a union was not a creation of law, but it served its purpose in those days better than wedding-bells and statutory enactments do in most cases today. However, Miles believed in ceremony, so he and Charlotte "jumped" several times back and forth over a broom repeating, "I marry you." . . .

STABILITY OF FAMILY TIES

In this account of the slave family it may appear that slavery in its most favorable aspects has been portrayed, although data which we have used have been drawn from all of the slave states. The object has not been to show up slavery either favorably or unfavorably but to discover those beginnings of the Negro family under the institution of slavery which gave stability to the family and built up a tradition that was handed down. All slaves could not boast with Josiah Henson that "when I was about twenty-two years of age, I married a very efficient, and, for a slave, a very well-taught girl belonging to a neighboring family, reputed to be pious and kind, whom I first met at the chapel I attended; and during nearly forty years that have since elapsed, I have had no reason to regret the connection, but many, to rejoice in it, and be grateful for it. She has borne me twelve children, eight of whom survive, and promise to be the comfort of my declining years."

The marital tie to many slaves was no more than what is given expression to by the slave in the following incident.

> "For what service particular did you want to buy?" inquired the trader of my friend. "A coachman." "There is one I think may suit you, Sir," said he; "George step out here." Forthwith a light-coloured Negro, with a fine figure and good face, bating an enormous pair of lips, advanced a step from the line, and looked with some degree of intelligence, though with an air of indifference upon his intended purchaser. "How old are you, George?" he inquired. "I don't recollect, Sir 'xactly—b'lieve I'm somewhere 'bout twenty-dree." "Where were you raised?" "On master R____'s farm in Wirginny." "Then you are a Virginian Negro?" "Yes, massa, me full blood Wirginny." "Did you drive your master's carriage?" "Yes, massa I drove ole missus' carriage more dan four years." "Have you a wife?" "Yes, massa, I lef' young wife in Richmond, but I got a new wife here in de lot. I wish you buy her massa, if you gwing to buy me."

But there is no question that the present Negro family took root under the institution of slavery. Bishop Gaines writing of his family says "the colored people generally held their marriage (if such unauthorized union may be called marriage) sacred, even while they were yet slaves. Many instances will be recalled by the older people of the South of the life-long fidelity and affection which existed between the slave and his concubine—the mother of his children. My own father and mother lived together for over sixty years. I am the fourteenth child of that union, and I can truthfully affirm that no marriage, however made sacred by the sanction of law, was ever more congenial and beautiful. Thousands of like instances might be cited to the same effect."

That there developed within the circle of the slave family enduring sentiments that held the members of the family together is attested by numerous cases. Between children whose parents were dead or had been sold the natural bond of sympathy and affection appears in their devotion and sacrifices for their relatives. A slave says concerning his early life, "My brother Jeff was the only kin I had that I knew anything about while I was coming up." Jeff ran off to the Yankees when the war started. "Jeff was gone and I sometimes cried because he was my only brother and I felt lonesome all the time." Finally Jeff came back for his brother but after leading him within the Union lines lost him during an engagement.

Booker Washington recalls his brother's generosity in regard to a shirt. "In connection with the flax shirt," said he, "my brother John, who is several years older than I, performed one of the most generous acts that I ever heard of one slave relative doing for another. On several occasions when I was being forced to wear a new flax shirt, he generally agreed to put it on in my stead and wear it for several days, till it was "broken in." Until I had grown to be quite a youth this single garment was all that I wore."

Runaway slaves were tracked because of their known devotion to the members of their family. The following is quoted from Savannah, Georgia, July 8, 1837.

> Ran away from the subscriber, his man Joe. He visits the city occasionally, where he has been *harbored by his mother and sister.* I will give one hundred dollars for proof sufficient to *convict his harborers.*
>
> *R. P. T. Mongin*

The regard of wives and husbands for each other is apparent according to the following advertisement which appeared in the Richmond *Enquirer,* Feb. 20, 1838.

> $50 REWARD.—Ran away from the subscriber his Negro man Pauladore, commonly called Paul. I understand GEN. R. Y. HAYNE *has purchased his wife and children* from H. L. PINCKNEY, Esq., and has them now on his plantation at Goose-creek, where, no doubt, the fellow is frequently *lurking.*
>
> *T. Davis*

. . . In the following account of the refugees who followed the

Union armies we have in the midst of the disorder the devotion of a man and his wife to their children.

> The hardships they underwent to march with the army are fearful, and the children often gave out and were left by their mothers exhausted and dying by the roadside and in the fields. Some even put their children to death, they were such a drag upon them, till our soldiers, becoming furious at their barbarious cruelty, hung two women on the spot. In contrast to such selfishness, she told us of one woman who had twelve small children—she carried one and her husband another and for fear she should lose the others she tied them all together by the hands and brought them all off safely, a march of hundreds of miles. The men have all been put to work in the quartermaster's department or have gone into the army, and the families are being distributed where they can find places for them.

In the literature on the Negro family during slavery there is constant reference to the regular visits of the father or husband to his family when they resided on different plantations. Probably one evidence of the strength of the family was the fact that the threat to sell the children, or the mother or the father away from the family was always a potent form of control. One slave recalled that his mistress wanted him to get married in order that he might become reconciled to slavery. The strength of the affectional bond between the father and his wife and children is clearly illustrated in the case of Ball's father who lost his family.

> My father never recovered from the effects of the shock, which this sudden and overwhelming ruin of his family gave him. He had formerly been of a gay social temper, and when he came to see us on Saturday night, he always brought us some little present such as the means of a poor slave would allow—apples, melons, sweet potatoes, or, if he could procure nothing else, a little parched corn, which tasted better in our cabin, because he had brought it. He spent the greater part of the time, which his master permitted him to pass with us, in relating such stories as he had learned from his companions, or in singing the rude songs common amongst the slaves of Maryland and Virginia. After this time, I never heard him laugh heartily, or sing a song. He became gloomy and morose in his temper, to all but me; and spent nearly all his leisure time with my grandfather, who claimed kindred with some royal family in Africa, and had been a great warrior in his native country.

The character of the slave family was affected to a large extent by the different aspects of the slave system. Where the slave trade was in full force there was no regard for the personality of the slave and no one has appeared a more hated figure than the slave trader.

Negroes became mere utilities and all the ties that bind men to other human beings were ignored. Cases of the treatment of the family relations of the slaves where business transactions were involved have been given. Occasionally an account indicates the little regard that was shown for slaves who were rooted up and placed on the market. "When I joined the coffle," said Charles Ball, "there was in it a Negro woman named Critty, who has belonged to one Hugh Benford. She was married, in the way that slaves are, but as she had no children, she was compelled to take a second husband. Still she did not have an offspring. This displeased her master, who sold her to Finney. Her anguish was intense, and within about four days from the time I saw her first, she died of grief. It happened in the night, whilst we were encamped in the woods."

The same disregard for the family relations of the slaves, which has been noted in the case of the large plantation, is found on the frontier of the plantation system. Lyell observed during his second visit to the United States that "the condition of the Negroes is least enviable in such out-of-the-way and half-civilized districts, where there are many adventurers and uneducated settlers, who have little control over their passions, and who, when they oppress their slaves, are not checked by public opinion as in more advanced communities."

Labor demands on the larger plantations which showed no consideration for the personalities of the slaves often created an inequality between numbers of the two sexes that led to complete demoralization. Said one observer, "Those who cannot obtain women (for there is a great disproportion between the numbers of the two sexes) traverse the woods in search of adventures, and often encounter those of an unpleasant nature. They frequently meet a patrole of the whites, who tie them up and flog them, and then send them home."

In the case of those slaves on the plantation where a patriarchial relationship had grown up we often find a stable family life that compares favorably with the family life in peasant communities.

> It was a rare thing, indeed, for slave girls to reach majority before being married or becoming mothers. Be it said to the credit of Sarah O. Hilleary that she taught those girls the value of a good name, and personally watched over them so carefully that it was known far and near. She allowed them to be married in her dining-room instead of in the cabin, and with ceremony. She always had to see and pass upon the man who was to marry one of her maids.

She did all she could to impress them with the importance of being clean, honest, truthful, industrious, and religious.

So loving, kind, faithful and obedient was Emily that her mother really overtaxed her with the care of her younger brothers and sisters, whenever she was not waiting upon "Miss Sallie." So happy and content was Emily that she did not marry until she was 26 years old. . . .

CONCLUSION

The examination of printed documents as well as those collected from ex-slaves gives evidence of a wide range of differences in the status of the Negro family under the institution of slavery. These differences are related to the character of slavery as it developed as an industrial and social system. Where slavery assumed a patriarchal character the favored position of the house servants, many of whom were mulattoes, facilitated the process by which the family mores of the whites were taken over. Thus close association of master class and the slaves often entailed such moral instruction and supervision of the behavior of the slave children that they early acquired high standards of conduct which seemed natural to them. Sexual relations between the white masters and the slave women did not mean simply a demoralization of African sex mores but tended to produce a class of mulattoes, who acquired a conception of themselves that raised them above the black field hands. In many cases these mulattoes either through emancipation or the purchase of their freedom became a part of the free class where an institutional form of the Negro family first took root.

On the other hand, the sexual relations between the masters and the slave women tended to give the mother in the slave family even a more dominant rôle than was the case ordinarily where the paternity of the father and his place in the family circle received recognition. Even where the Negro father was recognized and played a conspicuous part with the family he often had the status of a mere visitor when he was on another plantation. When he was on the same plantation his authority was always limited, and in a crisis the mother stood out as the more secure symbol of parental authority and affection.

Of fundamental importance for the stabilization of the slave family and the development within the family circle of enduring sentiments was the social life of the slaves themselves. Within their relatively autonomous social world there were distinctions of status and social functions. They had their own religious and moral leaders and in some communities a public opinion was powerful enough to restrain unapproved conduct.

Where the plantation system was breaking down and Negro artisans achieved a semi-free status and acquired property the slave family tended to become stabilized. In such cases the slave family was held together by more than the affectional bonds that developed naturally among its members through the association in the same household and the affection of parents for their offspring. However, even under the most favorable conditions of slavery the exigencies of the slave system made the family insecure in spite of the internal character of the family. In the case of field hands who were cut off from contacts with the whites and those slaves who were carried along as mere utilities in the advance of the plantation system family relations became completely demoralized.

6

From Day Clean to First Dark

Kenneth Stampp

From: *The Peculiar Institution* (New York: Alfred A. Knopf, 1956), pp. 54–60, 73–85. Footnotes renumbered. Copyright © 1956 by Kenneth Stampp. Reprinted by permission of Alfred A. Knopf, Inc.

Most slaveholders, themselves a minority in the South, held only a few slaves; yet three-quarters of the slaves belonged to those masters owning more than ten slaves. The majority of blacks lived on plantations containing more than twenty slaves, so that the slave experience was most likely to be on the plantation. Most of these slaves lived on cotton plantations, but those working on sugar, tobacco, rice, and hemp plantations shared a similar life style.

Plantation work is described by Kenneth Stampp in the following essay. He concludes that the tasks of the slaves were hard, with the working day beginning before sunrise and lasting until dark. As slavery was primarily a labor system, the planters and overseers attempted to extract as much labor as possible from their slaves. This meant that women and children were expected to carry their weight and even old and partially disabled slaves contributed what they could.

All told, the work day and the general life of the slave were under the tight control of the individual planter. Some of these, the so-called good masters, tried to treat their slaves well; but the decision to do so was based on personal and economic considerations, not the law. The slave codes offered few enforceable pro-

103

tections for the slave. The slave was primarily a work animal and his life was circumscribed by the zeal of the master to squeeze a profit out of him.

For the owner of a few slaves, labor management was a problem of direct personal relationships between individuals. For the owner of many, the problem was more difficult and required greater ingenuity. Both classes of masters desired a steady and efficient performance of the work assigned each day. They could not expect much cooperation from their slaves, who had little reason to care how much was produced. Masters measured the success of their methods by the extent to which their interest in a maximum of work of good quality prevailed over the slaves' predilection for a minimum of work of indifferent quality. Often neither side won a clear victory.

Slaveowners developed numerous variations of two basic methods of managing their laborers: the "gang system" and the "task system." Under the first of these systems, which was the one most commonly used, the field-hands were divided into gangs commanded by drivers who were to work them at a brisk pace. Competent masters gave some thought to the capacities of individual slaves and to the amout of labor that a gang could reasonably be expected to perform in one day. But the purpose of the gang system was to force every hand to continue his labor until all were discharged from the field in the evening.

Under the task system, each hand was given a specific daily work assignment. He could then set his own pace and quit when his task was completed. The driver's job was to inspect the work and to see that it was performed satisfactorily before the slave left the field. "The advantages of this system," according to a Georgia rice planter, "are encouragement to the laborers, by equalizing the work of each agreeable to strength, and the avoidance of watchful superintendence and incessant driving. As . . . the task of each [slave] is separate, imperfect work can readily be traced to the neglectful worker."[1]

The task system was best adapted to the rice plantation, with its fields divided into small segments by the network of drainage ditches. Outside the Low Country of South Carolina and Georgia planters occasionally used this system or at least experimented with it, but many of them found it to be unsatisfactory. For one thing, they could get no more work out of their stronger slaves than out

[1] *Southern Agriculturist,* VI (1833), p. 576.

of their weaker ones, since the tasks were usually standardized. The planters also found that the eagerness of slaves to finish their tasks as early as possible led to careless work. After using the task system for twenty years, an Alabama planter abandoned it because of evils "too numerous to mention." A South Carolina cotton planter, who also gave it up, noted with satisfaction that under the gang system his slaves did "much more" and were "not so apt to strain themselves."[2]

Actually, most planters used a combination of the two systems. Cotton planters often worked plow-hands in gangs but gave hoe-hands specific tasks of a certain number of cotton rows to hoe each day. Each hand was expected to pick as much cotton as he could, but he might be given a minimum quota that had to be met. Sugar, rice, and tobacco planters applied the task system to their coopers, and hemp growers used it with hands engaged in breaking or hackling hemp. Masters generally tasked their hands for digging ditches, cutting wood, or mauling rails.

Thus most slaves probably had some experience with both systems. From their point of view each system doubtless had its advantages and drawbacks. A strong hand might have preferred to be tasked if he was given an opportunity to finish early. But many slaves must have been appalled at the ease with which they could be held responsible for the quality of their work. The gang system had the disadvantages of severe regimentation and of hard driving which was especially onerous for the weaker hands. But there was less chance that a slave would be detected and held individually responsible for indifferent work. In the long run, however, the rigors of either system were determined by the demands of masters and overseers.

The number of acres a slaveholder expected each of his field-hands to cultivate depended in part upon how hard he wished to work them. It also depended upon the nature of the soil, the quality of the tools, and the general efficiency of the agricultural enterprise. Finally, it depended upon the crop. Cotton growers on flat prairies and river bottoms planted as many as ten acres per hand but rarely more than that. Those on hilly or rolling lands planted from three to eight acres per hand. Since a slave could ordinarily cultivate more cotton than he could pick, acreage was limited by the size of the available picking force. By the 1850s each hand was expected to work from nine to ten acres of sugar but seldom more than five

---

[2] James B. Sellers, *Slavery in Alabama* (University, Ala.) 1950), p. 67; Hammond Diary, entry for May 16, 1838.

acres of rice or three of tobacco, plus six or more of corn and other food crops.[3] The yield per acre and per hand varied with the fertility of the soil, the care in cultivation, the damage of insects, and the whims of the weather.

When calculating his yield per field-hand a slaveholder was not calculating his yield per slave, for he almost always owned fewer field-hands than slaves. Some of his slaves performed other types of work, and the very young and the very old could not be used in the fields. The master's diseased, convalescing, and partially disabled slaves, his "breeding women" and "sucklers," his children just beginning to work in the fields, and his slaves of advanced years were incapable of laboring as long and as hard as fulltime hands.

Most masters had systems of rating such slaves as fractional hands. Children often began as "quarter hands" and advanced to "half hands," "three-quarter hands," and then "full hands." As mature slaves grew older they started down this scale. "Breeding women" and "sucklers" were rated as "half hands." Some planters organized these slaves into separate gangs, for example, into a "sucklers gang." Children sometimes received their training in a "trash gang," or "children's squad," which pulled weeds, cleaned the yard, hoed, wormed tobacco, or picked cotton. Seldom were many more than half of a master's slaves listed in his records as field-hands, and always some of the hands were classified as fractional. Olmsted described a typical situation on a Mississippi cotton plantation: "There were 135 slaves, big and little, of which 67 went to the field regularly—equal, the overseer thought, to 60 able-bodied hands."[4]

The master, not the parents, decided at what age slave children should be put to work in the fields. Until they were five or six years old children were "useless articles on a plantation." Then many received "their first lessons in the elementary part of their education" through serving as "water-toters" or going into the

[3] These are generalized figures from a survey of many plantation records. See also *De Bow's Review,* II (1846), pp. 134, 138; X (1851), p. 625; Charles S. Sydnor *Slavery in Mississippi* (New York, 1933), pp. 13–14; Lewis C. Gray, *History of Agriculture in the Southern United States to 1860* (Washington, D.C., 1933), II, pp. 707–708; J. Carlyle Sitterson, *Sugar Country: The Cane Sugar Industry in the South, 1753–1950* (Lexington, Kentucky, 1953), pp. 127–128; Joseph Clarke Robert, *The Tobacco Kingdom* (Durham, N.C., 1938), p. 18.

[4] Frederick Law Olmsted, *A Journey in the Back Country* (New York, 1860), p. 47; Olmsted, *A Journey in the Seaboard Slave States* (New York, 1856), p. 433; *Southern Agriculturist,* VI (1833), pp. 571–573; Sydnor, *Slavery in Mississippi,* pp. 18–20; Sellers, *Slavery in Alabama,* p. 66.

fields alongside their mothers.[5] Between the ages of ten and twelve the children became fractional hands, with a regular routine of field labor. By the time they were eighteen they had reached the age when they could be classified as "prime field-hands."

Mature slaves who did not work in the fields (unless they were totally disabled or extremely old) performed other kinds of valuable and productive labor. Old women cooked for the rest of the slaves, cared for small children, fed the poultry, mended and washed clothes, and nursed the sick. Old men gardened, minded stock, and cleaned the stable and the yard.

Old or partially disabled slaves might also be put to spinning and weaving in the loom houses of the more efficient planters. The printed instructions in a popular plantation record book advised overseers to adopt this policy: "Few instances of good management will better please an employer, than that of having all the winter clothing spun and woven on the place. By having a room devoted to that purpose . . . where those who may be complaining a little, or convalescent after sickness, may be employed in some light work, and where all of the women may be sent in wet weather, more than enough of both cotton and woolen yarn can be spun for the supply of the place."[6] One planter reported that he had his spinning jenny "going at a round rate[.] Old Charles [is] Spinning and Esther reeling the thread. . . . Charles will in this way be one of my most productive laborers and so will several of the women[.]"[7] Thus a master's productive slaves were by no means limited to those listed as field-hands.

The bondsmen who were valued most highly were those who had acquired special skills which usually exempted them from field work entirely. This select group of slave craftsmen included engineers, coopers, carpenters, blacksmiths, brickmakers, stone masons, mechanics, shoemakers, weavers, millers, and landscapers. The excellence of the work performed by some of them caused slaveowners to make invidious comparisons between them and the free artisans they sometimes employed. An Englishman recalled an interview with the overseer on a Louisiana sugar plantation: "It

[5] [Joseph H. Ingraham], *The South-West. By a Yankee* (New York, 1835), II, p. 126; Charles S. Davis, *The Cotton Kingdom in Alabama* (Montgomery, 1939), p. 58.

[6] Thomas Affleck, *The Cotton Plantation Record and Account Book* (Louisville and New Orleans, 1847—).

[7] Gustavus A. Henry to his wife, December 3, 1846, Gustavus A. Henry Papers; Herbert A. Kellar (ed.), *Solon Robinson, Pioneer and Agriculturist* (Indianapolis, 1936), II, p. 203.

would have been amusing, had not the subject been so grave, to hear the overseer's praises of the intelligence and skill of these workmen, and his boast that they did all the work of skilled laborers on the estate, and then to listen to him, in a few minutes, expatiating on the utter helplessness and ignorance of the black race, their incapacity to do any good, or even to take care of themselves."[8]

Domestic servants were prized almost as much as craftsmen. The number and variety of domestics in a household depended upon the size of the establishment and the wealth of the master. They served as hostlers, coachmen, laundresses, seamstresses, cooks, footmen, butlers, housemaids, chambermaids, children's nurses, and personal servants. On a large plantation specialization was complete: "The cook never enters the house, and the nurse is never seen in the kitchen; the wash-woman is never put to ironing, nor the woman who has charge of the ironing-room ever put to washing. Each one rules supreme in her wash-house, her ironing-room, her kitchen, her nursery, her house-keeper's room; and thus . . . a complete system of domesticdom is established to the amazing comfort and luxury of all who enjoy its advantages."[9]

But the field-hands remained fundamental in the slave economy. Though their work was classified as unskilled labor, this of course was a relative term. Some visitors described the "rude" or "slovenly" manner in which slaves cultivated the crops, how "awkwardly, slowly, and undecidedly" they moved through the fields.[10] But other observers were impressed with the success of many masters in training field-hands to be efficient workers, impressed also by the skill these workers showed in certain crucial operations in the production of staple crops. Inexperienced hands had their troubles in sugar houses and rice fields, in breaking and hackling hemp, and in topping, suckering, sorting, and prizing tobacco. Even the neophyte cotton picker soon wondered whether this was unskilled labor, as one former slave testified: "While others used both hands, snatching the cotton and depositing it in the mouth of the sack, with a precision and dexterity that was incomprehensible to me, I had to seize the boll with one hand, and deliberately draw out the white, gushing blossom with the other." On his first day he managed to gather "not half the quantity required of the poorest picker."[11]

Field workers kept up a ceaseless struggle to make the lands

[8] William H. Russell, *My Diary North and South* (Boston, 1863), p. 273.

[9] Ingraham (ed.), *Sunny South,* pp. 179–181.

[10] Henry Watson, Jr., to Theodore Watson, March 3, 1831, Watson Papers; Olmsted, *Seaboard,* pp. 18–19.

[11] Solomon Northup, *Twelve Years a Slave* (Buffalo, 1853), pp. 178–179.

fruitful, against the contrary efforts of the insects and the elements. The battle seemed at times to be of absorbing interest to some of the slaves, conscripts though they were. In a strange and uneasy kind of alliance, they and their masters combatted the foes that could have destroyed them both.

. . . Mammy Harriet had nostalgic memories of slavery days: "Oh, no, we was nebber hurried. Marster nebber once said, 'Get up an' go to work,' an' no obserseer ebber said it, neither. Ef some on 'em did not git up when de odders went out to work, marster nebber said a word. Oh, no, we was nebber hurried."[12] Mammy Harriet had been a domestic at "Burleigh," the Hinds County, Mississippi, estate of Thomas S. Dabney. She related her story of slave life there to one of Dabney's daughters who wrote a loving volume about her father and his cotton plantation.

Another slave found life less leisurely on a plantation on the Red River in Louisiana: "The hands are required to be in the cotton field as soon as it is light in the morning, and, with the exception of ten or fifteen minutes, which is given them at noon to swallow their allowance of cold bacon, they are not permitted to be a moment idle until it is too dark to see, and when the moon is full, they often times labor till the middle of the night." Work did not end when the slaves left the fields. "Each one must attend to his respective chores. One feeds the mules, another the swine—another cuts the wood, and so forth; besides the packing [of cotton] is all done by candle light. Finally, at a late hour, they reach the quarters, sleepy and overcome with the long day's toil."[13] These were the bitter memories of Solomon Northup, a free Negro who had been kidnapped and held in bondage for twelve years. Northup described his experiences to a Northerner who helped him prepare his autobiography for publication.

Mammy Harriet's and Solomon Northup's disparate accounts of the work regimen imposed upon slaves suggest the difficulty of determining the truth from witnesses, Negro and white, whose candor was rarely uncompromised by internal emotions or external pressures. Did Dabney's allegedly unhurried field-hands (who somehow produced much cotton and one of whom once tried to kill the overseer) feel the same nostalgia for slavery days? How much was Northup's book influenced by his amanuensis and by the preconceptions of his potential northern readers?

And yet there is nothing in the narratives of either of these

[12] Susan Dabney Smedes, *Memorials of a Southern Planter* (Baltimore, 1887), p. 57.

[13] Northup, *Twelve Years a Slave,* pp. 166–168.

ex-slaves that renders them entirely implausible. The question of their complete accuracy is perhaps less important than the fact that both conditions actually did exist in the South. Distortion results from exaggerating the frequency of either condition or from dwelling upon one and ignoring the other.

No sweeping generalization about the amount of labor extracted from bondsmen could possibly be valid, even when they are classified by regions, or by occupations, or by the size of the holdings upon which they lived. For the personal factor transcended everything else. How hard the slaves were worked depended upon the demands of individual masters and their ability to enforce them. These demands were always more or less tempered by the inclination of most slaves to minimize their unpaid toil. Here was a clash of interests in which the master usually, but not always, enjoyed the advantage of superior weapons.

Not only must glib generalizations be avoided but a standard must be fixed by which the slave's burden of labor can be judged. Surely a slave was overworked when his toil impaired his health or endangered his life. Short of this extreme there are several useful standards upon which judgments can be based. If, for example, the quantity of labor were compared with the compensation the inevitable conclusion would be that most slaves were overworked. Also by present-day labor standards the demands generally made upon them were excessive. These, of course, were not the standards of the nineteenth century.

Another standard of comparison—though not an altogether satisfactory one—is the amount of work performed by contemporary free laborers in similar occupations. Independent farmers and artisans set their own pace and planned their work to fit their own convenience and interests, but they nevertheless often worked from dawn to dusk. Northern factory workers commonly labored twelve hours a day. This was arduous toil even for free laborers who enjoyed the advantages of greater incentives and compensation. Yet contemporaries did not think that slaves were overworked when their masters respected the normal standards of their day. Some slaveowners did respect them, and some did not.

Unquestionably there were slaves who escaped doing what was then regarded as a "good day's work," and there were masters who never demanded it of them. The aphorism that it took two slaves to help one to do nothing was not without its illustrations. After lands and slaves had remained in the hands of a single family for several generations, planters sometimes developed a patriarchal attitude toward their "people" and took pride in treating them indulgently. Such masters had lost the competitive spirit and the urge to increase their worldly possessions which had characterized their ancestors. To live gracefully on their declining estates, to smile tolerantly at the listless labor of their field-hands, and to be surrounded by a horde of pampered domestics were all parts of their code.

In Virginia, the easygoing manner of the patricians was proverbial. But Virginia had no monopoly of them; they were scattered throughout the South. Olmsted visited a South Carolina rice plantation where the tasks were light enough to enable reasonably industrious hands to leave the fields early in the afternoon. Slaves on several sea-island cotton plantations much of the time did not labor more than five or six hours a day. [14]

The production records of some of the small slaveholding farmers indicated that neither they nor their slaves exerted themselves unduly. These masters, especially when they lived in isolated areas, seemed content to produce little more than a bare subsistence. In addition, part of the town slaves who hired their own time took advantage of the opportunity to enjoy a maximum of leisure. The domestics of some wealthy urban families willingly helped to maintain the tradition that masters with social standing did not examine too closely into the quantity or efficiency of their work.

From these models proslavery writers drew their sentimental pictures of slave life. The specific cases they cited were often valid ones; their profound error was in generalizing from them. For this leisurely life was the experience of only a small fraction of the bondsmen. Whether they lived in the Upper South or Deep South, in rural or urban communities, on plantations or farms, the labor of the vast majority of slaves ranged from what was normally expected of free labor in that period to levels that were clearly excessive.

It would not be too much to say that masters usually demanded from their slaves a long day of hard work and managed by some means or other to get it. The evidence does not sustain the belief that free laborers generally worked longer hours and at a brisker pace than the unfree. During the months when crops were being cultivated or harvested the slaves commonly were in the fields fifteen or sixteen hours a day, including time allowed for meals and rest. [15] By antebellum standards this may not have been excessive, but it

[14] Olmsted, *Seaboard*, pp. 434–436; Guion G. Johnson, *A Social History of the Sea Islands* (Chapel Hill, 1930), pp. 124–125; E. Merton Coulter, *Thomas Spalding of Sapelo* (Baton Rouge, 1940), p. 85.

[15] Gray, *History of Agriculture*, I, pp. 556–557.

was not a light work routine by the standards of that or any other day.

In instructions to overseers, planters almost always cautioned against overwork, yet insisted that the hands be made to labor vigorously as many hours as there was daylight. Overseers who could not accomplish this were discharged. An Arkansas master described a work day that was in no sense unusual on the plantations of the Deep South: "We get up before day every morning and eat breakfast before day and have everybody at work before day dawns. I am never caught in bed after day light nor is any body else on the place, and we continue in the cotton fields when we can have fair weather till it is so dark we cant see to work, and this history of one day is the history of every day."[16]

Planters who contributed articles on the management of slaves to southern periodicals took this routine for granted. "It is expected," one of them wrote, "that servants should rise early enough to be at work by the time it is light. . . . While at work, they should be brisk. . . . I have no objection to their whistling or singing some lively tune, but no *drawling* tunes are allowed in the field, for their motions are almost certain to keep time with the music."[17] These planters had the businessman's interest in maximum production without injury to their capital.

The work schedule was not strikingly different on the plantations of the Upper South. Here too it was a common practice to regulate the hours of labor in accordance with the amount of daylight. A former slave on a Missouri tobacco and hemp plantation recalled that the field-hands began their work at half past four in the morning. Such rules were far more common on Virginia plantations than were the customs of languid patricians. An ex-slave in Hanover County, Virginia, remembered seeing slave women hurrying to their work in the early morning "with their shoes and stockings in their hands, and a petticoat wrapped over their shoulders, to dress in the field the best way they could."[18] The bulk of the Virginia planters were businessmen too.

Planters who were concerned about the physical condition of their slaves permitted them to rest at noon after eating their dinners in the fields. "In the Winter," advised one expert on slave manage-

[16] Gustavus A. Henry to his wife, November 27, 1860, Henry Papers.

[17] *Southern Cultivator*, VIII (1850), p. 163.

[18] William W. Brown, *Narrative of William W. Brown, a Fugitive Slave* (Boston, 1847), p. 14; Olmsted, *Seaboard*, p. 109; De Bow's Review, XIV (1853), pp. 176–178; Benjamin Drew, *The Refugee: or the Narratives of Fugitive Slaves in Canada* (Boston, 1856), p. 162.

ment, "a hand may be pressed all day, but not so in Summer. . . . In May, from one and a half to two hours; in June, two and a half; in July and August, three hours rest [should be given] at noon."[19] Except for certain essential chores, Sunday work was uncommon but not unheard of if the crops required it. On Saturdays slaves were often permitted to quit the fields at noon. They were also given holidays, most commonly at Christmas and after the crops were laid by.

But a holiday was not always a time for rest and relaxation. Many planters encouraged their bondsmen to cultivate small crops during their "leisure" to provide some of their own food. Thus a North Carolina planter instructed his overseer: "As soon as you have laid by the crop give the people 2 days but . . . they must work their own crops." Another planter gave his slaves a "holiday to plant their potatoes," and another "holiday to get in their potatoes." James H. Hammond once wrote in disgust: "Holiday for the negroes who fenced in their gardens. Lazy devils they did nothing after 12 o'clock." In addition, slave women had to devote part of their time when they were not in the fields to washing clothes, cooking, and cleaning their cabins. An Alabama planter wrote: "I always give them half of each Saturday, and often the whole day, at which time . . . the women do their household work; therefore they are never idle."[20]

Planters avoided night work as much as they felt they could, but slaves rarely escaped it entirely. Night work was almost universal on sugar plantations during the grinding season, and on cotton plantations when the crop was being picked, ginned, and packed. A Mississippi planter did not hesitate to keep his hands hauling fodder until ten o'clock at night when the hours of daylight were not sufficient for his work schedule.[21]

Occasionally a planter hired free laborers for such heavy work as ditching in order to protect his slave property. But, contrary to the legend, this was not a common practice. Most planters used their own field-hands for ditching and for clearing new ground. Moreover, they often assigned slave women to this type of labor as well as to plowing. On one plantation Olmsted saw twenty women operating heavy plows with double teams: "They were superintended by a male negro driver, who carried a whip, which he

[19] *Southern Cultivator*, VIII (1850), p. 163.
[20] Henry K. Burgwyn to Arthur Souter, August 6, 1843, Henry King Burgwyn Papers; John C. Jenkins Diary, entries for November 15, 1845; April 22, 1854; Hammond Diary, entry for May 12, 1832; *De Bow's Review*, XIII (1852), pp. 193–194.
[21] Jenkins Diary, entry for August 7, 1843.

frequently cracked at them, permitting no dawdling or delay at the turning."[22]

Among the smaller planters and slaveholding farmers there was generally no appreciable relaxation of this normal labor routine. Their production records, their diaries and farm journals, and the testimony of their slaves all suggest the same dawn-to-dusk regimen that prevailed on the large plantations.[23] This was also the experience of most slaves engaged in nonagricultural occupations. Everywhere, then, masters normally expected from their slaves, in accordance with the standards of their time, a full stint of labor from "day clean" to "first dark."

Some, however, demanded more than this. Continuously, or at least for long intervals, they drove their slaves at a pace that was bound, sooner or later, to injure their health. Such hard driving seldom occurred on the smaller plantations and farms or in urban centers; it was decidedly a phenomenon of the large plantations. Though the majority of planters did not sanction it, more of them tolerated excessively heavy labor routines than is generally realized. The records of the plantation regime clearly indicate that slaves were more frequently overworked by calloused tyrants than overindulged by mellowed patriarchs.

That a large number of southern bondsmen were worked severely during the colonial period is beyond dispute. The South Carolina code of 1740 charged that "many owners . . . do confine them so closely to hard labor, that they have not sufficient time for natural rest."[24] In the nineteenth century conditions seemed to have improved, especially in the older regions of the South. Unquestionably the antebellum planter who coveted a high rank in society responded to subtle pressures that others did not feel. The closing of the African slave trade and the steady rise of slave prices were additional restraining influences. "The time has been," wrote a planter in 1849, "that the farmer could kill up and wear out one Negro to buy another; but it is not so now. Negroes are too high in proportion to the price of cotton, and it behooves those who own them to make them last as long as possible."[25]

[22] Olmsted, *Back Country*, p. 81; Sydnor, *Slavery in Mississippi*, p. 12.

[23] See, for example, Marston Papers; Torbert Plantation Diary; *De Bow's Review*, XI (1851), pp. 369–372; Drew, *Refugee;* Frederick Douglass, *My Bondage and My Freedom* (New York, 1855), p. 215; Harrison A. Trexler, *Slavery in Missouri, 1804–1865* (Baltimore, Md., 1914), pp. 97–98.

[24] John C. Hurd, *The Law of Freedom and Bondage in the United States* (Boston, 1858–1862), I, p. 307; Ralph B. Flanders, *Plantation Slavery in Georgia* (Chapel Hill, N.C., 1933), p. 42.

[25] *Southern Cultivator*, VII (1849), p. 69.

But neither public opinion nor high prices prevented some of the bondsmen from suffering physical breakdowns and early deaths because of overwork. The abolitionists never proved their claim that many sugar and cotton growers deliberately worked their slaves to death every seven years with the intention of replacing them from profits. Yet some of the great planters came close to accomplishing that result without designing it. In the "race for wealth" in which, according to one Louisiana planter, all were enlisted, few proprietors managed their estates according to the code of the patricians.[26] They were sometimes remarkably shortsighted in the use of their investments.

Irresponsible overseers, who had no permanent interest in slave property, were frequently blamed for the overworking of slaves. Since this was a common complaint, it is important to remember that nearly half of the slaves lived on plantations of the size that ordinarily employed overseers. But planters could not escape responsibility for these conditions simply because their written instructions usually prohibited excessive driving. For they often demanded crop yields that could be achieved by no other method.

Most overseers believed (with good reason) that their success was measured by how much they produced, and that merely having the slave force in good condition at the end of the year would not guarantee re-employment. A Mississippi overseer with sixteen years of experience confirmed this belief in defending his profession: "When I came to Mississippi, I found that the overseer who could have the most cotton bales ready for market by Christmas, was considered best qualified for the business—consequently, every overseer gave his whole attention to cotton bales, to the exclusion of everything else."[27]

More than a few planters agreed that this was true. A committee of an Alabama agricultural society reported: "It is too commonly the case that masters look only to the yearly products of their farms, and praise or condemn their overseers by this standard alone, without ever once troubling themselves to inquire into the manner in which things are managed on their plantations, and whether he may have lost more in the diminished value of his slaves by over-work than he has gained by his large crop." This being the case, it was understandably of no consequence to the overseer that the old hands were "worked down" and the young

[26] Kenneth M. Clark to Lewis Thompson, December 29, 1859, Thompson Papers.

[27] *American Cotton Planter and Soil of the South*, II (1858), pp. 112–113.

ones "overstrained," that the "breeding women" miscarried, and that the "sucklers" lost their children. "So that he has the requisite number of cotton bags, all is overlooked; he is re-employed at an advanced salary, and his reputation increased."[28]

Some planters, unintentionally perhaps, gave overseers a special incentive for overworking slaves by making their compensation depend in part upon the amount they produced. Though this practice was repeatedly denounced in the antebellum period, many masters continued to follow it nevertheless. Cotton growers offered overseers bonuses of from one to five dollars for each bale above a specified minimum, or a higher salary if they produced a fixed quota. A Louisiana planter hired an overseer on a straight commission basis of $2.75 per bale of cotton and four cents per bushel of corn. A South Carolina rice planter gave his overseer ten percent of the net proceeds. And a Virginian offered his overseer "the seventh part of the good grain, tobacco, cotton, and flax" that was harvested on his estate. "Soon as I hear [of] such a bargain," wrote a southern critic, "I fancy that the overseer, determined to save his salary, adopts the song of 'drive, drive, drive.' "[29]

Masters who hired their slaves to others also helped to create conditions favoring ruthless exploitation. The overworking of hired slaves by employers with only a temporary interest in their welfare was as notorious as the harsh practices of overseers. Slaves hired to mine owners or railroad contractors were fortunate if they were not driven to the point where their health was impaired. The same danger confronted slaves hired to sugar planters during the grinding season or to cotton planters at picking time. Few Southerners familiar with these conditions would have challenged the assertion made before a South Carolina court that hired slaves were "commonly treated more harshly . . . than those in possession of their owner[s]."[30]

But the master was as responsible for the conduct of those who hired his slaves as he was for the conduct of the overseers he employed. Overworked slaves were not always the innocent victims of forces beyond his control; there were remedies which he sometimes failed to apply. A staunch defender of slavery described a set of avaricious planters whom he labeled "Cotton Snobs," or "Southern Yankees." In their frantic quest for wealth, he wrote indignantly, the crack of the whip was heard early and late, until their bondsmen

[28] *American Farmer*, II (1846), p. 78; *Southern Cultivator*, II (1844), pp. 97, 107.

[29] *North Carolina Farmer*, I (1845), pp. 122–123. Agreements of this kind with overseers are in the records of numerous planters.

[30] Helen T. Catterall, *Judicial Cases Concerning American Slavery and the Negro* (Washington, D.C., 1926–1937), II, p. 374.

were "bowed to the ground with over-tasking and over-toil."[31] A southern physician who practiced on many cotton plantations complained, in 1847, that some masters still regarded "their sole interest to consist in large crops, leaving out of view altogether the value of negro property and its possible deterioration." During the economic depression of the 1840s, a planter accused certain cotton growers of trying to save themselves by increasing their cotton acreage and by driving their slaves harder, with the result that slaves broke down from overwork. An Alabama newspaper attributed conditions such as these to "avarice, the desire of growing rich."[32]

On the sugar plantations, during the months of the harvest, slaves were driven to the point of complete exhaustion. They were, in the normal routine, worked from sixteen to eighteen hours a day, seven days a week.[33] Cotton planters who boasted about making ten bales per hand were unconsciously testifying that their slaves were overworked. An overseer on an Arkansas plantation set his goal at twelve bales to the hand and indicated that this was what his employer desired. On a North Carolina plantation a temporary overseer assured the owner that he was a "hole hog man rain or shine" and boasted that the slaves had not been working like men but "like horses." "I'd ruther be dead than be a nigger on one of these big plantations," a white Mississippian told Olmsted.[34]

Sooner or later excessive labor was bound to take its toll. In the heat of mid-summer, slaves who could not bear hard driving without sufficient rest at noon simply collapsed in the fields. In Mississippi a planter reported "numerous cases" of sunstroke in his neighborhood during a spell of extreme heat. His own slaves "gave out." On a Florida plantation a number of hands "fainted in the field" one hot August day. Even in Virginia hot weather and heavy labor caused "the death of many negroes in the harvest field."[35]

[31] Daniel R. Hundley, *Social Relations in Our Southern States* (New York, 1860), pp. 132, 187–188.

[32] *De Bow's Review*, I (1846), pp. 434–436; III (1847), p. 419; Selma *Free Press*, quoted in Tuscaloosa *Independent Monitor*, July 14, 1846.

[33] This is apparent from the records of sugar planters. See also Sitterson, *Sugar Country*, pp. 133–136; Olmsted, *Seaboard*, pp. 650, 667–668.

[34] P. Weeks to James Sheppard, September 20, 1854, James Sheppard Papers; Doctrine Davenport to Ebenezer Pettigrew, April 24, 1836, Pettigrew Family Papers; Olmsted, *Back Country*, pp. 55–57, 202.

[35] Jenkins Diary, entries for August 9, 1844; July 7, 1846; June 30, 1854; Ulrich B. Phillips and James D. Glunt (eds.), *Florida Plantation Records from the Papers of George Noble Jones* (St. Louis, 1927), p. 90; John B. Garrett Ms. Farm Journal, entry for July 19, 1830.

Working on a cotton plantation.
Source: Library of Congress.

Slaves cultivating sugar cane in Louisiana.
Source: Library of Congress

Slaves working in the fields. Slaves grew food as well as commercial staples.
Source: New York Historical Society (Reproduced on the cover.)

Slaves transporting cotton in North Carolina.
Source: New York Public Library

7

Simon Gray, Riverman
A Slave Who Was
Almost Free

John Hebron Moore

From: *Mississippi Valley Historical Review*, XLIX (December 1962), pp. 472–484. Footnotes deleted. Reprinted by permission.

Most slaves were engaged in work directly connected with agriculture. Roughly one-eighth were engaged in other activities. These slaves sometimes had skills they used on the plantations or were domestic servants. A considerable number, however, were not tied to the plantation. Instead, they worked in the cities, in the factories, on riverboats, in the mines, on construction gangs, and in a variety of other nonagricultural jobs. Beginning in the colonial period, for example, the southern iron industry used skilled and unskilled slave labor extensively. Prior to the 1840s the famous Tredegar Iron Works of Richmond, unlike most other iron works, had not used slaves. But in that decade slaves were hired, and from then until the abolition of slavery, the works depended upon slave labor.

It was in the cities that slaves obtained the greatest latitude under the system, especially the practice of hiring-out. Masters sometimes permitted their slaves to make their own hiring arrangements in return for part of the slave's wages. These slaves even found their own living accommodations and were often able to develop a secure family life. The line between the slave and the free black became blurred in the cities. Not that this represented enormous gains, for free blacks were despised and subjected to harsh laws which sometimes provided punishments usually limited to slaves. Still, the urban slaves were probably better off than those on the plantations. The case of Simon Gray, discussed in this selection is an exceptional example of the amount of latitude possible under slavery away from the plantation. Although a slave, Simon Gray was paid wages, was literate, made business trips for his employer, and was able to live apart from the other slaves.

Such unusual slaves were obviously a threat to the very nature of a slave society; a multitude of Simon Grays pointed in the direction of freedom. Accordingly, southern cities and states responded with restrictions aimed at preventing these loose arrangements and discouraging the development of urban and industrial slavery. There was work for the urban slaves to perform, but the white South was concerned about controlling them in the urban milieu once the day's tasks were done. The hiring-out system was apparently profitable, as were some types of industrial slavery, for they continued in spite of the regulations, as the case of Simon Gray shows.

In the lower Mississippi Valley numerous slaves were employed by the cypress lumber industry during the ante-bellum period. They worked in the sawmills, participated in logging operations, and served as crewmen on log rafts and lumber flatboats. While engaged in these various activities, Negroes often labored beside white employees of the lumber companies, performing the same duties as the whites. Furthermore, the character of the lumber industry prevented these slaves from being supervised as closely as field hands on cotton plantations, and many of them spent much of their time out from under the eyes of their employers. Under such conditions lumbermen tended to allow wide latitude to skilled slaves who had proved themselves trustworthy. This trend was especially apparent in the transportation phases of the business. By 1850 Negro slaves could be found on the Mississippi River and its tributaries in sole charge of rafts and flatboats. Slaves in such positions of authority could scarcely be distinguished in their daily lives from free men.

Simon Gray of Natchez was an outstanding example of the cypress lumber industry's quasi-free Negroes. This slave belonged to Andrew Donnan, a merchant and blacksmith, who hired him out to Andrew Brown, the senior partner of the firm of Andrew Brown and Company. Gray's name first appeared in the records of the company in 1835. At this time he was merely one of several slaves employed by Brown in his construction and sawmilling enterprises. He did not remain in the common labor category for long, however, for by 1838 he was directing a rafting crew engaged in bringing logs down from the Yazoo River basin to the Brown sawmill at Natchez. As head of a crew Gray was equipped with a pass signed by Brown which authorized him to travel free from interference by the legal authorities anywhere he wished on the "Yazoo or any other river, under good conduct." Brown at this time was also intrusting him with small sums of money for expenses for his crew, and was even permitting him to purchase timber from Yazoo River logmen for use of the mill. When Gray demonstrated his reliability and good judgment in these minor transactions, Brown allowed him to handle cash in large amounts. In one typical instance, the slave was given $800 to deliver to one of Brown's creditors, a task he carried out in routine fashion.

During 1844 the Brown lumber company enlarged the scope of its operations, and the resulting reorganization brought increased responsibility to Simon Gray. In that year, Andrew Brown, Jr., moved from Natchez to New Orleans, and there established a wholesale and retail outlet for the lumber his father was manufacturing at Natchez. Before making this move, young Brown, the sales manager of the company, had been disposing of the cypress lumber which the Natchez market could not absorb by peddling it from flatboats at towns and plantations between Natchez and New Orleans. Gray, when not rafting logs to the mill, had often accompanied Andrew Brown, Jr., on some of these "coasting" trips as his assistant. In this way, the slave learned both the art of flatboating and the business of retailing lumber. In due course he became quite proficient in these dual aspects of marketing cypress lumber. Consequently, when Andrew Brown, Jr., found that he must devote his full time to the New Orleans branch of the firm, he recommended to his father that Gray be allowed to handle the job of transporting the lumber to market. Andrew Brown soon afterward promoted the hired slave to the rank of flatboat captain, a position he retained until the Civil War.

The Negro captain quickly demonstrated that his employer's confidence in his seamanship was not misplaced. On his first voyage in command of a flatboat he brought his lumber-laden craft safely to its destination although it was leaking so badly that only the buoyancy of its cargo kept it afloat. After a second trip in which Gray navigated two flatboats to New Orleans without mishap, the younger Brown wrote from New Orleans that "Simon managed the boats very well last time. He is a first-rate fellow & can be as careful as anyone when he likes."

From 1845 until 1862 Simon Gray served as the Natchez lumber company's chief boatman. When the press of business required that two crews be used to supply the needs of the lumber yard in New Orleans, white men were employed temporarily as flatboat captains, but none of them ever succeeded in replacing the Negro. Andrew Brown, the founder and principal partner of the firm, continued to hold Gray in high regard despite occasional criticism of him by customers and New Orleans business associates.

As captain, Simon Gray exercised a degree of authority that is surprising to the modern student of slavery. His crews, usually numbering between ten and twenty men, were made up of both Negro slaves and white rivermen. Some of the slaves were the property of the company, while others, like Gray himself, were hired from their owners by the firm. The white crewmen, on the other hand, were employed by the Negro, who kept their records, paid their expenses, lent them money, and sometimes paid their wages. Consequently, they looked upon Gray as their employer. Curiously enough, the flatboat captain appears to have been more popular with his white crewmen than with the slaves. The latter sometimes complained to Andrew Brown, Jr., that Gray's manner was unduly overbearing, but the whites did not. Indeed, several of the white rivermen served under the Negro for a period of years. His unusual relations with white crewmen were a subject of comment among the members of the firm. On one occasion, William I. Key, a partner, reported from New Orleans that Gray had insisted on his paying the steamboat passage of some white rivermen from New Orleans to Natchez so that they could accompany him on his next trip. These crewmen Key described as the "meanest lot of *white men . . .* I ever saw."

Gray's flatboat voyages were of two general kinds. The one he undertook most frequently was a simple delivery of lumber from the Natchez mill to the New Orleans lumber yard. The other was the "coasting" trip, which received its name from the "German Coast" district above the Crescent City. On the New Orleans hauls, Gray's duties as captain were comparatively uncomplicated. At Natchez he supervised the loading of the cargoes into the flatboats, at the same time making a count of the number of linear feet of lumber of each variety placed on board. Small flatboats of the type used on the Mississippi approximated 70 by 18 feet, and could carry about 50,000 feet of plank, while very large ones of 170 by 20 feet could hold 200,000 feet. Brown usually furnished Gray with moderate-sized vessels of 100 by 18 feet which delivered 100,000 feet of lumber. On most of his trips, Gray handled two of these boats lashed together, employing a crew of twelve when weather and river conditions were favorable. Upon arriving in New Orleans, he moored his boats at the wharf, and turned them and their cargo over to representatives of the lumber yard there. The empty flatboats were not taken back to Natchez, but were sold to "breakers" who dismantled them in order to reclaim the planks. After delivering a cargo Gray returned to Natchez with his crew by steamboat to await the loading of another pair of flatboats. Ordinarily the trip from Natchez to New Orleans took him a week, but adverse weather and river currents could greatly prolong the voyage.

While on "coasting" trips, which often lasted from two to three weeks, Gray was compelled to exercise considerable initiative and independent judgment. The main object of these ventures was to deliver orders of lumber to customers at riverside plantations. When space was available, however, extra lumber was placed on the flatboat for Gray to sell at retail along the way. In addition to making deliveries he also solicited orders for the mill, quoted prices, extended credit to customers, and collected money owed to the lumber company. As a rule the Negro kept the necessary records himself, but he occasionally hired a clerk when the bookkeeping became burdensome. His memoranda and reports submitted to the company officials in New Orleans reveal that the Negro captain was as literate as most white men of the laboring class and that he was well versed in simple mathematics.

On lengthy retailing expeditions Gray was accustomed to submit reports about his progress by mail to the offices in New Orleans and Natchez. The following letter written from Plaquemine, Louisiana, on June 21, 1850, to Andrew Dott, a company clerk, is typical:

> I now write you these few lines to let you know that I am a little better than I was when I left. I have got along quite well with the boat so far and have delivered *Mr. Moss* bill [of lumber] according to order and taken a draft for the same. I stoped the boat from leaking in the evening [afternoon] of the 19th of this month. This bill [order] of Mr. Allens, it is to come with H. K. Moss next bill. I have not made any collections as yet but have the promis of some this morning This letter that I send in your care I want to send to my wife, if you please.
> Nothing more at preasant. I remain your umble servant &c.

The increasing number of privileges which Brown was according his Negro captain were not approved by William I. Key, Brown's partner, who had taken charge of the New Orleans lumber yard after the death of Andrew Brown, Jr., in 1848. Key objected particularly to Simon's being permitted to undertake retailing trips. As he was having continual difficulty in keeping his yards stocked with lumber, he wanted to abandon the German Coast trade altogether, so that all of the Natchez lumber could be sold in New Orleans. He maintained that he could obtain better prices for the cypress than Gray was obtaining from the planters, and that he could collect accounts in the city more easily. Furthermore, Key had grave doubts about Gray's honesty, which, however, were not shared by Andrew Brown. Although the Negro frequently brought the New Orleans office large amounts of cash which he had collected from his customers, Key nevertheless suspected him of grafting in small matters. These suspicions Key expressed to Dott in 1850: "That fellow Simon, there is no confidence can be placed in him. The very fact of his not wishing anyone with him that *will* act honestly is the very reason that we ought to have someone on every Boat that can keep a proper account of everything that occurs during the trip." He also complained that Simon was ignoring his orders. Despite repeated instructions to the contrary, the Negro persisted in advancing part of their pay to his white crewmen before reaching New Orleans. He also was inclined to delay reporting to the office after arriving in town, and he sometimes would deliberately, Key thought, miss the steamboat which was supposed to return him and his crew to Natchez.

In July 1850, Key detected Gray in an act he considered to be highly dishonest. Someone had warned him that the boatman was planning to bring a lumber flatboat belonging to a competitor from Natchez to New Orleans without obtaining authorization from the company. Alerted by this information, Key arranged to intercept the party on the river above the city. When they met he discovered that Gray was indeed transporting the load of lumber in question, using crews belonging to Brown's firm. The manager of the lumber yard was convinced that Gray intended to keep the matter secret, and that the boatman had been bribed. Key then complained bitterly to Brown—without effect—that "this thing of leaving Simon his own master has been going on too long and must be put an end to."

Instead of restricting Gray's movements because of Key's accusations, Brown accorded increased freedom to the Negro. In August 1850, he purchased "Simon's family" from Joseph W. Allen for the sum of $500. This Brown did only as an act of kindness for the Negro captain, for he made no subsequent use of the woman or her children. The Gray family thus united was domiciled by Brown in a rented house in Natchez, and the monthly rent was charged against the operating expenses of the firm. Further demonstrating his reliance upon the boatman, Brown sent Gray to Plaquemine, Louisiana, in 1852 to bring Dan Tucker, a slave whom Brown had purchased there, to Natchez. This, of course, was a task ordinarily reserved for responsible white men.

In 1853 Simon Gray became free in all but the legal sense of the word. Until this time Brown's company had been paying Andrew Donnan seventy-five cents per day for his services. In addition, Simon himself received a bonus of five dollars for each trip to New Orleans, plus a salary of eight dollars per month. Although the records are obscure on this point, it appears likely that Donnan gave Simon his freedom without going to the trouble to have a special act of emancipation passed by the state legislature. Whether this be true or not, Donnan ceased to receive payment for Simon's hire, and the Negro's monthly wages were increased from eight to twenty dollars. This latter sum was the wage which the lumber company was paying free white boatmen. In December 1854, Key's assistant in New Orleans wrote that Simon was leaving the city without "I am afraid, having made much progress in emancipation."

Even though Simon Gray continued to remain a slave in the eyes of the law, Andrew Brown nevertheless permitted the Negro to take part in private business enterprises when his services were not required by the company. The first of these ventures occurred in August 1855. At that time Gray purchased a flatboat in Natchez, filled it with a cargo of 1700 barrels of sand, and floated it to New Orleans. To help with the navigation of the flatboat, he hired Alfred, one of the slaves belonging to the sawmill. In New Orleans, Key disposed of the load for Gray by selling the sand to builders. A second cargo delivered in October brought twenty-five cents per barrel. As was usual in such cases, the sale was made on credit with 6 per cent interest being charged against the purchasers. Gray eventually grossed $487.44 from his second sand speculation, and in addition was able to dispose of his flatboat for sixty dollars. Out of his profits he had to pay the company for his and Alfred's time at the rate of one dollar per day each, and also had to settle with the owner of the sand bank from which he had obtained his commodity.

These sand trips were followed by many others over the next few years. On one of these completed in March 1856, Simon grossed $440.00 and netted $225.75. Another trip undertaken the next month was less profitable, for it netted him only $144.50. He continued in the business in spite of price fluctuations, and by June, 1856, had succeeded in accumulating more than five hundred dollars to his credit with the lumber company over and above the small sums he had withdrawn from time to time.

Gray apparently used this money to buy a son, Washington Gray, who had not been included in the purchase of "Simon's family" mentioned earlier. In any case, Andrew Brown acquired "Simon's boy Washington" for five hundred dollars. Subsequently, the mill paid Brown for the boy's services, but whether this money was then retained by him or given to Simon is not clear. In all probability, however, Brown was again accommodating his flatboat captain by acting in his behalf to accomplish an end forbidden by the slave code.

During the years in which Simon Gray was transporting sand to New Orleans, he also handled lumber flatboats and log rafts for the company as usual. He also took part in an unusual episode in March, 1856, when a log raft moored at the Natchez mill broke loose and drifted downstream. In such cases it was the custom to sell the logs to mills situated down-river; and Gray and a white employee were dispatched to overtake the raft and assume charge of it, but they failed to make contact. The runaway raft drifted past Baton Rouge and finally entered a small tributary of the Mississippi River, the Bayou Lafourche.

Meanwhile, William Key, in New Orleans, received word of the accident by telegraph. He hastened upriver on a steamboat in hopes of intercepting the raft, taking Jim Matthews, a slave who was Simon's counterpart in the rafting division of the company, with him. Failing to sight the raft below Baton Rouge, they returned to New Orleans, where they found Gray and the white workman waiting for them. The two men reported that they had traced the raft into the Bayou Lafourche and had found it tied up at Jacobs' wood yard. The owner of this establishment told them that a white man had sold the timber to him for $500 and then had departed for New Orleans. When Gray convinced Jacobs that the timber was the property of Andrew Brown, he offered the Negro and his white companion a reward of $250 if they would recover his money for him. They promptly left in pursuit of the swindler and overtook him on the wharf in New Orleans. When Brown's men accused the culprit of swindling Jacobs, he readily admitted his guilt, and gave them four hundred dollars on condition that they let him go free. When Gray returned the money to its rightful owner, Jacobs gave him fifty dollars as his share of the reward. To close the matter, Jacobs bought the raft again, this time from the proper owner.

Andrew Brown's various enterprises prospered greatly during the 1850s, reflecting a period of active building in New Orleans. Early in the decade, his firm erected a large steam-powered woodworking plant near the New Orleans lumber yard, and, under Key's shrewd direction, it soon was doing a rushing business in doors, windows, shutters, and woodwork for stairs and balusters. At the lumber yard, Key's chief problem became the maintenance of a stock of dry lumber sufficient to supply his customers. By 1856 it became apparent that the capacity of the Natchez mill was inadequate to meet the needs of the woodworking plant and lumber yard. Key was compelled to buy as many cargoes of pine and cypress at the wharf as he could contract for, as well as importing mahogany from Central America.

In Natchez, Andrew Brown also worked energetically to meet the increasingly pressing shortage of lumber. He rebuilt the sawmill on a larger scale and installed the most modern machinery obtainable in the North. When the renovation was completed he imported skilled sawyers from the Great Lakes region to operate his new machinery. In order to insure a better supply of logs, Brown entered into partnerships with numerous Yazoo Valley logmen, and bought large tracts of standing cypress timber. As these measures still did not correct the situation, he subsidized the erection of several small circular-saw mills along the Yazoo River and contracted for their entire output of cypress plank.

After 1856 Simon Gray became increasingly involved in the Yazoo Valley operations of the company. In January 1857, Brown intrusted the Negro with an urgent and delicate mission. He was to buy as much plank as he could from a sawmill in Yazoo City operated by Mayfield, Fuget and Company. The results of the subsequent negotiations he reported to Brown as follows:

> I have closed the trade for the lumber at $16 per M [thousand]. There is about 3000 feet 1 inch plank; the balance [is] 1¼, 1½ & 2 inch. I was just in time to get it. Mr. Klein had sent a man up and he arrived there in one hour after I had closed the bargain. He offered $18 for the lot. I have thought it best to go to Greenwood and see about [buying] the boat [to transport the lumber] and drop it down [to Yazoo City], and then will either come or send to you for hands [to serve as crew].

Gray's purchase consisted of 155,000 feet of cypress lumber, costing $2473.98. At New Orleans, Key's assistant noted that it was "rather shabby stuff" but welcome in the emergency nonetheless.

From this time until 1863, Simon Gray was largely employed in the Yazoo swamps. When there was sufficient water in the Yazoo River he transported cargoes of cypress lumber manufactured by the small sawmills under contract with Andrew Brown. At times when the stream was not navigable, he directed the activities of a crew working in the cypress brakes, "deadening" timber, rolling logs, building levees and dams, constructing "cribs" of logs, and in general performing all the host of tasks preparatory to rafting the logs to the sawmill at Natchez.

During much of 1858 and 1859 Gray was afflicted with ill health. He visited Hot Springs, Arkansas, to take the baths on numerous occasions, and in the course of these treatments spent nearly a thousand dollars. Apparently he had fallen victim to the occupational diseases of the riverman, malaria and rheumatism. In addition, he was wearing an "elastic stocking" to relieve varicose veins.

Despite these ailments and his advancing age, Simon was able gradually to resume his regular duties. During the summer and fall of 1860 he delivered numerous loads of lumber to New Orleans. By then he was also able to devote some attention to his own business interests. In January 1861, for example, Gray stopped his lumber flatboat at Baton Rouge and loaded on a sizable quantity of cordwood which he purchased there for $3.00 a cord. Upon reaching New Orleans the boatman disposed of his firewood at a profit of $1.30 per cord. Key, as usual, was displeased with Gray's business methods, and commented sourly that "Simon should bear a portion of the expenses" of the flatboat which carried his cordwood to New Orleans.

After the capture of New Orleans by the Federals cut the Natchez sawmill off from its market in the Crescent City, Andrew Brown moved almost all of his slaves from Natchez to his timber lands in the Yazoo basin for safekeeping. Gray, who had been working in the swamps for more than a year, was now joined by his wife and children, and they continued to live there until after the fall of Vicksburg. This Union victory in July 1863 evidently brought the Negro flatboat captain the freedom he desired, for his name disappears from the records of the lumber company after this date. In 1865, Andrew Brown included a debt owed him by Simon among a list of uncollectable accounts.

Almost every aspect of Simon Gray's career violates our modern conception of the lot of the slave in the lower South. Contrary to law and custom the Negro riverman was educated beyond the point reached by the ordinary white workingman. He was permitted to travel about almost as freely as if he had not been a slave. He was paid a regular wage throughout most of his career, and he was able to live in privacy with his family apart from his fellows. More surprisingly, he frequently bought and sold as an agent of his employer and was able to exercise authority effectively over other employees of the company, both black and white. Gray even owned and made use of firearms with full consent of his employer. In short, the restrictions of slavery rested lightly upon this Natchez Negro.

Gray's status differed from other slaves in the employ of Andrew Brown only in degree. For example, Jim Matthews, a slave who belonged to the firm, pursued a career quite similar to that of Simon Gray. Beginning as a common laborer in the sawmill, he gradually worked his way upward to a position of authority and comparative independence. As early as the 1840s Matthews was commanding rafting crews, paying their expenses, and keeping simple records of their time. Although the raftsman never received a regular wage like the flatboat captain, he did receive pay for extra work performed at night or on holidays, and he often sold logs to the company which he had salvaged from the river. Like Simon, Jim did not take advantage of his liberties to flee to the North. Not until July 1863 did he leave his duties with the lumber company.

Other slaves employed by Brown in less responsible positions also enjoyed an unusual status. Not a few of them were literate, and one of this group, William Thompson, made use of his ability to read and write to escape from slavery. Forging a travel permit, he journeyed upriver to freedom and eventually made his way to Canada. After finding employment as fireman on a railway locomotive there, Thompson wrote a letter to his old friend Jim Matthews in care of his former master—a letter, by the way, which was delivered. In this communication he described living conditions in Canada, and inquired about his mother's health. Most significantly, he asked in most affectionate terms for news about Andrew Brown and his family. All of Brown's slaves were provided with excellent food, clothing, and medical attention. As in the case of Gray and Matthews they received pay for extra work at the rate of a dollar a day in addition to a cash bonus at Christmas, and they were seldom punished. Indeed, in most respects their lot was quite different from that of the ordinary cotton plantation field hand.

Whether the treatment accorded the slaves employed by Andrew Brown's lumbering firm was typical of non-agricultural enterprises in the lower Mississippi Valley is not yet determined. The testimony of another resident of the area, Horace S. Fulkerson, implies, however, that the privileges these industrial workers enjoyed were not unusual. In his *Random Recollections of Early Days in Mississippi*, written soon after the Civil War, Fulkerson discussed the construction business carried on by George, William, and Thomas Weldon. These Irish brothers specialized in building bridges, jails, courthouses, factories, and other large structures. Their working force consisted of nearly a hundred slaves, some of whom were skilled craftsmen. In fact, John Jackson, their architect, was a Negro, and it was he who designed the Warren County courthouse which still stands in Vicksburg. According to Fulkerson, the Weldons were extremely lenient with their slaves. The Weldon brothers were long-time friends, customers, and business associates of Andrew Brown, and it is entirely possible that the methods of both firms in handling Negro labor conformed to the rule of industry in the lower South. Though these examples are isolated instances, they nevertheless suggest that historians should examine more closely the role of slaves in industry.

Skilled slaves—coopers making barrels.
Source: Virginia State Library

A slave being flogged. Slaves sometimes were used to punish their fellow slaves.
Source: Library of Congress

8

The Lash
and the Law

Richard C. Wade

From: *Slavery in the Cities: The South, 1820–1860* by Richard C. Wade (New York: Oxford University Press, 1964), pp. 180–194. Copyright © 1964 by Oxford University Press, Inc. Reprinted by permission. Footnotes deleted.

It might be tempting to conclude from a selection such as the one on Simon Gray that slavery seldom revealed its coercive side. And yet, by its very nature it was based on a set of strict rules backed ultimately by the whip, the branding iron, and the gallows.

Rules governing slave behavior were incorporated into the slave codes. These were first formulated in the mid-seventeenth century and were often borrowed in large part from the codes of the Caribbean sugar colonies. Besides defining, and severely constricting, the slaves' civil status, they also constituted a criminal code. As a criminal code they were invariably harsher than even the stringent laws that applied to whites in these years. Slaves who committed crimes could be branded or mutilated. For black bondsmen, moreover, there was a long list of offenses for which the punishment was hanging. In addition to murder, of course, manslaughter, rape or attempted rape, rebellion, poisoning, and arson were accounted capital offenses for slaves. The most common punishment for slave violations, however, was whipping, and the whipping post, either at the plantation or at the town jail, was a common feature in the slave states.

It is hard to say precisely how large physical punishment loomed in the daily life of the average slave. We know that there were plantations and households where slaves were seldom punished, whether because masters were lenient or because they had terrified their chattels into obedience. There were others, clearly, where the whip and the branding iron were commonly employed. A large proportion of the advertisements for runaway slaves indicated that the fugitive had either been severely flogged or branded for some past offense.

Additional evidence for the harsh punishment of slaves comes from the court records. Southern law did attempt to prevent outright brutality. Unfortunately, the rules against cruelty were generally little more than pious declarations. Neither slaves nor free blacks could testify against whites, so that it required a white man's evidence to convict a brutal slave master or overseer. Given the coercive power of white opinion, which held that Southerners must present a united front in support of slavery, it was very difficult to get such evidence. Nevertheless, the court records of every slave state contain examples of white men brought before the courts on the testimony of other white men for treating their slaves brutally.

The slave codes as they applied to the plantation have received most of the historians' attention. Yet, in some ways, the codes were most actively employed in the cities and towns of the Old South. On the plantation the master's word was law, and the punishment of the plantation slave rested squarely in his hands. In the towns and cities the public authorities counted for more. In the following selection by Richard Wade we see that while the city provided more freedom for the slave, it also subjected him more directly to the operations of strict rules of behavior and inevitably to punishment.

"It has long seemed to us," ran a characteristic comment of one of the South's urban leaders, "that there is a spirit of insubordination among the colored gentry that requires checking. There is a carelessness, a disrespect, and *'devil may care'* sort of independence, and absence of wholesome restraint, a neglect of common propriety and courtesy of manner, which is becoming almost intolerable." Of course, this observer omitted " 'de fuss color'd circle' " in his remarks, since they were "justly noted for real politeness and oblingingness" of manners. "But take off the respectable upper crust, and you shall find enough material, which would be seriously improved by the application of a few good, sound affectionate floggings." The correction, however, should not be vengeful. "We mean floggings on principle, not in passion, and such administration of the birch as any idle, disobedient, churlish, good for nothing child deserves at the hands of its parents. Something is wanting to 'rectify the alignment of these sables,' and the sooner it is done the better."

If whites believed that discipline in the cities was dangerously loose, the Negroes thought it tight enough. The symbols of servitude surrounded bondsmen almost everywhere they went. It was not only that they were slaves owned by another person, but their color carried a general stigma. "*Color* raises the presumption of slavery," a Missouri judge had asserted flatly in enunciating the familiar equation. Hence even when outside the immediate supervision of the master or employer, the blacks were made aware of their status.

Every contact between the races, casual as well as formal, reminded Negroes of their inferiority. In ordinary conversation they were expected to show deference to all whites. Even the tone of voice and use of words could be offensive. Being "out of place"—a phrase which covered the whole range of etiquette—might bring a quick reprisal on the spot or a trip to the Mayor's Court and a "correction" in the municipal jail. "In the city," a runaway remembered, "a black man must get off the side-walk if he meets a white man, or stop on the curb-stone and raise his hat: if he meets a lady and gentleman he must step clean off the walk and raise his hat."

Years of the system conditioned both blacks and whites to acceptance of this sense of social distance. Northern Negroes, who had their own reasons to know discrimination, found the extent of racial deference in Dixie vexing. G. E. Stephens, a sailor whose ship stopped over in Charleston, fumed on hearing bondsmen refer to the children of their owners as "Master and Mistress." When he reprimanded one of them, she was "astonished" and said "those children were entitled to this distinction." The visitor ruefully concluded that, "the Blacks here invariably believe that white men are superior not only mentally, but physically."

The subtle inhibitions were just as revealing as the more obvious ones. Blacks, for example, could not smoke in public. The rationale was often baldly stated. "The negroes, habitually careless, care not where they throw their cigars; whether on the ground, in a pile of shavings, or under a bale of cotton," the *New Orleans Bee* asserted, adding that this objection did not take into account "the offensiveness to some, of coming into contact with a negro's cigar puff." A Savannah editor found the habit of "Puffing cigar smoke into the faces of passers-by" an "offense against good manners." Alexander, "a brawny-shouldered black negro," came before a Richmond judge after having been picked up while "strutting along a public street with a lighted cigar in his mouth" and was lectured on racial propriety and proper subservience.

Many blacks became inured to this relationship, and no doubt believed it natural. Yet others never could. The records of the courts are replete with punishment for "being out of place." "John, a mulatto," ran a typical sentence, "was disorderly and saucy in the market, showed a large amount of independence" and got "20 heavy stripes for his impudence." A drayman, Ben, received 39 lashes, another account noted, "for not remembering the courtesy due a white man, both in word and deed." In another case "a negro girl was sentenced to twenty-five lashes for using insulting language to a white lady and otherwise acting disorderly." Occasionally a bondsman would reject the whole business. A Mobile slave, for example, found himself in great trouble for saying that "negroes are equal to whites," though the judge went "lightly" on him because he admitted to being "three sheets to the wind" at the time.

This etiquette was, of course, common to both city and country. But it took on special importance in town because there the races mingled most frequently, black and white dealt with each other constantly, and the social distance had to be maintained in the face of physical proximity. Ordinances might provide a legal blueprint for these numberless encounters and the courts punish any transgressions; yet the functioning of daily affairs rested on the broader subjugation of Negro to white, and observances in the smallest matters seemed almost as crucial as acceptance of slavery itself. Hence the slave—indeed, the free colored person too—was never allowed to forget his servitude whenever a white man was near.

When smaller, informal restraints broke down, the slave was confronted with the organized power of the white community. A lenient owner might permit a wider freedom, but in so doing he invited the intervention of local authorities. "If the masters of families do not check . . . [the] impudence and abandon in their dependents," a Savannah observer advised, "it is time for the City Marshal and constables to take the matter in hand." And "in hand" usually meant a more rigid enforcement.

Municipal interference occasionally protected the slaves from the worst excesses of a brutal owner. In one case, after a particularly grisly episode, a judge explained the rationale: "It is admitted on all hands that the treatment of slaves is a delicate subject, and our laws in their wisdom have left the subject to the discretion of the master; but when masters degenerate into relentless and bloody tyrants . . . then indeed does the self defense of the community" require that measures be taken against the white. Not only did the "dictates of humanity" suggest such a course, but, more practically, it would "induce the blacks to rely upon the justice of free inhabitants to remove any causeless severity which may be exercised toward them."

Still the usual thrust of the official machinery was against the slave. The constables by day and the watch by night made the supervision of Negroes a special concern. Slaves found their ubiquitous presence a constant danger. At any time one might stop a black, ask for his papers, and frisk his clothing. A small matter or a slight infraction could end in a trip to jail. Resistance was foolish, an attempt to run away was worse. The prudent slave acquiesced in any encounter with the man on the beat and hoped nothing would happen. After curfew, it was particularly important not to be discovered away from the premises without proper authorization. The public might complain that the patrols were inefficient and ineffective, still, they arrested often enough to keep the colored community alert, if not always in awe.

The fear of being picked up was considerable, in part because the next step was the jail. Prisons for either race were hardly attractive; and for Negroes conditions were especially bad. To be sure, a visitor might find one "neat and clean," yet this was never characteristic. A grand jury in New Orleans in 1837 brought in a report that could have been filed in almost any city in any year. While one of the town's three jails was adequate, the other two were worse than "dreadful" accounts had indicated. In the Second Municipality, Negroes were kept in five "dens" which measured ten feet square with a small door fifteen inches wide providing the only outlet. The temperature outside was between 90 and 95 degrees, while the rooms were much hotter and filled with "filth and abominable odors." The second cell contained three slaves; the third had seven "light women" either slaves or free persons of color and "one *white* (comment on such indiscriminate imprisonment is not thought necessary *in this state*)"; the fourth apartment held six men. This last, "the largest and lightest, and best ventilated," housed fourteen slaves, "most of them naked by choice." Because it faced Lafayette Square, the presentment found the prison absolutely intolerable.

Conditions were not much better elsewhere. In the same city a few years later, a committee of the First Municipality issued a sharp rebuke to its jailor when it found the walls without whitewash, great overcrowding, sick slaves mingling with the healthy, and others idling about when they should have been on public work gangs. A Louisville grand jury made a similar indictment in 1834, describing the cells as "most filthy, offensive and disgusting." In one they found "twenty four persons crowded into one room twenty-two feet square." Those who claimed that bondsmen would just as soon go to jail as work had obviously never been in one.

Patrolmen and jails were only the beginning of woe for the slave entangled with the law. No explanation of his arrest need be given him, and conditions in prison would almost certainly be shoddy. However, he would not languish there long. Masters insisted that their property not be detained needlessly. Hence in the morning the bondsman faced the judge. Of course, no trial in a meaningful sense followed. The slave had no right to plead, none to call a witness, indeed, no right to speak unless the presiding officer asked a question. Curiously, however, his bondage might be some protection. His owner could insist on proof, or at least a statement of why his chattel was in court. On a rare occasion a master would carry a case to a higher tribunal.

But the routine presumed guilt, and the owner often did not bother to appear. The only question to be decided was the sentence. At this point the magistrate often questioned the black, especially to find out if any circumstances should be considered in fixing the punishment. Sometimes, the slave protested innocence but seldom with any success. "However jealously a negro seeks to affect innocence, the eye always betrays guilt and a great evil capacity," the Richmond *Whig* explained. "Bill, the slave of Mrs. Elizabeth Johnson, who stole the coat and five dollars from Richard, slave of T. Cauthorn, who works on board the canal boat Glazebrook, was ordered thirty by the Mayor on yesterday, in disregard of the most solemn protestations of innocence on the part of Bill. There was an amount of villainy reflected in his eyes that could well contradict all the protestations he could utter for a month."

The anxiety of the slaves in municipal courts sprang from hard experience. Occasionally, the punishment could be simply demeaning rather than bruising. Bishop Whipple once came upon a slave in a pillory, his head "mounted with a fool's cap, a paper pinned to his breast—'Stolen $5.00.'" Others he saw working as scavengers in the street, chained to each other as "punishment for some offence." But the workhouse, irons, and even branding could be ingredients of the sentence. Above all there was whipping. "Negroes will be negroes in cunning, stupidity or stubbornness," a Richmond court reporter mused after listening to Mayor Mayo dispose of the "ordinary run of misbehavior by colordom, . . . so it is impossible to think of changing their nature, unless by the lash, which is a great institution for stretching negroes' skin and making them grow good."

No other penalty carried the same meaning or so embodied the social relations of the "peculiar institution." The lash in the white hand on the black back was a symbol of bondage recognized by both races. "No man should ever use a cowhide on a white man," the *Richmond Enquirer* contended. "It is a cutting insult never forgiven by the cowhided party, because white human nature revolts at such a degrading chastisement." A Charleston grand jury embedded its objection in a still broader context. Noting that blacks looked on intently whenever whites were whipped, it explained that they were "activated" by two sympathies: one was "of sorrow for the suffering of the criminal without reference to the justice of his punishment," and, secondly, "self gratulation in the degradation of the white by the same punishment to their own level."

Whipping, then, was more than an ordinary punishment; it was meant to express a particular relationship as well. It served the system of bondage by permitting stiff penalties without depriving the master of his chattel's labor for any extended period. And, just as important, it came to be a social gesture embodying discipline, deterrence, and degradation. These purposes were clearly stated, and magistrates developed methods to give emphasis to one or another function. "A flogging in the Market is always given as a mark of disgrace, in contradistinction to a flogging in the Work House which is characterized by its *severity*," a Charleston constable explained. "In the former instance, the exposure is more considered than the Laceration of the criminal's body." Moreover, the blacks understood this. "It is a well known fact," the same authority added, "that every negro in this community regards a whipping in the Market as the greatest disgrace which can befall them."

The distinction was more significant for the masters than slaves. They found whipping in either setting a dreadful thing. James Watkins, a Baltimore bondsman picked up for being out after hours, described the ordinary punishment from the victim's end. His friend, arrested at the same time, was called first. Watkins heard "a dreadful scream" and became very uneasy "knowing that my turn came next." After being called, he stated, "I was told to strip off my clothes, and was then placed on a wooden frame, my head down, and the other part of my body up." The jailor then "got a long paddle which was perforated with a number of holes, about a quarter of inch in diameter, and laid it on the fleshy part of my body with great violence." Lumps formed and broke with successive strokes. "These blows were repeated six times, and the torture was such I never experienced either before or since."

Watkin's stripes might have been severe, but the number was fewer than the usual sentence. Judges generally prescribed much nearer the upper limit even in minor cases. The minutes of Richmond's Hustings Court for 1825, for instance, recite typical penalties for theft: for stealing three dollars, twenty lashes; three blankets, fifteen; four dollars, twenty-five; a calico dress, fifteen; a pair of boots, thirty-nine; one featherbed, ten. In Mobile the Mayor's Court thirty years later encompassed still another customary range of punishments: ten lashes for "keeping Christmas by getting drunk"; fifteen for "impudence"; twenty-five for "insolent language"; twenty for imbibing the "expressed juice of corn"; twenty-five for being "out of place"; thirty-nine for a "charge too indelicate to be published."

In other instances the penalty ran well beyond the legal limit, though it would be executed at different times. In such a case a Charleston girl, for example, was accused of making "several attempts to fire" a building; her sentence: "to receive twenty lashes on the first three Fridays of three successive months, and to remain two hours in the stocks each time; then to remain five years in solitary confinement." If the owner thought this excessive, he could take her out of the state after the first year. In other decisions the magistrate indicated a higher severity by directing that the lashes be "laid on hard."

In some places, too, at least for a period, burning on the hand was added to the stripes. A Richmond magistrate ordered a slave to be "burnt" and receive fifteen stripes on his bare back at the public whipping post for "stealing thirty dollars." In the same year of 1825, more than a dozen other sentences involved this same punishment. Finally, a decade later, the court ordered the practice abolished, since it was "cruel and unsuited to the age" and "the effect upon that class of people on whom it is inflicted for the correction of crimes is at least doubtful." Like whipping, burning was designed to combine severity with servitude, and the resultant scar was to be a constant reminder to the Negro of his "place."

In short, the character of the punishment was as important as its harshness. In the countryside, master or overseer wielded the lash on their own slaves with much less regard to social ritual. Only when a bondsman was sent to a nearby plantation or court house for correction did outside considerations enter. In the towns, on the other hand, the patrol, the courts, and the custom of using the municipal jailor became widespread. In such a situation, a large part of ordinary discipline devolved upon the whipping post and workhouse. What was private on plantations became public. Hence, punishment often became an event charged with a broader significance than the mere chastisement of a single black.

An episode in Charleston in 1837 neatly caught the social over-tones. Two slaves had been adjudged guilty of theft, Sarah for steal-ing thirteen yards of linen and a "negro fellow" for a "similar offense." Her sentence was two whippings of twenty stripes and two weeks solitary confinement in the workhouse; his was "a like num-ber of lashes." But the administration of the penalties differed. "*Sarah* walked free and unshackled in advance of the crowd" which had gathered for the affair. She carried a piece of watermelon, "look-ing much more like a favored slave, rewarded for good conduct with dainties for her stomach, than a thief returning from public punish-ment, to be incarcerated in a solitary cell." The man "was severely chastised, tied and carried (as he deserved) among the hisses of the mob like a felon, to the workhouse."

Some whites criticized the constable for his handling of the proceedings, and in the discussion that followed the rationale for public discipline was laid bare. "Civis," who claimed that this was the first "public execution" he had ever seen, contended that the jailor applied the punishment on Sarah so delicately that he virtually extinguished the sentence. "The ceremony occupied about 90 sec-onds, a small whip being lightly dropped upon the shoulders of this favored brunette, . . . I have seen a gauze-wing fly who would have kept his hold upon the neck of my horse in defiance of such an admonition." Moreover, other Negroes gathered around whose sympathy "was poured forth without measure." Sarah thus won the "glories of martyrdom" and "paraded through the crowd, conscious and proud of the punishment, not inflicted on her by the law, but the law by her."

"Civis" had a direct remedy. "If the negroes are to be whipped," he proposed, "they ought to be carried to the workhouse, not suffered to be marched through the streets and highways in open defiance of decency and law—and for a moment at least, they should be separated from the caresses and comfortings of their accomplices in vice." Another Charlestonian joined in this view, though not on the score of harshness, for he "did not consider the good effect to be derived from corporal punishment dependent as much upon its severity as upon its publicity." But "Justice" did think "she should have been tied and carried through the streets, as an example and warning to others of her color, who are too prone to follow in her footsteps."

Constable John Myer responded with the official view. Answer-ing the charge that Sarah's lashes had been light, he observed that he had used cowhide and had no doubt that "Civis" would have "quailed under the severity of their infliction." But more significantly he argued that public punishment was more effective than tougher treatment. Slaves would "cheerfully submit (notwithstanding the severity) to a punishment of twice the number of stripes in the Workhouse," he contended, "rather than be tied to the public post, exposed to the gaze of every bystander, and liable, forever afterwards, to have the finger of scorn pointed at them as one who had been flogged in the Market." Negroes, not a party to this debate, might well have found it without real meaning, yet the nature of the discussion suggested what whites intended to express with the lash and the whipping post.

The whip itself conveyed enough terror to the slave, but the public whipping posts served to institutionalize the cruelty. They were, in the bitter words of a former slave, "the monuments of the religion and greatness of Southern cities." The installation itself was an elaborate contraption which reminded many of a medieval rack. There were variations, of course, but Mobile's contained most of the usual elements. "It was constructed like a sash frame," wrote a traveler: "The lower board on which the feet of the unfortunate being were to stand, could be pushed up or down, to accommodate the height of the individual. Upon it is a block, through which the legs are passed. The neck and arms passed through another." Designed for both personal punishment and public disgrace, usually located at the market in the heart of town, it was for the black the grotesque embodiment of the slave regime.

The lash and the whipping post were the pivots of the system of discipline in Dixie's cities, but beyond, and always at hand, were other instruments of control. The workhouse, usually equipped with solitary cells and occasionally a treadmill, provided an alternative to the judge who delivered an extended sentence. Available too were irons, the historic emblem of bondage. And, of course, in the last extremity the hangman stood ready to dispatch the dangerous and intractable. Since none of these punishments was confined to blacks, they were seldom identified with the system of slavery. Yet the Negro community had every reason to see them in the context of that institution.

Indeed, the argument for the treadmill was usually put in terms of discipline. In the midst of the Vesey crisis in 1822, "City Rustic" suggested that Charleston adopt the device *"as a punishment amongst our domestics."* Addressing himself to "every owner of town Negroes," he said it would be especially important "to the female owners of slaves, whose humanity but too often stands between the Negro and the well merited visits to the Workhouse." The "good effects to be derived from this excellent invention," he predicted, "would be incalculable. No lady even, would hesitate to send a lazy insolent waiting man, or a sulky seamstress, to the refreshing exercise of a week's walk in the Stepping-Mill." Moreover, "our male and female dandies, *and even some ladies who are not dandies,* could find their silk stockings and corsets considerably more lasting through its influence."

Its establishment later in the decade met some of these requirements. The Duke of Saxe-Weimar found that whippings had been reduced, since the device made it possible to punish twenty-four people simultaneously, and women could be included with the men. In addition, he was told, "the negroes entertain a strong fear of the treadmills, and regard flogging as the lighter evil! Of about one hundred and sixty, who, since the erection of the treadmill, have been employed on them, only six have been sent back a second time." Basil Hall was less impressed with this "sort of Bridewell," and thought it would never replace the lash as "an essential part of the system of slavery." At any rate, not enough cities adopted the practice to permit it to become a competing symbol to the whipping post.

Irons, too, played a role in the system of discipline. There was nothing unique in their use in the cities since they appeared wherever the institution went. In fact, this punishment was probably employed more sparingly in the towns than elsewhere. Whites often criticized the practice, sometimes bitterly. A St. Louisan, for example, complained of the "shocking spectacle" of seeing "an unfortunate Female Slave crawling about the house in the ordinary business of the kitchen and compelled to drag along the grating manacles." He then asked why "the humane citizens" of the town should be "compelled to witness a scene at which barbarians should blush." Still the books of the blacksmith employed by the municipal government in the same town carried such entries: "putting on three pair of hand irons, $2; . . . Ironing Negro hand and foot, $1; . . . putting irons on negro, $.50." In addition, the authorities shackled runaways, jailors used the device when so instructed by judges or masters and whenever they found a prisoner difficult to mange. Certainly for the slave, the relationship between irons and servitude was uncomfortably clear.

Behind all these measures stood the gallows, the ultimate exercise of power. The hangman, of course, handled whites as well as blacks and probably he saw no connection between his craft and slavery. The noose could be swung over a limb in the countryside as well as dropped from an elaborate frame at the edge of town. Yet the subtleties in both instances counted. The level of tolerance for crimes was much lower for colored people and especially slaves, and an execution in the city was always more of a public event than in remoter areas. Hence capital punishment occupied a crucial position in the disciplinary system. This display of final authority, even though used only occasionally, was the ultimate and swift response to any who sought too boldly to move across the broad line dividing the races.

To be really effective, the act, or at least its result, had to be very public. It would serve no deterrent purpose if a slave was whisked away and disposed of quietly. Hence the jailyard usually formed the setting for the grim proceedings. On special occasions when the whites considered either the slave or the offense particularly threatening, the execution was conducted in a way to strike fear into the whole colored community. In 1822, for example, those presumably implicated in the Vesey plot went to the gallows in full view of the city. In another instance in Richmond a "promiscuous assemblage of persons, variously estimated from five to ten thousand," watched Giles put to death. The *Enquirer* noted that at the end the prisoner warned "his fellow servants to shun his course of wickedness," thus vindicating the publicity that attended the spectacle.

The list of crimes for which a magistrate might prescribe death for a slave was long, and it included many small offenses. Yet the courts hesitated to invoke it for trivial matters since owners would protest the loss of property. Even when bondsmen were sent to the gallows for insurrection, the master might sue for damages. In addition, in some cases where the judge prescribed hanging, the owner was given the privilege of "transporting" his chattel, which meant selling the slave elsewhere. Nevertheless, custom and law lodged in the court this weapon to be used not only to satisfy some accepted sense of justice, but as a tool of racial discipline as well. And in every city the hangman was employed often enough to remind the blacks of this residual authority. . . .

part V

The Slave's Response

Selling a mother from her child.
Source: New York Public Library

Chasing a fugitive slave.
Source: New York Historical Society

Slaves fighting for their freedom.
Source: Library of Congress

A desperate slave mother. Slave women sometimes destroyed their children rather than see them remain slaves.
Source: New York Public Library

9

Slavery and Personality

Stanley Elkins

From: *Slavery, A Problem in American Institutional and Intellec-
tual Life* (Chicago, Ill.: University of Chicago Press, 1959),
pp. 81–139. Footnotes deleted.

*Slavery was not so consistent or remorseless as to provide no leeway
for the exceptionally talented and enterprising few. Nevertheless,
the South's peculiar institution was in general brutal and exploitive.
It subjected its victims to hard, repetitive labor, it disrupted their
family life, and it degraded them into salable chattels. But these, in
some ways, are all external penalties. What did the system do to
the morale and personality of its victims? Did it break their spirits
and make them docile; or did it generate rage, making them militant
and aggressive?*

*Historians have answered this interesting question in a number
of different ways. In the selection that follows Stanley Elkins accepts
the view that the system demoralized the slave. Elkins believes that
human nature is readily molded by environment. He is impressed
by the frequency of large-scale slave revolts in Latin America and
the relative absence of such resistance in the United States. He takes
seriously contemporary reports of the irresponsible, childlike, even
sunny nature, of the slave's personality. He concludes that the black
man was by nature neither childish nor docile, but that slavery as it
developed in this country was peculiarly damaging to human personality. Arguing from the experience of the Nazi concentration
camps, he suggests that the docility of the North American slave, as
exemplified in the "Sambo" type, can be explained as a natural
human response to a "total" system of control and coercion. Slaves
disliked the system they were subjected to, but deprived of the*

institutional protection that existed in Latin America in the shape of the Catholic Church and the Spanish crown, the slave in the United States was reduced to utter dependence on his master. While many blacks obviously escaped the psychological damage this involved, many others were reduced to something approaching the childlike level of a Sambo.

Elkins' thesis has touched a sensitive nerve. It suggests to some people that the degrading stereotype of the "happy darky" is valid, and that in some way slavery for black men was a benign institution. Such a conclusion would be unfair to Elkins. Surely no harsher indictment of slavery could be made than to insist that the system unmanned its victims and reduced them to childishness. Recent work testing the validity of Elkins' view of the comparative severity of Anglo-Saxon and Latin slavery has been contradictory. So have investigations of the nature of slave personality. In the end Elkins' view may be totally invalidated. But at the moment there are few hypotheses concerning slavery that are more intriguing and subtle or more suggestive for understanding the effects of slavery on those caught in its toils.

An examination of American slavery, checked at certain critical points against a very different slave system, that of Latin America, reveals that a major key to many of the contrasts between them was an institutional key: The presence or absence of other powerful institutions in society made an immense difference in the character of slavery itself. In Latin America, the very tension and balance among three kinds of organizational concerns–church, crown, and plantation agriculture—prevented slavery from being carried by the planting class to its ultimate logic. For the slave, in terms of the space thus allowed for the development of men and women as moral beings, the result was an "open system": a system of contacts with free society through which ultimate absorption into that society could and did occur with great frequency. The rights of personality implicit in the ancient traditions of slavery and in the church's most venerable assumptions on the nature of the human soul were thus in a vital sense conserved, whereas to a staggering extent the very opposite was true in North American slavery. The latter system had developed virtually unchecked by institutions having anything like the power of their Latin counterparts; the legal structure which supported it, shaped only by the demands of a staple-raising capitalism, had defined with such nicety the slave's character as chattel that his character as a moral individual was left in the vaguest of legal obscurity. In this sense American slavery operated as a "closed" system—one in which, for the generality of slaves in their nature as men and women, *sub specie aeternitatis,* contacts with free society could occur only on the most narrowly circumscribed of terms. The next question is whether living within such a "closed system" might not have produced noticeable effects upon the slave's very personality.

The name "Sambo" has come to be synonymous with "race stereotype." . . . The characteristics that have been claimed for the type come principally from Southern lore. Sambo, the typical plantation slave, was docile but irresponsible, loyal but lazy, humble but chronically given to lying and stealing; his behavior was full of infantile silliness and his talk inflated with childish exaggeration. His relationship with his master was one of utter dependence and childlike attachment: it was indeed this childlike quality that was the very key to his being. Although the merest hint of Sambo's "manhood" might fill the Southern breast with scorn, the child, "in his place," could be both exasperating and lovable.

Was he real or unreal? What order of existence, what rank of legitimacy, should be accorded him? Is there a "scientific" way to talk about this problem? For most Southerners in 1860 it went without saying not only that Sambo was real—that he was a dominant plantation type—but also that his characteristics were the clear product of racial inheritance. That was one way to deal with Sambo, a way that persisited a good many years after 1860. But in recent times, the discrediting, as unscientific, of racial explanations for any feature of plantation slavery has tended in the case of Sambo to discredit not simply the explanation itself but also the thing is was supposed to explain. Sambo is a mere stereotype—"stereotype" is itself a bad word, insinuating racial inferiority and invidious discrimination. . . .

There ought, however, to be . . . a . . . way of dealing with the Sambo picture, some formula for taking it seriously. The picture has far too many circumstantial details, its hues have been stroked in by too many different brushes, for it to be denounced as counterfeit. Too much folk-knowledge, too much plantation literature, too much of the Negro's own lore, have gone into its making to entitle one in good conscience to condemn it as "conspiracy." One searches in vain through the literature of the Latin-American slave systems for the "Sambo" of our tradition—the perpetual child incapable of maturity. How is this to be explained? If Sambo is not a product of race (that "explanation" can be consigned to oblivion) and not simply a product of "slavery" in the abstract (other societies have had slavery), then he must be related to our own peculiar variety of it.

And if Sambo is uniquely an American product, then his existence, and the reasons for his character, must be recognized in order to appreciate the very scope of our slave problem and its aftermath. . . .

Let the above, then, be a preface to the argument of the present essay. It will be assumed that there were elements in the very structure of the plantation system—its "closed" character—that could sustain infantilism as a normal feature of behavior. These elements, having less to do with "cruelty" per se than simply with the sanctions of authority, were effective and pervasive enough to require that such infantilism be characterized as something much more basic than mere "accommodation." It will be assumed that the sanctions of the system were in themselves sufficient to produce a recognizable personality type.

. . . [It need not] be claimed that the "Sambo" type, even in the relatively crude sense employed here, was a universal type. It was, however, a plantation type, and a plantation existence embraced well over half the slave population. Two kinds of material will be used in the effort to picture the mechanisms whereby this adjustment to absolute power—an adjustment whose end product included infantile features of behavior—may have been effected. One is drawn from the theoretical knowledge presently available in social psychology, and the other, in the form of an analogy, is derived from some of the data that have come out of the German concentration camps. . . .

[This] . . . body of material, involving an experience undergone by several million men and women in the concentration camps of our own time, contains certain items of relevance to the problem here being considered. The experience was analogous to that of slavery and was one in which wide-scale instances of infantilization were observed. . . .

While the widespread existence of "Sambo" on the ante-bellum plantation is being taken for granted, it is also taken for granted that no set of characteristics, Sambo-like or otherwise, may possibly be accounted for in terms of "race" or "inborn nature." But "race" is not the only explanation that has been offered for Negro character. Another, very much like it but based on assumptions about the "primitive" nature of African tribal culture, has also enjoyed considerable currency. In fact, with a warrant presumably more scientific, the "culture argument" managed to keep its respectability rather longer than did the one based on race, and to a great extent simply replaced it. But here, too, "inferiority" was in some sense taken as given and was in turn "explained" by generalizations about the low and savage state of the African tribal cultures from which the majority of slaves were originally taken.

. . . But . . . no true picture, cursory or extended, of African culture seems to throw any light at all on the origins of what would emerge, in American plantation society, as the stereotyped "Sambo" personality. The typical West African tribesman was a distinctly warlike individual; he had a profound sense of family and family authority; he took hard work for granted; and he was accustomed to live by a highly formalized set of rules which he himself often helped to administer. If he belonged to the upper classes of tribal society—as did many who later fell victim to the slave trade—he might have had considerable experience as a political or military leader. He was the product, in any case, of cultural traditions essentially heroic in nature.

Something very profound, therefore, would have had to intervene in order to obliterate all this and to produce, on the American plantation, a society of helpless dependents.

We may suppose that every African who became a slave underwent an experience whose crude psychic impact must have been staggering and whose consequences superseded anything that had ever previously happened to him. Some effort should therefore be made to picture the series of shocks which must have accompanied the principal events of that enslavement.

The majority of slaves appear to have been taken in native wars, which meant that no one—neither persons of high rank nor warriors of prowess—was guaranteed against capture and enslavement. Great numbers were caught in surprise attacks upon their villages, and since the tribes acting as middlemen for the trade had come to depend on regular supplies of captives in order to maintain that function, the distinction between wars and raiding expeditions tended to be very dim. . . . Under the glaring sun, through the steaming jungle, they were driven along like beasts tied together by their necks; day after day, eight or more hours at a time, they would stagger barefoot over thorny underbrush, dried reeds, and stones. Hardship, thirst, brutalities, and near starvation penetrated the experience of each exhausted man and woman who reached the coast. . . .

The episode that followed—almost too protracted and stupefying to be called a mere "shock"—was the dread Middle Passage, brutalizing to any man, black or white, ever to be involved with it. The holds, packed with squirming and suffocating humanity, became stinking infernos of filth and pestilence. Stories of disease, death, and cruelty on the terrible two-month voyage abound in the testimony which did much toward ending the British slave trade forever.

The final shock in the process of enslavement came with the Negro's introduction to the West Indies. Bryan Edwards, describing the arrival of a slave ship, writes of how in times of labor scarcity crowds of people would come scrambling aboard, manhandling the slaves and throwing them into panic. . . .

The thoroughness with which African Negroes coming to America were detached from prior cultural sanctions should thus be partly explainable by the very shock sequence inherent in the technique of procurement. But it took something more than this to produce "Sambo," and it is possible to overrate—or at least to over-generalize—this shock sequence in the effort to explain what followed. A comparable experience was also undergone by slaves coming into Latin America, where very little that resembled our "Sambo" tradition would ever develop. We should also remember that, in either case, it was only the first generation that actually experienced these shocks. It could even be argued that the shock sequence is not an absolute necessity for explaining "Sambo" at all. . . .

A certain amount of the mellowness in Ulrich Phillips' picture of antebellum plantation life has of necessity been discredited by recent efforts not only to refocus attention upon the brutalities of the slave system but also to dispose once and for all of Phillips' assumptions about the slave as a racially inferior being. And yet it is important—particularly in view of the analogy about to be presented —to keep in mind that for all the system's cruelties there were still clear standards of patriarchal benevolence inherent in its human side, and that such standards were recognized as those of the best Southern families. . . .

Introducing, therefore, certain elements of the German concentration-camp experience involves the risky business of trying to balance two necessities—emphasizing both the vast dissimilarities of the two regimes and the essentially limited purpose for which they are being brought together, and at the same time justifying the use of the analogy in the first place. . . .

The system of the concentration camps was expressly devised in the 1930s by high officials of the German government to function as an instrument of terror. The first groups detained in the camps consisted of prominent enemies of the Nazi regime; later, when these had mostly been eliminated, it was still felt necessary that the system be institutionalized and made into a standing weapon of intimidation—which required a continuing flow of incoming prisoners. The categories of eligible persons were greatly widened to include all real, fancied, or "potential" opposition to the state. They were often selected on capricious and random grounds, and together they formed a cross-section of society which was virtually complete: criminals, workers, businessmen, professional people, middle-class Jews, even members of the aristocracy. The teeming camps thus held all kinds—not only the scum of the underworld but also countless men and women of culture and refinement. During the war a specialized objective was added, that of exterminating the Jewish populations of subject countries, which required special mass-production methods of which the gas chambers and crematories of Auschwitz-Birkenau were outstanding examples. Yet the basic technique was everywhere and at all times the same: the deliberate infliction of various forms of torture upon the incoming prisoners in such a way as to break their resistance and make way for their degradation as individuals. These brutalities were not merely "permitted" or "encouraged"; they were prescribed. Duty in the camps was a mandatory phase in the training of SS guards, and it was here that particular efforts were made to overcome their scruples and to develop in them a capacity for relishing spectacles of pain and anguish. . . .

One part of the prisoner's being was thus, under sharp stress, brought to the crude realization that he must thenceforth be governed by an entire new set of standards in order to live. Mrs. Lingens-Reiner puts it bluntly: "Will you survive, or shall I? As soon as one sensed that this was at stake everyone turned egotist." ". . . I think it of primary importance," writes Dr. Cohen, "to take into account that the superego acquired new values in a concentration camp, so much at variance with those which the prisoner bore with him into camp that the latter faded." But then this acquisition of "new values" did not all take place immediately; it was not until some time after the most acute period of stress was over that the new, "unreal" self would become at last the "real" one.

"If you survive the first three months you will survive the next three years." Such was the formula transmitted from the old prisoners to the new ones, and its meaning lay in the fact that the first three months would generally determine a prisoner's capacity for survival and adaptation. "Be inconspicuous"; this was the golden rule. The prisoner who called attention to himself, even in such trivial matters as the wearing of glasses, risked doom. Any show of bravado, any heroics, any kind of resistance condemned a man instantly. There were no rewards for martyrdom: not only did the martyr himself suffer, but mass punishments were wreaked upon his fellow inmates. To "be inconspicuous" required a special kind of alertness—almost an animal instinct—against the apathy which tended to follow the initial shocks. To give up the struggle for survival was to commit "passive suicide"; a careless mistake meant death. There were those, however, who did come through this phase and who managed an adjustment to the life of the camp. It was the striking contrasts between this group of two- and three-year veterans and the perpetual stream of newcomers which made it possible for men like Bettelheim and Cohen to speak of the "old prisoner" as a specific type.

The most immediate aspect of the old inmates' behavior which struck these observers was its *childlike* quality. "The prisoners developed types of behavior which are characteristic of infancy or early youth. Some of these behaviors developed slowly, others were immediately imposed on the prisoners and developed only in intensity as time went on." Such infantile behavior took innumerable forms. The inmates' sexual impotence brought about a disappearance of sexuality in their talk, instead, excretory functions occupied them endlessly. They lost many of the customary inhibitions as to soiling their beds and their persons. Their humor was shot with silliness and they giggled like children when one of them would expel wind. Their relationships were highly unstable. "Prisoners would, like early adolescents, fight one another tooth and nail . . . only to become close friends within a few minutes." Dishonesty became chronic. "Now they suddenly appeared to be pathological liars, to be unable to restrain themselves, to be unable to make objective evaluation, etc." "In hundreds of ways," writes Colaço Belmonte, "the soldier, and to an even greater extent the prisoner of war, is given to understand that he is a child. . . . Then dishonesty, mendacity, egotistic actions in order to obtain more food or to get out of scrapes reach full development, and theft becomes a veritable affliction of camp life." This was all true, according to Elie Cohen, in the concentration camp as well. Benedikt Kautsky observed such things in his own behavior: "I myself can declare that often I saw myself as I used to be in my school days, when by sly dodges and clever pretexts we avoided being found out, or could 'organize' something." Bruno Bettelheim remarks on the extravagance of the stories told by the prisoners to one another. "They were boastful, telling tales about what they had accomplished in their former lives, or how they succeeded in cheating foremen or guards, and how they sabotaged the work. Like children they felt not at all set back or ashamed when it became known that they had lied about their prowess."

This development of childlike behavior in the old inmates was the counterpart of something even more striking that was happening to them: *"Only very few of the prisoners escaped a more or less intensive identification with the SS."* As Mr. Bettelheim puts it: "A prisoner had reached the final stage of adjustment to the camp situation when he had changed his personality so as to accept as his own the values of the Gestapo." The Bettelheim study furnishes a catalogue of examples. The old prisoners came to share the attitude of the SS toward the "unfit" prisoners; newcomers who behaved badly in the labor groups or who could not withstand the strain became a liability for the others, who were often instrumental in getting rid of them. Many old prisoners actually imitated the SS; they would sew and mend their uniforms in such a way as to make them look more like those of the SS—even though they risked punishment for it. "When asked why they did it, they admitted that they loved to look like . . . the guards." Some took great enjoyment in the fact that during roll call "they really had stood well at attention." There were cases of nonsensical rules, made by the guards, which the older prisoners would continue to observe and try to force on the others long after the SS had forgotten them. Even the most abstract ideals of the SS, such as their intense German nationalism and antiSemitism, were often absorbed by the old inmates—a phenomenon observed among the politically well-educated and even among the Jews themselves. The final quintessence of all this was seen in the "Kapo"—the prisoner who had been placed in a supervisory position over his fellow inmates. These creatures, many of them professional criminals, not only behaved with slavish servility to the SS, but the way in which they often outdid the SS in sheer brutality became one of the most durable features of the concentration-camp legend.

To all these men, reduced to complete and childish dependence upon their masters, the SS had actually become a father-symbol. "The SS man was all-powerful in the camp, he was the lord and master of the prisoner's life. As a cruel father he could, without fear of punishment, even kill the prisoner and as a gentle father he could scatter largesse and afford the prisoner his protection." The result, admits Dr. Cohen, was that "for all of us the SS was a father image. . . ." The closed system, in short, had become a kind of grotesque patriarchy.

It is hoped that the very hideousness of a special example of slavery has not disqualified it as a test for certain features of a far milder and more benevolent form of slavery. But it should still be possible to say, with regard to the individuals who lived as slaves within the respective systems, that just as on one level there is every difference between a wretched childhood and a carefree one, there are, for other purposes, limited features which the one may be said to have shared with the other.

Both were closed systems from which all standards based on prior connections had been effectively detached. A working adjustment to either system required a childlike conformity, a limited choice of "significant others." Cruelty per se cannot be considered the primary key to this; of far greater importance was the simple "closedness" of the system, in which all lines of authority descended from the master and in which alternative social bases that might have supported alternative standards were systematically suppressed. The individual, consequently, for his very psychic security, had to picture his master in some way as the "good father." . . .

For the Negro child, in particular, the plantation offered no really satisfactory father-image other than the master. The "real" father was virtually without authority over his child, since discipline, parental responsibility, and control of rewards and punishments all rested in other hands; the slave father could not even protect the mother of his children except by appealing directly to the master. Indeed, the mother's own role loomed far larger for the slave child than did that of the father. She controlled those few activities— household care, preparation of food, and rearing of children—that were left to the slave family. For that matter, the very etiquette of plantation life removed even the honorific attributes of fatherhood from the Negro male, who was addressed as "boy"—until, when the vigorous years of his prime were past, he was allowed to assume the title of "uncle."

. . . For the master, the role most aptly fitting such a relationship would naturally be that of the father. As a father he could be either harsh or kind, as he chose, but as a *wise* father he would have, we may suspect, a sense of the limits of his situation. He must be ready to cope with *all* the qualities of the child, exasperating as well as ingratiating. He might conceivably have to expect in this child— besides his loyalty, docility, humility, cheerfulness, and (under supervision) his diligence—such additional qualities as irresponsibility, playfulness, silliness, laziness, and (quite possibly) tendencies to lying and stealing. Should the entire prediction prove accurate, the result would be something resembling "Sambo."

The social and psychological sanctions of role-playing may in the last analysis prove to be the most satisfactory of the several approaches to Sambo, for, without doubt, of all the roles in American life that of Sambo was by far the most pervasive. The outlines of the role might be sketched in by crude necessity, but what of the finer shades? The sanctions against overstepping it were bleak enough, but the rewards—the sweet applause, as it were, for performing it with sincerity and feeling—were something to be appreciated on quite another level. The law, untuned to the deeper harmonies, could command the player to be present for the occasion, and the whip might even warn against his missing the grosser cues, but could those things really insure the performance that melted all hearts? Yet there was many and many a performance, and the audiences (whose standards were high) appear to have been for the most part well pleased. They were actually viewing their own masterpiece. Much labor had been lavished upon this chef d'oeuvre, the most genial resources of Southern society had been available for the work; touch after touch had been applied throughout the years, and the result—embodied not in the unfeeling law but in the richest layers of Southern lore—had been the product of an exquisitely rounded collective creativity. And indeed, in a sense that somehow transcended the merely ironic, it was a labor of love. "I love the simple and unadulterated slave, with his geniality, his mirth, his swagger, and his nonsense," wrote Edward Pollard. "I love to look upon his countenance shining with content and grease; I love to study his affectionate heart; I love to mark that peculiarity in him, which beneath all his buffoonery exhibits him as a creature of the tenderest sensibilities, mingling his joys and his sorrows with those of his master's home." Love, even on those terms, was surely no inconsequential reward. . . .

Might the process, on the other hand, be reversed? It is hard to imagine its being reversed overnight. The same role might still be played in the years after slavery—we are told that it was—and yet it was played to more vulgar audiences with cruder standards, who paid much less for what they saw. The lines might be repeated more and more mechanically, with less and less conviction; the incentives to perfection could become hazy and blurred, and the excellent old piece could degenerate over time into low farce. There could come a point, conceivably, with the old zest gone, that it was no longer worth the candle. The day might come at last when it dawned on a man's full waking consciousness that he had really grown up, that he was, after all, only playing a part.

. . . Why should it be, turning once more to Latin America, that there one finds no Sambo, no social tradition, that is, in which slaves were defined by virtually complete consensus as children incapable of being trusted with the full privileges of freedom and adulthood? There, the system surely had its brutalities. The slaves arriving there from Africa had also undergone the capture, the sale, the Middle

Passage. They too had been uprooted from a prior culture, from a life very different from the one in which they now found themselves. There, however, the system was not closed.

Here again the concentration camp, paradoxically enough, can be instructive. There were in the camps a very small minority of the survivors who had undergone an experience different in crucial ways from that of the others, an experience which protected them from the full impact of the closed system. These people, mainly by virtue of wretched little jobs in the camp administration which offered them a minute measure of privilege, were able to carry on "underground" activities. In a practical sense the actual operations of such "undergrounds" as were possible may seem to us unheroic and limited: stealing blankets; "organizing" a few bandages, a little medicine, from the camp hospital; black market arrangements with a guard for a bit of extra food and protection for oneself and one's comrades; the circulation of news; and other such apparently trifling activities. But for the psychological balance of those involved, such activities were vital; they made possible a fundamentally different adjustment to the camp. To a prisoner so engaged, there were others who mattered, who gave real point to his existence—the SS was no longer the *only* one. . . .

It was just such a difference—indeed, a much greater one—that separated the typical slave in Latin America from the typical slave in the United States. Though he too had experienced the Middle Passage, he was entering a society where alternatives were significantly more diverse than those awaiting his kinsman in North America. Concerned in some sense with his status were distinct and at certain points competing institutions. This involved multiple and often competing "significant others." His master was, of course, clearly the chief one—but not the only one. There could, in fact, be a considerable number: the friar who boarded his ship to examine his conscience, the confessor; the priest who made the rounds and who might report irregularities in treatment to the *procurador*; the zealous Jesuit quick to resent a master's intrusion upon such sacred matters as marriage and worship (a resentment of no small consequence to the master); the local magistrate, with his eye on the king's official protector of slaves, who would find himself in trouble were the laws too widely evaded; the king's informer who received one-third of the fines. For the slave the result was a certain latitude; the lines did not all converge on one man; the slave's personality, accordingly, did not have to focus on a single role. He was, true enough, primarily a slave. Yet he might in fact perform multiple roles. He could be a husband and a father (for the American slave these roles had virtually no meaning); open to him also were such activities as artisan, peddler, petty merchant, truck gardener (the law reserved to him the necessary time and a share of the proceeds, but such arrangements were against the law for Sambo); he could be a communicant in the church, a member of a religious fraternity (roles guaranteed by the most powerful institution in Latin America—comparable privileges in the American South depended on a master's pleasure). These roles were all legitimized and protected *outside* the plantation; they offered a diversity of channels for the development of personality. Not only did the individual have multiple roles open to him as a slave, but the very nature of these roles made possible a certain range of aspirations should he some day become free. He could have a fantasy-life not limited to catfish and watermelons; it was within his conception to become a priest, an independent farmer, a successful merchant, a military officer. The slave could actually—to an extent quite unthinkable in the United States—conceive of himself *as a rebel*. Bloody slave revolts, actual wars, took place in Latin America; nothing on this order occurred in the United States. But even without a rebellion, society here had a network of customary arrangements, rooted in antiquity, which made possible at many points a smooth transition of status from slave to free and which provided much social space for the exfoliation of individual character. . . .

The American slave system, compared with that of Latin America, was closed and circumscribed, but, like all social systems, its arrangements were less perfect in practice than they appeared to be in theory. It was possible for significant numbers of slaves, in varying degrees, to escape the full impact of the system and its coercions upon personality. The house servant, the urban mechanic, the slave who arranged his own employment and paid his master a stipulated sum each week, were all figuratively members of the "underground." Even among those working on large plantations, the skilled craftsman or the responsible slave foreman had a measure of independence not shared by his simpler brethren. Even the single slave family owned by a small farmer had a status much closer to that of house servants than to that of a plantation labor gang. For all such people there was a margin of space denied to the majority; the system's authority-structure claimed their bodies but not quite their souls. . . .

It is of great interest to note that although the danger of slave revolts (like Communist conspiracies in our own day) was much overrated by touchy Southerners, the revolts that actually did occur were in no instance planned by plantation laborers but rather by

Negroes whose qualities of leadership were developed well outside the full coercions of the plantation authority-system. Gabriel, who led the revolt of 1800, was a blacksmith who lived a few miles outside Richmond; Denmark Vesey, leading spirit of the 1822 plot at Charleston, was a freed Negro artisan who had been born in Africa and served several years aboard a slavetrading vessel; and Nat Turner, the Virginia slave who fomented the massacre of 1831, was a literate preacher of recognized intelligence. Of the plots that have been convincingly substantiated (whether they came to anything or not), the majority originated in urban centers.

For a time during Reconstruction, a Negro elite of sorts did emerge in the South. Many of its members were Northern Negroes, but the Southern ex-slaves who also comprised it seem in general to have emerged from the categories just indicated. Vernon Wharton, writing of Mississippi, says:

> A large portion of the minor Negro leaders were preachers, lawyers, or teachers from the free states or from Canada. Their education and their independent attitude gained for them immediate favor and leadership. Of the natives who became their rivals, the majority had been urban slaves, blacksmiths, carpenters, clerks, or waiters in hotels and boarding houses; a few of them had been favored body-servants of affluent whites.

The William Johnsons and Denmark Veseys have been accorded, though belatedly, their due honor. They are, indeed, all too easily identified, thanks to the system that enabled them as individuals to be so conspicuous and so exceptional and, as members of a group, so few.

10

Day to Day Resistance to Slavery

Raymond A. Bauer and Alice H. Bauer

From: *Journal of Negro History*, XXVII (October 1942), pp. 388–419. Some footnotes deleted and renumbered. Copyright © 1942 by The Association for the Study of Negro Life and History, Inc.

There were a number of slave revolts in the United States and there were still more near-revolts. But even if Elkins is right in general, does this mean that all slaves acquiesced in the system of bondage or that every slave was docile all the time? It is surely hard to believe that even a "total" system does not slip occasionally, and that even the most docile victim does not sometimes strike back. Admittedly the weak often do not dare to resist their oppressors openly; but the weak, as any parent or army officer knows, have ways of retaliating indirectly against the strong. They do this in covert ways that are difficult to detect and difficult to stop.

In this selection Raymond and Alice Bauer describe how slaves were able to express their anger at the slave regime and to frustrate the white men who had imposed it on them. While the Bauers do not say so directly, their story suggests a possible explanation for the Sambo personality that Elkins finds among the slaves: one excellent way to bedevil the masters was to be lazy, inefficient, and uncomprehending. It might not earn the respect of the slaveholder, but it would often effectively express the slave's opposition and perhaps enable him to escape from some of the normal burdens of his status. At all events, as the Bauers indicate, contemporaries recognized that the apparent clumsiness and stupidity of many blacks was sham, put

on to avoid work or punishment. Obviously this "day to day resist-
ance" could not destroy the slave system, but it certainly made it
less efficient and less profitable, and also less intolerable to its
victims.

I

    The tradition that has grown up about Negro slavery is that the
slaves were docile, well adapted to slavery, and reasonably content
with their lot. . . . This concept is gradually being changed as the
study of slave revolts, and of the social tension caused by the constant threat of revolt progresses. In answer to the question, " 'Are the
masters afraid of insurrection?' (a slave) says, 'They live in constant
fear upon this subject. The least unusual noise at night alarms them
greatly. They cry out, 'What is that?' 'Are the boys all in'?"

    The purpose of this paper is to study a less spectacular aspect
of slavery—the day to day resistance to slavery, since it is felt that
such a study will throw some further light on the nature of the
Negro's reaction to slavery. Our investigation has made it apparent
that the Negroes not only were very discontented, but that they
developed effective protest techniques in the form of indirect retaliation for their enslavement. Since this conclusion differs sharply
from commonly accepted belief, it would perhaps be of value if a
brief preliminary statement were made of how belief so at variance
with the available documentary materials could gain such
acceptance.

    The picture of the docile, contented Negro slave grew out of
two lines of argument used in antebellum times. The proslavery
faction contended that the slaves came of an inferior race, and that
they were happy and contented in their subordinate position, and
that the dancing and singing Negro exemplified their assumption.
Abolitionists, on the other hand, tended to depict the Negro slave
as a passive instrument, a good and faithful worker exploited and
beaten by a cruel master. As one reads the controversial literature
on the slavery question, it soon becomes apparent that both sides
presented the Negro as a docile creature; one side because it wished
to prove that he was contented, the other because it wished to prove
that he was grossly mistreated. Both conceptions have persisted to
the present time. Writers who romanticize the "Old South" idealize
the condition of the slaves, and make of them happy, willing servi-
tors, while those who are concerned with furthering the interests of
the Negroes are careful to avoid mention of any aggressive tenden-

cies which might be used as a pretext for further suppressing the Negroes.

Many travelers in the South have accepted the overt behavior of the slaves at its face value. The "yas suh, Cap'n," the smiling, bowing, and scraping of the Negroes have been taken as tokens of contentment. [James] Redpath's conversations with slaves indicated how deep seated this behavior was. This point of view, however, neglects the fact that the whites have always insisted on certain forms of behavior as a token of acceptance of inferior status by the Negro. The following quotation from [John] Dollard is pertinent:

> An informant already cited has referred to the Negro as a "Dr. Jekyll and Mr. Hyde." He was making an observation that is well understood among Negroes—that he has a kind of dual personality, two rôles, one that he is forced to play with white people and one the "real Negro" as he appears in his dealings with his own people. What the white southern people see who "know their Negroes" is the rôle that they have forced the Negro to accept, his caste role.

The conceptual framework within which this paper is written is that the Negro slaves were forced into certain outward forms of compliance to slavery; that, except for the few who were able to escape to the North, the Negroes had to accept the institution of slavery and make their adjustments to that institution. The patterns of adjustment which we have found operative are: slowing up of work, destruction of property, malingering and self-mutilation. . . .

II

The Negroes were well aware that the work they did benefited only the master. "The slaves work and the planter gets the benefit of it." "The conversation among the slaves was that they worked hard and got no benefit, that the masters got it all." It is thus not surprising that one finds many recurring comments that a slave did not do half a good day's work in a day. A northerner whom [Sir Charles] Lyell met in the South said:

> Half the population of the south is employed in seeing that the other half do their work, and they who do work accomplish half what they might do under a better system.

An English visitor, with a very strong proslavery bias corroborates this:

> The amount of work expected of the field hand will not be more than one half of what would be demanded of a white man; and even that will not be properly done unless he be constantly overlooked.

Statements of other writers are to the same effect:

> It is a common remark of those persons acquainted with slave-labour, that their proportion is as one to two. This is not too great an estimate in favour of the free-labourer; and the circumstances of their situation produce a still greater disparity.
>
> A capitalist was having a building erected in Petersburg, and his slaves were employed in carrying up the brick and mortar for the masons on their heads: a Northerner, standing near, remarked to him that they moved so indolently that it seemed as if they were trying to see how long they could be in mounting the ladder without actually stopping. The builder started to reprove them, but after moving a step turned back and said: "It would only make them move more slowly still when I am not looking at them, if I should hurry now. *And what motive have they to do better?* It's no concern of theirs how long the masons wait. I am sure if I was in their place, I shouldn't move as fast as they do.

A well-informed capitalist and slave-holder remarked,

> In working niggers, we always calculate that they will not labor at all except to avoid punishment, and they will never do more than just enough to save themselves from being punished, and no amount of punishment will prevent their working carelessly or indifferently. It always seems on the plantations as if they took pains to break all the tools and spoil all the cattle that they possibly can, even when they know they'll be directly punished for it.

Just how much of this was due to indifference and how much due to deliberate slowing up is hard to determine. Both factors most probably entered. A worker who had to devote himself to a dull task from which he can hope to gain nothing by exercising initiative soon slips into such a frame of mind that he does nothing more than go through the motions. His chief concern is to escape from the realities of his task and put it in the back of his mind as much as possible.

There is, indeed, a strong possibility that this behavior was a form of indirect aggression. While such an hypothesis cannot be demonstrated on the basis of the available contemporary data, it is supported by Dollard's interpretation of similar behavior which he found in southern towns.

> If the reader has even seen Stepin Fetchit in the movies, he can picture this type of character. Fetchit always plays the part of a well-

accommodating lower-class Negro, whining, vacillating, shambling, stupid, and moved by very simple cravings. There is probably an element of resistance to white society in the shambling, sullenly slow pace of the Negro; it is the gesture of a man who is forced to work for ends not his own and who expresses his reluctance to perform under these circumstances.

Certainly description after description emphasizes the mechanical plodding of the slave workers:

> John Lamar wrote, "My man Ned the carpenter is idle or nearly so at the plantation. He is fixing gates and, like the idle groom in Pickwick, trying to fool himself into the belief that he is doing something—He is an eye servant."
>
> Those I saw at work appeared to me to move very slowly and awkwardly, as did those engaged in the stables. These also were very stupid and dilatory in executing any orders given them, so that Mr. C. would frequently take the duty off their hands into his own, rather than wait for them, or make them correct their blunders; they were much, in these respects, what our farmers call *dumb Paddees*— that is, Irishmen who do not readily understand the English language, and who are still weak and stiff from the effects of the emigrating voyage. At the entrance gate was a porter's lodge, and, as I approached I saw a black face peeping at me from it, but both when I entered and left, I was obliged to dismount and open the gate myself.
>
> Altogether, it struck me—slaves coming here as they naturally did in comparison with free laborers, as commonly employed on my own and my neighbors' farms, in exactly similar duties—they they must have been difficult to direct efficiently, and that it must be irksome and trying to one's patience, to have to superintend their labor.

To what extent this reluctant labor was the rule may be appreciated when it is pointed out that a southern doctor classified it under the name *Dysaethesia Aethiopica* as a mental disease peculiar to Negroes. [Frederick Law] Olmsted quotes this Dr. Cartwright as follows:

> "From the careless movements of the individual affected with this complaint, they are apt to do much mischief, which appears as if intentional, but it is mostly owing to the stupidness of mind and insensibility of the nerves induced by the disease. Thus, they break, waste, and destroy everything they handle—abuse horses and cattle —tear, burn, or rend their own clothing, and, paying no attention to the rights of property, steal others to replace what they have destroyed. They wander about at night, and keep in a half nodding state by day. They slight their work—cut up corn, cotton and tobacco, when hoeing it, as if for pure mischief. They raise disturbances with their overseers, and among their fellow servants, without cause or

motive, and seem to be insensible to pain when subjected to punishment.

> . . . The term 'rascality' given to this disease by overseers, is founded on an erroneous hypothesis, and leads to an incorrect empirical treatment, which seldom or never cures it."

There are only two possible interpretations of the doctor's statement. Either the slaves were so extraordinarily lazy that they gave the appearance of being mentally diseased, or the doctor was describing cases of hebephrenic schizophrenia. Either situation is startling. The phenomenon was obviously widespread, and if it was actually a mental disease it certainly would indicate that Negroes did not become "easily adjusted to slavery."

Whatever the case, it is certain that the slaves consciously saved their energy. Olmsted, who always had his eye open for such incidents, reported:

> The overseer rode among them, on a horse, carrying in his hand a raw-hide whip, constantly directing and encouraging them; but, as my companion and I, both, several times noticed, as often as he visited one line of the operations, the hands at the other end would discontinue their labor, until he turned to ride toward them again.

The few statements on this point we have by ex-slaves seem to indicate that the slaves as a group made a general policy of not letting the master get the upper hand.

> I had become large and strong; and had begun to take pride in the fact that I could do as much hard work as some of the older men. There is much rivalry among slaves, at times, as to which can do the most work, and masters generally seek to promote such rivalry. But some of us were too wise to race with each other very long. Such racing, we had the sagacity to see, was not likely to pay. We had times out for measuring each other's strength, but we knew too much to keep up the competition so long as to produce an extraordinary day's work. We knew that if, by extraordinary exertion, a large quantity of work was done in one day, the fact, becoming known to the master, might lead him to require the same amount every day. This thought was enough to bring us to a dead halt whenever so much excited for the race.

Writer after writer, describing incidents in which slaves were compelled to assist in punishing other slaves states that they did so with the greatest of reluctance.

> The hands stood still;—they knew Randall—and they knew him also take a powerful man, and were afraid to grapple with him. As soon as Cook had ordered the men to seize him, Randall turned to

them, and said—"Boys, you all know me; you know that I can handle any three of you, and the man that lays hands on me shall die. This white man can't whip me himself, and therefore he has called you to help him." The overseer was unable to prevail upon them to seize and secure Randall, and finally ordered them all to go to their work together.

In some cases it was noted that the slave resisting punishment took pains not to treat his fellows with any more than the absolute minimum of violence.

With such demonstrations of solidarity among the slaves it is not surprising to find a slave telling of how he and his fellows "captured" the institution of the driver. The slave Solomon Northrup was such a driver. His task was to whip the other slaves in order to make them work.

> "Practice makes perfect," truly; and during eight years' experience as a driver I learned to handle the whip with marvelous dexterity and precision, throwing the lash within a hair's breadth of the back, the ear, the nose without, however, touching either of them. If Epps was observed at a distance, or we had reason to apprehend he was sneaking somewhere in the vicinity, I would commence plying the lash vigorously, when, according to arrangement, they would squirm and screech as if in agony, although not one of them had in fact been grazed. Patsey would take occasion, if he made his appearance presently, to mumble in his hearing some complaints that Platt was whipping them the whole time, and Uncle Abram, with an appearance of honesty peculiar to himself would declare roundly I had just whipped them worse than General Jackson whipped the enemy at New Orleans.

Williams, another slave whose task was to drive his fellows, said:

> He was at these periods terribly severe to his hands, and would order me to use up the cracker of my whip every day upon the poor creatures who were toiling in the field; and in order to satisfy him, I used to tear it off when returning home at night. He would then praise me for a good fellow and invite me to drink with him.

The amount of slowing up of labor by the slaves must, in the aggregate, have caused a tremendous financial loss to plantation owners. The only way we have of estimating it quantitatively is through comparison of the work done in different plantations and under different systems of labor. The statement is frequently made that production on a plantation varied more than 100 percent from time to time. Comparison in the output of slaves in different parts of the South also showed variations of over 100 percent. Most significant is the improvement in output obtained under the task, whereby the slaves were given a specific task to fulfill for their day's work, any time left over being their own. Olmsted gives us our best information on this point:

> These tasks certainly would not be considered excessively hard by a northern laborer; and, in point of fact, the more industrious and active hands finished them often by two o'clock. I saw one or two leaving the field soon after one o'clock, several about two; and between three and four, I met a dozen women and several men coming home to their cabins, having finished their day's work.
>
> Under this "Organization of Labor" most of the slaves work rapidly and well. In nearly all ordinary work, custom has settled the extent of the task, and it is difficult to increase it. The driver who marks it out, has to remain on the ground until it is finished, and has no interest in overmeasuring it; and if it should be systematically increased very much, there is danger of a general stampede to the swamp, a danger the slave can always hold before his master's cupidity.
>
> It is the custom of tobacco manufacturers to hire slaves and free negroes at a certain rate of wages each year. A task of 45 pounds per day is given them to work up, and all they choose to do more than this, they are paid for—payment being made once a fortnight; and invariably this over-wages is used by the slave for himself, and is usually spent in drinking. licentiousness, and gambling. The man was grumbling that he had saved but $20 to spend at the holidays. One of the manufacturers offered to show me by his books, that nearly all gained by over-work $5 a month, many $20 and some as much as $28.
>
> He (the speaker) was executor of an estate in which, among other negroes, there was one very smart man, who, he knew perfectly well, ought to be earning for the estate $150 a year, and who could if he chose, yet whose wages for a year being let out by the day or job, had amounted to but $18, while he had paid for medical attendance upon him $45.

The executor of the estate finally arranged for this man to work out his freedom, which he readily accomplished.

A quantitative estimate can be made from another situation which Olmsted observed. Rain during a previous day had made certain parts of the work more difficult than others. The slaves were therefore put on day work, since it would not be possible to lay out equitable tasks.

> Ordinarily it is done by tasks—a certain number of the small divisions of the field being given to each hand to burn in a day; but owing to a more than usual amount of rain having fallen lately, and some other causes, making the work harder in some places than in

others, the women were now working by the day, under the direction of a "driver," a negro man, who walked about among them, taking care they had left nothing unburned. Mr. X inspected the ground they had gone over, to see whether the driver had done his duty. It had been sufficiently well burned, but not more than a quarter as much ground had been gone over, he said, as was usually burned in tasked work,—and he thought they had been very lazy, and reprimanded them for it.

Most revealing of all is this statement:

"Well, now, old man," said I, "you go and cut me two cords today?" "Oh, massa! two cords! Nobody could do dat. Oh! massa, dat is too hard! Neber heard o' nobody's cuttin' more 'n a cord o' wood in a day, round heah. No nigger couldn't do it." "Well, old man, you have two cords of wood cut to-night or to-morrow morning you shall get two hundred lashes—that's all there is about it. So look sharp." And he did it and ever since no negro ever cut less than two cords a day for me, though my neighbors never get but one cord. It was just so with a great many other things—mauling rails—I always have two hundred rails mauled in a day; just twice what it is the custom of the country to expect of a negro, and just twice as many as my negroes had been made to do before I managed them myself.

These estimates, let it be recollected in conclusion, are all deliberately and carefully made by gentlement of liberal education, who have had unusual facilities of observing both at the North and the South.

The slaves were well aware of their economic value, and used it to good advantage. The skilled laborers among the slaves knew their worth, and frequently rebelled against unsatisfactory work situations. Slaves who were hired out would run away from the masters who had hired them, and then either return home, or remain in hiding until they felt like returning to work.

The slave, if he is indisposed to work, and especially if he is not treated well, or does not like the master who has hired him, will sham sickness—even make himself sick or lame—that he need not work. But a more serious loss frequently arises, when the slave, thinking he is worked too hard, or being angered by punishment or unkind treatment, "getting the sulks,' 'takes to "the swamp," and comes back when he has a mind to. Often this will not be till the year is up for which he is engaged, when he will return to his owner, who, glad to find his property safe, and that it has not died in the swamp, or gone to Canada, forgets to punish him, and immediately sends him for another year to a new master.

"But, meanwhile, how does the negro support life in the swamp?" I asked.

"Oh, he gets sheep and pigs and calves, and fowls and turkey; sometimes they will kill a small cow. We have often seen the fires, where they were cooking them, through the woods in the swamp yonder. If it is cold, he will crawl under a fodder stack, or go into the cabins with some of the other negroes, and in the same way, you see, he can get all the corn, or almost anything else he wants."

"He steals them from his master?"

"From anyone: frequently from me. I have had many a sheep taken by them."

"It is a common thing, then?"

"Certainly it is, very common, and the loss is sometimes exceedingly provoking. One of my neighbors here was going to build, and hired two mechanics for a year. Just as he was ready to put his house up, the two men, taking offense at something, both ran away, and did not come back at all, till their year was out, and then their owner immediately hired them out again to another man."

One plantation overseer wrote to the plantation owner concerning a carpenter he had hired out to one G. Moore:

Not long before Jim run away G More (sic.) wanted him to make some gates and I sent him theireselves (sic.) and he run away from him and cum home and then he left me withow (sic.) a cause.

Even the threat of a whipping did not deter such slaves from running off for a time when they were displeased. The quotation from Olmsted below is typical of a constantly recurring pattern of statements:

The manager told me that the people often ran away after they have been whipped or something else had happened to make them angry. They hide in the swamp and come into the cabins at night to get food. They seldom remain away more than a fortnight and when they come in they are whipped.

Some of the resistance took on the aspects of organized strikes:

Occasionally, however, a squad would strike in a body as a protest against severities. An episode of this sort was recounted in a letter of a Georgia overseer to his absent employer: "Sir: I write you a few lines in order to let you know that six of your hands has left the plantation—every man but Jack. They displeased me with their work and I give some of them a few lashes, Tom with the rest. On Wednesday morning they were missing. I think they are lying out until they can see you or your Uncle Jack." The slaves could not negotiate directly at such a time, but while they lay in the woods they might make overtures to the overseer through slaves on a neighboring plantation as to terms upon which they would return to work, or they might await their master's posthaste arrival and appeal to him for a redress of grievances. Humble as their demeanor might be, their power of renewing the pressure by repeating their act could not be ignored.

John Holmes, an escaped slave, told how he ran off and hid in the swamp after an overseer attempted to whip him.

> At last they told all the neighbors if I would come home, they wouldn't whip me. I was a great hand to work and made a great deal of money for our folks.

The same overseer had further trouble with the slaves.

> She (a slave) was better with her fists, and beat him, but he was better at wrestling and threw her down. He then called the men to help him, but all hid from him in the brush where we were working. . . . Then (later) the calculation was to whip us every one, because we did not help the overseer. . . . That night every one of us went away into the woods. . . . We went back, but after a while (the overseer) came back too, and stayed the year out. He whipped the women but he did not whip the men, of fear they would run away.

III

The indifference of the slaves to the welfare of the masters extended itself to a complete contempt for property values. The slaves were so careless with tools that they were equipped with special tools, and more clumsy than ordinary ones:

> "The nigger hoe" was first introduced into Virginia as a substitute for the plow, in breaking up the soil. The law fixes its weight at four pounds,—as heavy as the woodman's axe. It is still used, not only in Virginia, but in Georgia and the Carolinas. The planters tell us, as the reason for its use, that the negroes would break a Yankee hoe in pieces on the first root, or stone that might be in their way. An instructive commentary on the difference between free and slave labor!
> The absence of motive, and the consequent want of mental energy to give vigor to the arm of the slave is the source of another great drawback upon the usefulness of his labour. His implements or tools are at least one-third (in some instances more than twofold) heavier and stronger than the northern man's to counteract his want of skill and interest in his work. A Negro hoe or scythe would be a curiosity to a New England farmer.

Not only tools but live stock suffered from the mistreatment by the slaves. Olmsted found not only the "nigger hoe" but even discovered that mules were substituted for horses because horses could not stand up under the treatment of the slaves.

. . . . I am shown tools that no man in his senses, with us, would allow a laborer, to whom he was paying wages, to be encumbered with; and the excessive weight and clumsiness of which, I would judge, would make work at least ten per cent greater than those ordinarily used with us. And I am assured that, in the careless and clumsy way they must be used by the slaves, anything lighter or less crude could not be furnished them with good economy, and that such tools as we constantly give our laborers and find profit in giving them, would not last out a day in a Virginia corn-field—much lighter and more free from stones though it be than ours.

So, too, when I ask why mules are so universally substituted for horses on the farm, the first reason given, and confessedly the most conclusive one, is, that horses cannot bear the treatment they always must get from negroes; horses are always soon foundered or crippled by them but mules will bear cudgeling, and lose a meal or two now and then, and not be materially injured, and they do not take cold or get sick if neglected or overworked. But I do not need to go further than to the window of the room in which I am writing, to see, at almost any time, treatment of cattle that would insure the immediate discharge of the driver, by almost any farmer owning them in the North.

Redpath verifies Olmsted's statement—by telling how he saw slaves treat stock. It is important to note that Redpath was a strong abolitionist and most sympathetic toward the slaves.

He rode the near horse, and held a heavy cowhide in his hand, with which from time to time he lashed the leaders, as barbarous drivers lash oxen when at work. Whenever we came to a hill, especially if it was very steep, he dismounted, lashed the horses with all his strength, varying his performances by picking up stones, none of them smaller than half a brick, and throwing them with all his force, at the horses' legs. He seldom missed.

The wagon was laden with two tons of plaster in sacks.

This is a fair specimen of the style in which Negroes treat stock.

The indifference to live-stock is well illustrated by an incident which Olmsted recounts:

I came, one afternoon, upon a herd of uncommonly fine cattle as they were being turned out of a field by a negro woman. She had given herself the trouble to let down but two of the seven bars of the fence, and they were obliged to leap over a barrier at least four feet high. Last of all came, very unwillingly, a handsome heifer, heavy with calf; the woman urged her with a cudgel and she jumped, but lodging on her belly, as I came up she lay bent, and, as it seemed, helplessly hung upon the top bar. . . . The woman struck her severely and with a painful effort she boggled over.

In the Sea Islands off the coast of Georgia, [Fanny] Kemble reported that the slaves started immense fires, destroying large sections of woods through carelessness or maliciousness.

> The "field hands" make fires to cook their midday food wherever they happen to be working, and sometimes through their careless neglect, but sometimes, too, undoubtedly on purpose, the woods are set fire to by these means. One benefit they consider . . . is the destruction of the dreaded rattlesnakes.

The slaves on [M. G.] Lewis' West Indies plantation let cattle get into one of his best cane-pieces because they neglected to guard them, being more interested in a dance which was going on. They were fully aware that the cattle were ruining the sugar cane, but kept right on singing and dancing. Lewis was able to get only a handful of house servants to drive the cattle out of the cane, and that not until the cane-piece was ruined.

One tobacco planter complained that his slaves would cut the young plants indiscriminately unless they were watched. When it became late in the season and there was need of haste to avoid frost they would work only the thickest leaving the sparser ones untouched. Another planter said that he could cultivate only the poorer grades of tobacco because the slaves would not give necessary attention to the finer sort of plants. An English visitor said:

> The kitchens and out-offices are always at the distance of several yards from the principal dwelling. This is done as well to guard against the house-Negroes through carelessness setting the houses on fire, for they generally sit over it half the night, as to keep out their noise. (sic.)

The full import of these practices strikes home fully only when they are read in the words of the original observers. Olmsted's comments, and the ease with which he found incidents to illustrate them, are most valuable. So important is his testimony that we must once more quote him at some length.

> Incidents, trifling in themselves, constantly betray to a stranger the bad economy of using enslaved servants. The catastrophe of one such occurred since I began to write this letter. I ordered a fire to be made in my room, as I was going out this morning. On my return, I found a grand fire—the room door having been closed and locked upon it "out of order." Just now, while I was writing, down tumbled

upon the floor, and rolled away close to the valance of the bed, half a hod-full of ignited coal, which had been so piled upon the diminutive grate, and left without a fender or any guard, that this result was almost inevitable. If I had not returned at the time I did, the house would have been fired.

On the rice plantation which I have particularly described, the slaves were, I judge, treated with at least as much discretion and judicious consideration of economy, consistently with humane regard to their health, comfort, and morals, as on any other in all the Slave States; yet I could not avoid observing—and I certainly took no pains to do so, nor were any special facilities offered me for it—repeated instances of that waste and misapplication of labor which it can never be possible to guard against, when the agents of industry are slaves. Many such evidences of waste it would not be easy to specify; and others, which remain in my memory after some weeks, do not adequately account for the general impression that all I saw gave me; but there were, for instance, under my observation gates left open and bars left down, against standing orders; rails removed from fences by the negroes (as was conjectured, to kindle their fires with), mules lamed, and implements broken, by careless usage; a flat boat, carelessly secured, going adrift on the river; men ordered to cart rails for a new fence depositing them so that a double expense of labor would be required to lay them, more than would have needed if they had been placed, as they might have almost as easily been, by a slight exercise of forethought . . . making statements which their owner was obliged to receive as sufficient excuse, though, he told me, he felt assured they were false—all going to show habitual carelessness, indolence, and mere eye-service.

But not only did the Negro slaves refuse to work, and not only did they destroy property, but they even made it impossible for planters to introduce new work techniques by feigning clumsiness. They prevented the introduction of the plow in this way on many plantations. Olmsted here cites many instances. Lewis, quoted in *Plantation Documents*, found the same thing to be true in Jamaica.

It appears to me that nothing could afford so much relief to the negroes, under the existing system of Jamaica, as the substituting of labor of animals for that of slaves in agriculture wherever such a measure is practicable. On leaving the island, I impressed this wish of mine upon the mind of my agents with all my power; but the only result has been the creating a very considerable expense in the purchase of ploughs, oxen and farming implements; the awkwardness and still more the obstinacy of the few negroes, whose services were indispensable, was not to be overcome: they broke plough after plough, and ruined beast after beast, till the attempt was abandoned in despair.

IV

Malingering was a well-known phenomenon throughout the slave states. The purpose of feigning illness was generally to avoid work, although occasionally a slave who was being sold would feign a disability either to avoid being sold to an undesirable master, or to lower his purchase price so as to obtain revenge on a former master. The women occasionally pretended to be pregnant, because pregnant women were given lighter work assignments and were allowed extra rations of food.

In a situation such as this in which physical disability was an advantage, one would expect much malingering. One might also expect to find functional mental disorders, hysterical disorders which would get one out of work. There is some evidence that many had such functional disorders.

> There are many complaints described in Dr. Cartwright's treatise, to which the Negroes, in slavery, seem to be peculiarly subject.
>
> "Negro-consumption," a disease almost unknown to medical men of the Northern States and of Europe, is also sometimes fearfully prevalent among the slaves. "It is of importance," says the Doctor, "to know the pathognomic signs in its early stages, not only in regard to its treatment but to detect impositions, as negroes, afflicted with this complaint are often for sale; the acceleration of the pulse, on exercise, incapacitates them for labor, as they quickly give out, and have to leave their work. This induces their owners to sell them, although they may not know the cause of their inability to labor. Many of the negroes brought South, for sale, are in the incipient stages of this disease; they are found to be inefficient laborers, and sold in consequence thereof. The effect of superstition —a firm belief that he is poisoned or conjured—upon the patient's mind, already in a morbid state (dyaesthesia), and his health affected from hard usage, overtasking or exposure, want of wholesome food, good clothing, warm, comfortable lodging, with the distressing idea (sometimes) that he is an object of hatred or dislike, both to his master or fellow-servants, and has no one to befriend him, tends directly to generate that erythism of mind which is the essential cause of negro consumption" . . . "Remedies should be assisted by removing the *original cause* [Cartwright's italics] of the dissatisfaction or trouble of mind, and by using every means to make the patient comfortable, satisfied and happy."

Of course it is impossible to determine the extent of these disorders. Assuming that Dr. Cartwright's assumption was correct, very few observers would be qualified to make an adequate diagnosis, and a very small proportion of these would be inclined to accept his interpretation. After all, functional disorders are in many cases almost impossible to tell from real disorders or from feigning, and since the behavior which Cartwright describes could very easily be interpreted on another, and easier, level by a less acute observer.

Of the extent to which illness was feigned there can, however, be little doubt. Some of the feigning was quite obvious, and one might wonder why such flagrant abuses were tolerated. The important thing to remember is that a slave was an important economic investment. Most slave owners sooner or later found out that it was more profitable to give the slave the benefit of the doubt. A sick slave driven to work might very well die.

> But the same gentleman admitted that he had sometimes been mistaken and had made men go to work when they afterwards proved to be really ill; therefore, when one of his people told him he was not able to work, he usually thought, "very likely he'll be all the better for a day's rest, whether he's really ill or not," and would let him off without being very particular in his examination. Lately he had been getting a new overseer, and when he was engaging him he told him that this was his way. The overseer replied, "It's my way too, now; it didn't used to be, but I had a lesson. There was a nigger one day at Mr.——'s who was sulky and complaining; he said he couldn't work. I looked at his tongue, and it was right clean, and I thought it was nothing but damned sulkiness so I paddled him, and made him to go to work; but, two days after, he was under ground. He was a good eight hundred dollar nigger, and it was a lesson to me about taming possums, that I ain't going to forget in a hurry."

So one might find situations like this:

> At one, which was evidently the "sick house" or hospital, there were several negroes, of both sexes, wrapped in blankets, and reclining on the door steps or on the ground, basking in sunshine. Some of them looked ill, but all were chatting and laughing as I rode up to make inquiry.

The situation turned in on itself. The masters were always suspicious of the sick slaves, so that slaves who were moderately sick accentuated their symptoms in order to make out a convincing case.

> It is said to be nearly as difficult to form a satisfactory diagnosis of negroes' disorders, as it is of infants', because their imagination of symptoms is so vivid, and because not the smallest reliance is to be placed on their accounts of what they have felt or done. If a man is really ill, he fears lest he should be thought to be simulating, and therefore exaggerates all his pains, and locates them in whatever he supposes to be the most vital parts of his system.
> Frequently the invalid slaves will neglect or refuse to use the

remedies prescribed for their recovery. They will conceal pills, for instance, under their tongue, and declare they have swallowed them, when, from their producing no effect, it will be afterwards evident that they have not. This general custom I heard ascribed to habit acquired when they were not very disagreeably ill and were loth to be made quite well enough to have to go to work again.

Fortunately in this field we have some quantitative estimates which enable us to appreciate fully the extent of these practices. [Charles] Sydnor has digested the records of sickness on various plantations. From the Wheeles plantation records he found that of 1429 working days 179 were lost on account of sicknes, a ratio of almost one to seven. On the Bowles' plantation, in one year 159½ days were missed on account of sickness but only five days were on Sundays. This is a recurrent pattern, everybody sick on Saturday, and scarcely anybody sick on Sunday. On the Leigh plantation, where thirty persons were working there were 398 days of sickness. In examining this record Sydnor discovered that the rate of sickness was greatest at the times of the year when there was the most work to be done. Olmsted says that he never visited a plantation on which twenty Negroes were employed where he did not find one or more not at work on some trivial pretext.

Lewis' anecdote is typical:

On Saturday morning there were no fewer than forty-five persons (not including children) in the hospital; which makes nearly a fifth of my whole gang. Of these the medical people assured me that not above seven had anything whatever the matter with them.... And sure enough on Sunday morning they all walked away from the hospital to amuse themselves, except about seven or eight.

Sometimes the feigning did not work, as is shown by two incidents that Olmsted relates:

A Mr. X asked if there were any sick people.

"Nobody, oney dat boy Sam, sar."

"What Sam is that?"

"Dat little Sam, sar; Tom's Sue's Sam, sar."

"What's the matter with him?"

"Don' spec der's nothing much de matter wid him nof, sar. He came in Sa'dy, complaining he had de stomach-ache, an' I give him some ile, sar, "spec he mus" be well dis time, but he din go out dis mornin."

"Well, I see to him.

Mr. X went to Tom's Sue's cabin, looked at the boy and concluded that he was well, though he lay abed, and pretended to cry with pain, ordered him to go out to work.

A planter asked the nurse if anyone else was sick.

"Oney dat woman Caroline."

"What do you think is the matter with her?"

"Well, I don't think there is anything de matter wid her, masser; I mus answer you for true, I don't tink anything de matter wid her, oney she's a little sore from dat whipping she got."

The manager found the woman groaning on a dirty bed and after examining her, scolded her and sent her to work.

The prevalence of malingering may be better appreciated when one realizes that despite the fact that Olmsted refers to it throughout four volumes of his works, in one place he has five whole pages of anecdotes concerning it.

Pretending to be pregnant was a type of escape in a class by itself, since the fraud must inevitably have been discovered. This in itself may give us some insight into the Negroes' attitude toward the relative advantages of escaping work and of escaping punishment. Just as the slave who ran off into the woods for a temporary relief from work, the pseudo-pregnant woman must have realized in advance that she would inevitably be punished.

I will tell you of a most comical account Mr.——has given me of the prolonged and still protracted pseudo-pregnancy of a woman called Markie, who for many more months than are generally required for the process of continuing the human species, pretended to be what the Germans pathetically and poetically call "in good hope" and continued to reap increased rations as the reward of her expectation, till she finally had to disappoint the estate and receive a flogging.

One woman sought to escape from the consequences of her fraud. The results were quite tragic:

A young slave woman, Becky by name, had given pregnancy as the reason for a continued slackness in her work. Her master became skeptical and gave notice that she was to be examined and might expect the whip in case her excuse were not substantiated. Two days afterwards a Negro midwife announced that Becky's baby had been born; but at the same time a neighboring planter began search for a child nine months old which was missing from his quarter. This child was found in Becky's cabin, with its two teeth pulled and the tip of its navel cut off. It died, and Becky was convicted only of manslaughter.

An outstanding example of malingering is given by [S.] Smedes, a writer who insisted so emphatically on the devotion of the slaves to their masters.

The cook's husband, who for years had looked on himself as

nearly blind, and therefore unable to do more than work about her, and put her wood on the fire, sometimes cutting a stick or two, made no less than eighteen good crops for himself when the war was over. He was one of the best farmers in the country.

The most effective means of retaliation against an unpopular master which the slave had at his command was by feigning disability on the auction block. How often this was done we do not know, but [Ulrich B.] Phillips accepts it as a recognized pattern.

> Those on the block often times praised their own strength and talents, for it was a matter of pride to fetch high prices. On the other hand if a slave should bear a grudge against his seller, or should hope to be bought only by someone who would expect but light service he might pretend a disability though he had it not.

[J. W.] Coleman offers the same opinion:[1]

Similar actions were not unknown in slave sales. Frequently on such occasions there is a strong indisposition in such creatures to be sold, and that by stratagem to avoid sale, they may frequently feign sickness, or magnify any particular complaint with which they are affected.

As was customary at a public auction of slaves, the auctioner announced that Mr. Anderson, the master, would give a bill of sale for his slave with the usual guarantee—"sound of mind and body and a slave for life." While there began a lively bidding among the Negro traders, George suddenly assumed a strange appearance—his head was thrown back, his eyes rolled wildly, his body and limbs began to twitch and jerk in an unheard of manner.

What's the matter with your boy, Mr. Anderson?" one of the traders asked the owner, who, astonished and puzzled, drew nearer the block. But Mr. Anderson did not answer the question. George was now foaming at the mouth, and the violent twitching and jerking increased precipitously.

"What's the matter with you, boy?" gruffly demanded the trader. "O, I 'es fits I has!" exclaimed George, whereupon his body doubled up and rolled off the block.

Of course the auction was hastily terminated. George was hustled off to jail, and a doctor sent for, but, after a careful examination the medical man was somewhat mystified as to the slave's actual condition. He advised the master to leave George in the jailer's custody for a while, promising to look in on him the next morning. Under his master's instruction, the wily slave was put to bed in the debtor's room, where he soon sank, apparently, into a sound sleep.

[1] Coleman, J. W., *Slavery Times in Kentucky*. Chapel Hill, N. C.: University of North Carolina Press, 1940, pp. 129–130. Copyright © 1940 by the University of North Carolina Press. Reprinted by permission of the publisher.

Next morning when the jailer brought in breakfast, he found the bed empty. George was gone, and nothing was heard of him again until word came, several weeks later, that he was safe in Canada.

Or, again, we read:

A young girl, of twenty years or thereabouts, was the next commodity put up. Her right hand was entirely useless—dead," as she aptly called it. One finger had been cut off by a doctor, and the auctioneer stated that she herself chopped off the other finger—her forefinger—because it hurt her, and she thought that to cut it off would cure it.

"Didn't you cut your finger off?" asked a man, "kase you was mad?"

She looked at him quietly, but with a glance of contempt, and said:

"No, you see it was a sort o' sore, and I thought it would be better to cut it off than be plagued with it."

Several persons around me expressed the opinion that she had done it willfully, to spite her master or mistress, or to keep her from being sold down South.

Another instance is described as follows:

As I came up, a second-rate plantation hand of the name of Noah, but whom the crier persisted in calling "Noey," was being offered, it being an administrator's sale. Noey, on mounting the steps, had assumed a most drooping aspect, hanging his head and affecting the feebleness of old age. He had probably hoped to have avoided sale by a dodge, which is very common in such cases. But the first bid—$1000—startled him, and he looked eagerly to the quarter whence it proceeded. "Never mind who he is, he has got the money. Now, gentlemen, just go on; who will say fifty." And so the crier proceeds with his monotonous calling. "I ain't worth all that, mass'r; I ain't much count no how," cried Noey energetically to the first bidder. "Yes you are, Noey—ah, $1000, thank you, sir," replies the crier.

The strength of Negro resistance to slavery becomes apparent in the extent to which the slaves mutilated themselves in their efforts to escape work. A girl on Lewis' plantation who had been injured tied pack thread around her wounds when they started to heal and then rubbed dirt in them. In her anxiety to avoid work she gave herself a very serious infection. But this action was mild compared to that of others.

General Leslie Coombs, of Lexington, owned a man named Ennis, a house carpenter. He had bargained with a slave-trader to take him and carry him down the river. Ennis was determined not to go. He took a broadaxe and cut one hand off; then contrived to lift the axe, with his arm pressing it to his body, and let it fall upon the other, cutting off the ends of the fingers.

"*But some on 'em would rather be shot then be took, sir,*" he added simply.

A farmer living near a swamp confirmed this account, and said he knew of three or four being shot on one day.

Planters had much trouble with slaves fresh from Africa, the new slaves committing suicide in great numbers. Ebo landing in the Sea Islands was the site of the mass suicide of Ebo slaves who simply walked in a body into the ocean and drowned themselves. A planter writing on the handling of slaves mentions the difficulty of adjusting the Africans to slavery. He advocates mixing them in with seasoned slaves.

> It too often happens that poor masters, who have no other slaves or are too greedy, require hard labor of these fresh negroes, exhaust them quickly, lose them by sickness and more often by grief. Often they hasten their own death; some wound themselves, other stifle themselves by drawing in the tongue so as to close the breathing passage, others take poison, or flee and perish of misery and hunger.

The one problem of Negro resistance to slavery which is most enticing is that of the attitude of slave mothers toward their children. There are frequent references in the literature to Negro women who boasted about the number of "niggers they hade for the massah," but breeding was probably quite secondary to sex activity. It would be interesting to discover the motives behind this apparent pleasure in presenting babies to the master. Some of the women may have been sincere in their pride. What makes this problem peculiarly important is the presence of much indirect evidence that, the Negro mothers either had no affection for their children, or did not want them to be raised as slaves.

We know quite well that African Negroes are . . . able to take care of their children, and that the slave women efficiently tended the children of the plantation mistress. Yet one runs across comment after comment that the Negro mothers were ignorant, and careless, and did not know how to care for their own offspring. Typical of such statements is this:

> The Negro mothers are often so ignorant and indolent, that they cannot be trusted to keep awake and administer medicine to their own children; so that the mistress has often to sit up all night with a sick Negro child.

Guion Johnson states that plantation owners in the Sea Islands offered the mothers rewards to take good care of their children. They were paid for those who survived the first year! This at least would indicate that there was something to be desired in their attitude toward their children.

Occasionally one runs across a reference to a slave mother killing her child, but the statements are almost invariably incomplete. For instance, [Helen H.] Catterall has a record of a trial, the details of which are: "The prisoner was indicted for murder of her own child," no more. Or a plantation overseer writes, "Elizabeth's child died last night. She smothered it somehow." There is no indication as to whether or not the smothering was deliberate.

Several cases, where it was certain that parents killed their children to keep them from slavery, have been described. They are important enough to be given in detail.

> Of all the cases of slave rendition, the saddest and probably the most circulated at the time was that of Margaret Garner. Winter was the best time for flight across the Ohio River, for when it was frozen over the difficulties of crossing were fewer. Simeon Garner, with his wife Margaret and two children, fled from slavery in Kentucky during the cold winter of 1856 and after crossing the frozen stream at night, made their ways to the house of a free Negro in Cincinnati.
>
> Quickly tracing the fugitive Negroes to their hideout in Cincinnati, the armed pursuers, after some resistance, broke down the door and entered the house. There they found Margaret, the mother, who, preferring death to slavery for her children, had striven to take their lives, and one child lay dead on the floor. The case was immediately brought into court, where despite the efforts made by sympathetic whites, rendition was ordered. On their return to slavery, Margaret in despair attempted to drown herself and child by jumping into the river but even the deliverance of death was denied her, for she was recovered and soon thereafter sold to a trader who took her to the cotton fields of the Far South.
>
> Not only were slaves known to take the lives of their masters or overseers, but they were now and then charged with the murder of their own children, sometimes to prevent them from growing up in bondage. In Covington a father and mother, shut up in a slave baracoon and doomed to the southern market, "when there was no eye to pity them and no arm to save," did by mutual agreement "send the souls of their children to Heaven rather than have them descend to the hell of slavery," and then both parents committed suicide.
>
> "Take off your shoes, Sylva," said Mrs. A., "and let this gentleman see your feet."
>
> "I don't want to," said Sylva.
>
> "But I want you to," said her mistress.

"I don't care if you do," replied Sylva sullenly.

"You must," said the mistress firmly.

The fear of punishment impelled her to remove the shoes. Four toes on one foot, and two on the other were wanting! "There!" said the mistress, "my husband, who learned the blacksmith's trade for the purpose of teaching it to the slaves, to increase their market value, has, with his own hands, pounded off and wrung off all those toes, when insane with passion. And it was only last week that he thought Sylva was saucy to me, and he gave her thirty lashes with the horse whip. She was so old that I could not bear to see it, and I left the house.

"Sylva says," Mrs. A. continued, "that she has been the mother of thirteen children, every one of whom she has destroyed with her own hands, in their infancy, rather than have them suffer slavery"!

V

The patterns of resistance to slavery studied in this paper are: (1) deliberate slowing up of work; (2) destruction of property, and indifferent work; (3) feigning illness and pregnancy; (4) injuring one's self; (5) suicide; (6) a possibility that a significant number of slave mothers killed their children.

The motivation behind these acts was undoubtedly complex. The most obvious of the motives was a desire to avoid work. It has been demonstrated that the slaves were acutely conscious of the fact that they had nothing to gain by hard work except in those instances where they were working under the task system. The destruction of property and the poor quality of the slaves' work was mainly due to their indifference to their tasks. There is enough evidence that they could, and did, work hard and well when sufficiently motivated to refute any contention that the Negro slaves were congenitally poor workers.

Many of the slaves reacted to the institution of slavery in a far more drastic fashion than could be manifested by a mere desire to avoid work. Some of these slaves committed suicide; others killed members of their families, usually their children, in order that they might not grow up as slaves.

Possibly the most significant aspect of these patterns of resistance is the aggression against the white masters they imply. Unfortunately, however, though this aspect may be the most significant, it is the least subject to proof. On the plane of logic, there is every reason to believe that a people held in bondage would devise techniques such as have been described above as an indirect means of retaliation. The statement of Dollard, previously quoted, indicates that such techniques (slowness, inefficiency, etc.) are used at the present time as a means of indirect aggression.

The material presented here suggests the need for a reconsideration of the concept of the Negro's easy adjustment to slavery. He was not a cheerful, efficient worker, as has been assumed. Rather, he was frequently rebellious, and almost always sullen, as any person faced with a disagreeable situation from which he cannot escape will normally be. Nor, can the belief that racial inferiority is responsible for inefficient workmanship on his part be supported. For such deficiencies of his workmanship as he manifested, or, indeed, may still be manifested, are seen to be explainable in terms that are in no sense to be couched in the conventional mold of inherent racial differences.

part VI

Slavery and Society

11

Slavery as an Obstacle to Economic Growth in the United States
A Panel Discussion

Douglas Dowd, Eli Ginzberg, and Stanley Engerman

From: *The Journal of Economic History*, XXVII (December 1967), pp. 531–544. Footnotes deleted. Reprinted by permission.

As we have already noted, American slavery was originally designed to solve an economic problem—labor scarcity in a new land. Eventually it also became a system of social control and race adjustment. But it never ceased, of course, to serve an essentially economic function. Did it serve that function well or did it serve it badly?

The question is important for several reasons. It is important to economists because it touches on the interesting issue of the social requirements of economic progress. Can a society with an unfree labor force attain rapid and sustained economic growth? It is important to students of American history because it implies some important things about the Civil War and its origins. One group of historians has used the economic failings of slavery as an apology for the slave South and an indictment of the South's abolitionist antagonists. As the argument goes, white Southerners did not make a profit out of human misery, but actually lost money. They only continued the peculiar institution because they did not know how to end it without violence and severe social disruption. Slavery was declining by 1860 and, if left alone by antislavery extremists, would have disappeared or been fundamentally transformed without the holocaust of civil war. On the other side, another group of historians insists that slavery was profitable. It would have survived indefinitely. Only the antislavery movement and the Civil War, regrettable as it was, could have ended the evil system.

Finally, there is a third group of historians who combine both views in a special way. Although scarcely sympathetic to slavery or the slave South, these scholars also insist that slavery was unprofitable. Whatever profits were made by individual planters, the South as a whole lost by slavery. Only by constant geographic expansion to new, fertile lands could the plantation system survive and the Southern economy flourish. Unfortunately, the North, and most emphatically the northern Republican party, would not tolerate further expansion of slave territory. The only escape from the dilemma for the South was secession and, inadvertently, cataclysmic civil war.

The selection that follows is excerpted from a symposium of economists and economic historians who gathered to discuss the question of "slavery as an obstacle to economic growth. . . ." The starting point of their discussion was the important 1958 essay of Alfred Conrad and John Meyer on the economics of the South's pre-Civil War slave system. This closely reasoned article sought to test statistically the premise of slavery's unprofitability. It concluded that both individual slaveholders and the South as a whole earned a good return on investments in cotton grown by slave labor. In the three sections from this symposium Conrad and Meyer are both attacked and supported. As these sections suggest, the issue of the economic implications of slavery has still not been resolved to everyone's satisfaction, and we may expect continuing discussion in the years to come.

DOUGLAS DOWD: Whether in the slavery or the new economic history controversies of the past decade, one moves to a feeling that the participants are often talking past one another, talking to themselves and to what may loosely be thought of as their respective adherents. The new economic historians, it may be said, put one in mind of rather light-hearted evangelists; while those who dissent from their innovations seem, by comparison, stuffy, oldfashioned, fearful of the new truths, perhaps of truth itself.

As is well-known, when controversies take on such characteristics, it is because procedures and conclusions, rather than assumptions and aims, form the stuff of the controversy. Only apparently are the discussions concerned, then, with the same subject matter, for the parameters are different, and they are different because—quite appropriately for both parties—the purposes are different. The slavery controversy provides a useful basis for an exploration of this question, not least because it came as the opening gun of the new economic history, a decade ago, when Messrs. Conrad and Meyer presented their twin papers on methodology and on slavery to the joint EHA-NBER [Economic History Association—National Bureau of Economic Research] meetings and I served as a critic.

Then, as still today, I puzzled over what Conrad and Meyer were trying to show. If they were attempting to demonstrate that Ulrich B. Phillips (in his *American Negro Slavery, inter alia*) was wrong, there was much more than the profitability of slavery on which to focus, for by the time they wrote Phillips had been quite thoroughly discredited on both narrow and broad questions, perhaps most completely by Kenneth Stampp (in his *Peculiar Institution*). I had thought, by then, that contemporary historians had come to view Phillips and his works more as sociological than as historical materials; documents, almost, revealing how a partisan of the Lost Cause viewed the evolution of that society. And was it not generally accepted by students of the South that writers like Phillips took the position that slavery was unprofitable because to do otherwise would muddy the more fundamental justifications for the system?

There is often something to be said for precise refutations of mistaken notions, to be sure. But what can be said that is positive diminishes to the degree that a general analysis would do. It is of course reasonably obvious that in any functioning social system, slave or otherwise, there will be incomes that are high at the top and decrease as one moves to the bottom of the social scale; and that power will be roughly proportionate to income and wealth. What is less obvious are the costs of a given system—costs in terms of alternatives foregone, as well as the social and human costs of the existent reality.

For the American South, it surely was good business sense that led planters to emphasize cotton cultivation, slaveholding, and slave-breeding; and good business sense was also good economic sense, if the short run and the interests of those in power are taken as guiding criteria. But when we speak of economic development it is not business sense or economic sense for the short run as viewed by those in power that are, or should be, taken as the appropriate referents for judgment; for then we are speaking not only of structural realities and changes in the economy, but also of far-reaching social and political structures and changes.

As I said a decade ago, one cannot evaluate the meaning of slavery as though it were merely one kind of a labor force rather than another. Slavery normally implies and requires, and especially in the United States implied and required, a slavery-dominated society as much as a society dominating slaves. In turn, this meant that whatever business considerations might support the continuation of the slave-cum-cotton system, these were immeasurably reinforced by the social and political imperatives—ever more on the defensive in the *ante-bellum* South—of maintaining a slave society. Is this not made more evident when we examine the post-Civil War development of the South?

I should have thought it would be unnecessary to raise these questions once more, except that here we are meeting again on the subject; and, more vividly, we are aware of new work tending to move in the same directions as the earlier work of Conrad and Meyer. I have been away from the United States for a year, having just returned a week ago. Consequently, I have been unable to read Stanley Engerman's latest contributions on the South, slavery, and the Civil War. But may I not assume that Robert Fogel represented Mr. Engerman accurately in his article on the new economic history? There it is said:

> The retarded development of the South during the last third of the nineteenth century and the first half of the twentieth was due not to stagnation during the slave era, but to the devastation caused by the Civil War. As Stanley Engerman points out, if *ante-bellum* growth-rates had continued through the war decade, southern *per capita* income would have been twice the level that actually prevailed in 1870. So disruptive was the war that it took the South some thirty years to regain the *per capita* income of 1860 and another sixty years to reach the same relative position in national *per capita* income that it enjoyed at the close of the *ante-bellum* era. The case for the abolition of slavery thus appears to turn on issues of morality and equity rather than on the inability of a slave system to yield a high rate of economic growth (p. 647).

In a paper delivered to this Association in 1956, in which I attempted to explain the late nineteenth- and early twentieth-century retardation of the southern economy, I did not say, nor do I recall anyone else having said, that southern stagnation was due to "stagnation during the slave era." But I do recall arguing that it was the consequence of slave society, in all its ramifications, that explains that stagnation. To reopen that argument here and now would be impossible, as well as unrewarding, just as it would be impossible to come to grips even partially with all the questions that arise from the works of Messrs. Conrad, Meyer, Fogel, Engerman, and others now cultivating the new vineyards. But perhaps our brief excursion can provide a basis for fruitful discussions in the meeting today.

Perhaps I am mistaken, but I believe I am correct in seeing the new economic history as an attempt to incorporate the methodology of neoclassical economics and the procedures of econometrics with the materials and the questions of economic history—with the added notion that economic history will thereby be strengthened, made more scientific. In its essence this entails the central use of partial equilibrium analysis. Such an approach may or may not be appropriate for the analysis of questions of narrow focus and very short time periods, where the pound of *ceteris paribus* [all things being equal] can serve as a temporary safe haven for "other things." Can it do so when we concern ourselves with changes taking a long period, and that neither begin nor end with economic, let alone quantitative, matters?

It was of utmost significance that slavery in the United States could not be maintained without vitally affecting "all other things," whether that slavery was profitable or not. As Stanley M. Elkins has so capably shown in his *Slavery*, American Negro slavery was the very "worst" the world had known, in its nature and in its consequences, whether it be compared with ancient or contemporaneous slavery (in, for example, Brazil or the Caribbean). What does "worst" signify in this context, and why should it have been so? Slaves have always and everywhere been cruelly treated (and always with exceptions), and black slaves especially. Even so, their treatment, their rights, or total lack of rights), their "family" lives, the depths to which racism sank, the manner in which the present and long-distant future of black slaves (even, as we know, their past) was distorted and doomed—in social, psychological, political, and of course economic terms—in the United States reached the lowest of depths. Why should this be so, in the land of the free and the home of the brave? Was not economic individualism adhered to in the South? It surely was, extending even to trafficking in human beings as commodities. Did not the Enlightenment, did not Christianity, extend into the American South? Most assuredly, but as with economic individualism, certain exotic notions had to be grafted onto otherwise healthy plants. To achieve such exoticism took a mighty effort, an effort that became obsessive, compulsive, and sickening not just to those who lived under the system, but also to those who lived from it and with it and for it.

Which brings me to the postwar period, if a bit abruptly, with Mr. Engerman's contributions in mind. Without asking how *ante-*

bellum growth rates could have continued indefinitely; without asking, that is, how the South could have maintained its power in the nation while it also maintained slavery (with or without westward expansion); without asking whether or not there was some determining relationship between the Civil War and the socioeconomic system of the South and its power struggle with the North; without asking any of these questions, let us point to some questions that relate growth to development, and war destruction to growth, and development.

Keeping in mind the well-recognized distinctions between growth and development, between quantitative and qualitative change (and keeping in mind, too, their connections), let us examine the notion of "*antebellum* growth rates continuing through the war decade" and even more, beyond that time. By 1860, the South showed few significant signs of moving away from its dependence on slaves and cotton. The signs that such a concentration might be something less than promising had begun to appear already during the Civil War; but what were then mere whispers turned into a roar in the years after 1870. Were the falling cotton prices (among other prices) in the last quarter of the century a function largely, if at all, of the Civil War? Is there any reasonable basis to assume either (1) that slave-breeding would have maintained the supply of slaves within economically viable magnitudes, or (2) that political realities would have allowed the reopening of the external trade? Has anyone specified how the maintenance of slavery (and the power of those who would so maintain it) in the United States in the late nineteenth century might be made compatible with economic development? Or how its forceful abolition (apart from the Civil War) would have been accomplished? Or its peaceful abolition, by those squarely dependent upon it? Is there any ground for believing that the kinds of structural (economic, political, social) changes that are implied by economic development would have ensued in a South whose economy could no longer "thrive" on the basis of agriculture (for the majority of either its white or its black population)? And, given that the slaves were in fact (legally) emancipated, how does one explain the persistence of all the essential qualities of *antebellum* southern society in *post-bellum* southern society, down to the very recent past? Civil war damage? But is it not difficult to believe that for eighty years the southern economy was retarded by war destruction, in the light of what we have seen of so many other war-damaged economies in our own lives? Can the answers to any of these questions be turned to the advantage of the relevant conclusions of the new economic history? Or to its procedures? Can we learn nothing about our own economic development from our studies of the complex interrelationships of development (or its lack) in the contemporary underdeveloped world.

Furthermore, and in a different vein: What is the point of the analyses that have occupied these studies? "The case for the abolition of slavery" *of course* "turns on issues of morality and equity rather than on the inability of a slave system to yield a high rate of economic growth." To state otherwise would be to say, one presumes, that an economically viable slave system is to be recommended to . . . whom? The underdeveloped countries? Of course not, and the sneers of the new economic historians to such a query are appropriate. But then what is the point? If students of the South had earlier believed the system was profitable, what then, besides elegance, was the point of going on? Or did we have to be told, once more, that the Civil War was terribly destructive? Are we going back to Ranke, "simply" recording the facts, with technical trimmings? Or are there more vital tasks facing social scientists today; more vital, more demanding, more promising.

Of course slavery was profitable. And of course imperialism has been profitable. And of course the status quo in today's underdeveloped countries is profitable. Profitable, in all cases, to investors, whose definitions of profit do not go beyond the balance sheet and the income statement, and whose definitions of propriety are quite identical with their definitions of property. And of course slavery damaged both whites and blacks in the long run (and most, also, in the short run). And imperialism damages most citizens of both metropolis and colony, in the long run; and similarly with underdevelopment. Nor is it difficult to show that the damage that accrues from such systems is not solely, or mostly, economic; it is social, psychological, political, cultural, As it is also true that economic development both requires and brings about social, political, psychological, and cultural changes.

We are concerned in these meetings with obstacles to economic development, a focus that requires us to look at reality. That is a considerable improvement over the earlier inclinations of economists to develop and to use abstract models that, if they had any application at all, were relevant only to highly industrialized, politically stable societies, operating within basically capitalist institutions. But improvements do not constitute sufficiencies; and especially they do not if their effect is to fragmentize an area of inquiry that requires broadening, deepening, and an enhanced sense of relevance.

Because in practice the meaning of economic development extends out and down so broadly and deeply, the analysis of development, not to say its implementation, must be as broad and as deep. This is to say that "experts" in economic development must take on the staggering task of attempting to understand the functioning of *societies,* and the manner in which *social* change takes place. One of my criticisms of the new economic history, and not only in its manifestations as regards the South, is that its methods, its thrust, are in exactly the opposite direction from that so desperately needed in the field today. Market relationships (for capital, commodities, labor) are indeed central to the functioning of an economy, as the heart is to the body. But the heart functions in relationship with a nervous system, and a circulatory system, and, among other things, in an environment. If the problem is a heart murmur, perhaps —no more than perhaps—total concentration on the heart itself will do. But those who will understand a cardiac condition, and prescribe for it, require themselves to understand the body in all its essential functions and characteristics. The lack of economic development is a problem in today's world that does not fall within the purview of the man who thinks in terms of heart murmurs. And the South had a cardiac condition in the nineteenth century.

To say that slavery was profitable and yet it inhibited economic development is not to say that slavery but that slave society in the United States in the nineteenth century, during and after its existence, inhibited economic development. But this is to say something else: Both before and after emancipation, social, economic, and political power in the South was held by those who had helped to create, and fought to maintain, slavery; nor was there a lack of interested parties in the North either before or after the War. For the South to develop economically, it was essential—and it is essential —either for a social upheaval within the South to take place and/or for steady pressures, positive and negative, to be introduced from "outside." Power—its sources and its uses has to be changed; that is, its possessors have to be changed.

What is true for the South is true for other societies that would develop. To detail such changes, let alone to understand, advocate, and support them, on a country-by-country basis is not only to move out from partial equilibrium analysis, but to move into the swirl and turbulence that characterize the world. And that suggests the stance of the committed and concerned social scientist—distasteful though such an idea is to our profession—more than that of the cheerful and comfortable economist.

ELI GINZBERG: Let me suggest to you how someone who has been working for the last thirty years on human resources in connection with economic development thinks about the argument at hand. I am well placed to do so at the moment because I've just finished a book called *People and Progress in East Asia*. It has nothing to do with slavery. I have, however, remembered my chapter titles, and they may serve as a kind of mirror for the discussion at hand. The first point is, if you're going to have economic development, it must be tied in with the concept of nationhood with the exercise of some kind of governmental power that is effective over a region. The one thing we know about the American slave system is that it finally operated in such a way as to destroy the Union for a time. So some connection must be made between discussions of profitability and the destruction of the Union. Professor Conrad did mention that possibly slavery would have been profitable had it been contained in the original states, but we know that's just what the slave owners would not settle for. Lincoln offered them that as a compromise; they refused to accept it, from which I deduce that maybe they knew their interests best and thought they would die on the vine if they accepted the offer. That was Lincoln's estimate, and that's why he made the offer. I think, therefore, you just cannot deal with such short-run approaches without settling the question into at least the national frame.

The second point I wish to make is that economic development has something to do with the standards of living of the mass of the population. There were large numbers of slaves in the South, and in some states they were in the majority. Now I suppose you can have very rapid development with very substantial inequalities of income. I submit that probably sooner or later fundamental conflict arises here. We may have misled many developing countries by failing to understand the importance of energizing rural life and giving the people who have a contribution to make to increased output some share in a better life. This is just what slavery did not do. I have no doubt, therefore, that in the short run it was profitable for the slave owners to exploit their slaves, but I would argue that, for the long run, this was really not a profitable way to expand the economy at something like an optimum level.

Let's take the question of education in the South. We know that it was forbidden to educate a slave. Not only does this mean that few of them were educated, but that it was a crime to do so. That means that the South inhibited economic development by insisting that it would not make use of the latent potential of a large part of its labor force. One of the most important aspects of the acquisition of skills is that it depends largely on the individual having some incentive to increase his skills, so that he and his family can get some advantage from it. It is my understanding that in a system of slavery this was generally impossible. We know there were a few slaves in the cities who made a deal with their masters but they were exceptional. In the nature of the case there was no incentive for the bulk of the Negro population in the South to improve themselves. In fact, they got into very bad habits of doing as little as possible, except under maximum coercion. Once again, it is perfectly possible to argue that slavery was a profitable system. The question is: how profitable, for whom, and for how long? And on those three counts I would say history is clear. Slavery broke up the Union, it had to be expanded in order to stay profitable, and it was a poor way of using the human resources of the region.

Let's take the question of management or entrepreneurship. We know that thought control became such an essential part of the South that anybody who dissented had to leave the South. I submit again that is a bad way to run the economy. Hitler did it, but not very successfully. If one of the systems of coercion that is needed to operate an economy is the suppression of dissent, that economy is in a bad way. And we know that many able people of the South left the South, if they could possibly get away. The whole tendency of the system was antidevelopmental, except within the narrow context of "getting a few more dollars out of your slaves." That's not sufficient because economic development requires specialization and more specialization. And that's exactly what was impossible with an agricultural system like this. You could use the land for ten years, twenty years, thirty years, forty years, and then you finally had to get new land. Slaves could not be used in a factory system because factory employment and slavery did not mix. There were, of course, a few slaves in the mines and a few out on contract. On the whole, the system of social control was in fundamental conflict with long-term economic development. I think that is the critical point. I would like to remind you that the first legal case on slavery in the history of the United States that I have been able to uncover was in 1629 in Jamestown. The issue had very little to do with economics, but much to do with social control. This was a case of punishing a white man who had slept with a *Negro* woman. The colonists understood quite well at that point in time that it was only through very rigid social controls that they could maintain the kind of society they wanted to maintain. I remind you finally that the title of my book, *The Troublesome Presence*, comes from a quotation of Abraham Lincoln in his eulogy of Henry Clay. Lincoln said that Henry Clay sought to remove the "troublesome presence" of the *free* Negro from the backs of the slave owners. I submit that if the only way you can have economic development is to ship a labor force back to Africa, you may be in trouble.

. . . .

STANLEY ENGERMAN: I would like to reply briefly to some of the comments made by Professor Dowd. In my judgment the Conrad and Meyer argument about whether slavery was profitable to the planters and the planter class is now agreed upon by most people. The statistical work and the reasoning seem to be largely accepted. The focus of the debate has become the question of Southern growth rates, the importance of the slave system in Southern growth before the Civil War and its lingering effects after the Civil War. One important series, the importance of which is often overlooked, is the series of regional income estimates prepared by Richard Easterlin. Professor Easterlin, no doubt, has certain reservations about placing considerable weight on these estimates, but the direction in which they lead is quite suggestive.

There are really two questions. One can discuss how rapid were the growth rates that did occur in the period 1840–1860. This, of course, is the question which Professor Easterlin has asked and to which he wants an answer. The second question, the one which is implied by Professor Dowd, is, given the land-labor endowment, and given certain things which we feel about the relationship between slavery and entrepreneurship, how rapidly *could* this Southern economy grow? The really difficult questions are the questions which downplay Southern development and try to argue that development could have been more rapid. This may be true; no one has yet simulated the Southern economy in the absence of slavery; no one has asked what would have happened. One point to note, however, is the much more stringent requirement being imposed upon the South than on the North.

The question of income distribution—whether it was more or less equal in the North than in the South—is still unresolved and very few data are available. If one accepts the suggestion made by Professor Kuznets that with the development of urban areas you get a more skewed distribution than in agricultural areas, it's not clear that the South and the North differed greatly in income distribution. Perhaps more important, the relationship between income distribution and growth is still debatable. It might be argued that the South would have grown more rapidly if there had been no conspicuous consumption; but in the North there was much conspicuous consumption. The building of mansions was not solely a Southern problem; it was certainly occurring in the North.

There were art collections in the North and various other forms of what, from the point of view of economic growth, may be called social waste. If you ask of the South: "What is the maximum amount of capital formation which could have occurred in the absence of conspicuous consumption?" and don't ask that question about the North, you will get a rather misleading answer.

The third point is the question of the efficiency of the labor force. Paul Gates, discussing Northern agriculture after the Civil War, has reported farmers' complaints about the hired hands, the gist of which was that the hired hands were lazy, they didn't show up when you wanted them, they couldn't work with machinery, they destroyed the animals, and so on. To raise these questions about the slaves in the South and not apply the same stringent criteria to the North seems to me misleading. We know from the Easterlin data that the South was growing rapidly from 1840 to 1860, and this estimate includes both whites and Negroes in the population base. We also know that, including Negroes, Southern per capita income was higher than in the Western agricultural areas. The picture of the prewar South as a stagnant, poor society is belied by the evidence.

A question has been raised about income distribution and whether the South had such a poor income distribution that growth was inconceivable in the long run. The evidence that we have now on income distribution is insufficient to support that conclusion. The only estimate which I have ever seen on income distribution in the South in the traditional sources is the estimate from *The Cotton Kingdom* prepared by William E. Dodd. It is not clear how the data were prepared, and the implications are so astounding that it is hard to believe that they have any validity. That extreme conclusion doesn't appear to be correct. What we have at the moment (awaiting the results of research now under way) is in effect no information. I may suggest, however, that many statements about income distribution in the South before the Civil War are made in apparent ignorance of the income distribution which existed in the 1920s and the 1930s, and still exists today. [Eugene] Genovese, for example, attempts to show the small size of the market in the South by arguing that Southern income distribution was skewed because the top 6 percent of the landowners in his sample of Mississippi counties had 33 percent of the land. A number of adjustments must of course be made, but data on wealth distribution in the 1920s suggest that the top 2 percent of the families then had about 32 or 33 percent of national wealth. Questions of income distribution and its effect on economic growth are still open.

The final remark I wish to make about Professor Dowd's comments has to do with another implication of the Easterlin results. Easterlin has no estimate for 1870, but he does have regional relatives for 1880, 1900, and 1920. It appears from these estimates, linked to mine, that from 1870 to 1920 the South was growing as rapidly as the rest of the country, and that the South started to converge on the national average after 1920. The questions would be, first, should we have expected earlier convergence, as is apparently implicit in the argument? And secondly, what occurred in the South to prevent a catching-up? To argue that, starting from 1870, the Southern economy was stagnant is belied again by the Easterlin data. How did growth occur? The South still had close to a world monopoly in cotton, in the sense that it was by far the largest producer; and the demand for cotton was expanding in this period. The South grew from 1870 to 1900 in roughly the same way as it had grown before. It grew because of a rise in the demand for cotton in the world market and the continuing profitability of cotton.

One final point about westward expansion: In most arguments which an economist will accept it is agreed that there was sufficient land in the old boundaries of the South on which to expand, but that land values were such that it was more profitable to expand outward. There is little reason to suggest that once outward expansion was precluded it was impossible to reinvest and redevelop the existing soil.

Slavery disintegrates under the impact of the Civil War.
Source: Virginia State Library

Reading the Emancipation Proclamation.
Source: Library of Congress.

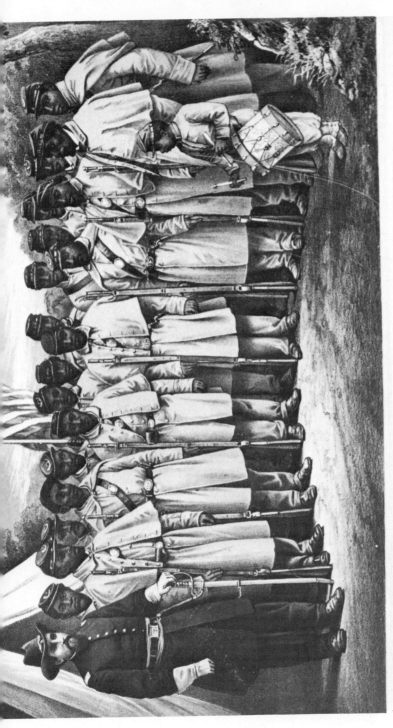

COME AND JOIN US BROTHERS

Black troops during the Civil War.
Source: Chicago Historical Society.

12

The Coming of the "Yankees"

Bell I. Wiley

From: *Southern Negroes, 1861–1865* (New Haven, Conn.: Yale University Press, 1965), pp. 3–23. Some footnotes deleted and renumbered. Copyright © 1938 by Yale University Press, 1965 by Bell I. Wiley.

For most southern blacks the final chapter of the slave experience was the arrival of blue-clad Union regiments. This event occurred for some slaves rather early as federal forces quickly penetrated the Upper South and seized some coastal regions. For others it awaited the Union occupation army after Appomattox. Whenever it happened it was a time of tremendous jubilation for the slaves.

During the war itself slaves deep within the Confederacy had been watchful and expectant, but quiet. Whatever coercive power southern society had possessed before was now compounded as the Confederate States became an armed camp. Beyond this, however, was the uncertainty concerning Union goals. At the outset the Lincoln administration had carefully avoided offending the border slave states by denying any intention to attack slavery. Union victory under these circumstances held out little hope for the black man, and he had no reason to risk his safety for the Union cause.

After September 1862 the picture changed drastically. By then the Lincoln administration had come to believe that destroying slavery would damage the South and that the black man might prove useful in defeating the rebellion. The ensuing preliminary Emancipation Proclamation and the recruiting of black soldiers for the Union *army taken together convinced many slaves that they had a stake in Confederate defeat. Thousands fled to the Federal lines as Yankee armies advanced southward. Other thousands enlisted in the United States forces, although they were not accorded equal treatment with white recruits. In a relatively short period of time, as Bell Wiley shows in this selection, the institution of slavery crumbled. The slave, after two hundred years, had finally taken his fate into his own hands and helped destroy the institution that had oppressed him.*

From the launching of the first "on to Richmond" drive in July, 1861, until the surrender of Lee at Appomattox, the conflict between North and South was a war of invasion on the one hand and a war of resistance on the other. In 1861 Federal penetration of the Confederacy was limited to a small portion of northern Virginia and seacoast areas of the Carolinas. During that year life for the Negroes in the South went on in much the same manner as before. True, there was a great deal of excitement in the air, much beating of drums, and much waving of flags. "Ole missus'" eyes often betrayed weeping and "ole massa" was exceedingly quiet and thoughtful after "young massa" rode away. But there was a full crop of cotton in the fields; and the fact that a war was under way somewhere in the distance did not retard the growth of grass in the cotton rows or diminish the number of chores around the house. There was much work to be done and all through the South the Negroes went about the performance of their daily tasks. Even after the invasion of northern Virginia, western Tennessee, northern Mississippi, and other peripheral portions of the South, the life of the Negro in the interior was not appreciably altered. The second and third years of the war brought greater impingements on food, clothing, and labor, but the necessary adjustments were made gradually and with very little disturbance.

The coming of the "Yankees," however, whether to northern Virginia in 1861, to western Tennessee in 1862, or to central Georgia in 1864, wrought immediate and radical changes in the life of the slaves; and the effects of invasion on all areas were very much alike. When the Federals approached, many planters removed their Negroes to the interior. If time permitted, they frequently rented plantations and arranged in advance for the transfer of slaves and other movable property. There was a tendency, however, for owners to postpone their departure as long as possible, thinking to get more of their crops gathered before the Federals arrived, or hoping that a turn in the fortunes of war might relieve them of the necessity of removal. In some cases, masters and slaves lingering too long were caught unawares by the cry "Yankees coming"; the result was a disordered flight.

Reluctance of planters to remove their slaves sometimes provoked military authorities to compel them to transfer the ablebodied males to places beyond the reach of the Union army. This was due to the initiation by the Federal government of the policy of employing the Negroes in military pursuits. "Every sound male black left for the enemy," wrote Kirby Smith to Sterling Price, "becomes a soldier whom we have afterward to fight." [1] Facilities for transportation of slaves were provided by the military authorities. [2]

The planter usually selected his more valuable slaves—domestic servants and field hands—for removal and left the old and decrepit ones behind for the "Yankees." Children were taken or left, according to the dictates of sentiment or circumstances. Sometimes when an owner had to leave members of his family at the plantation in the path of the enemy, he selected a few of his most faithful slaves to remain with them to help look after the affairs of the farm. In some cases, slaves who were suspected of disloyal designs were removed first. The overseer of Mulberry Hill Plantation in Virginia wrote the owner: "I . . . sent Dave to Lynchburg thinken it a safer place than here, for at that time there were 10,000 Yankeys at Buffaloe." [3]

"Running the negroes," as their movement was generally designated, was a practice much in vogue in the South, especially after the Federals began their extensive campaigns of 1862. Travelers on the highways often met great droves of slaves, moving from the coast to the "up country" in South Carolina, from Mobile to the environs of Montgomery, from Mississippi to Alabama, to Louisiana, or even to Texas. It was estimated that two thousand slaves were removed from Washington and Tyrrell counties to the interior of North Carolina within a ten-day period in the fall of 1862. A short time later a Texas newspaper reported that trains of from fifty to sixty wagons, belonging to refugees from Louisiana, were often seen on the highways. [4] These caravans of refugees were inter-

---

[1] *Official Records of the Union and Confederate Armies,* Ser. 1, XXII, pt. 2, 990, Sept. 4, 1863. The *Official Records* will be cited hereafter as *O. R.*

[2] W. W. Scott, ed., *Two Confederate Items,* p. 11.

[3] Wallace to McDowell, May 8, 1862, Mulberry Hill Plantation Letters (MSS. in private possession).

[4] *The True Issue* (La Grange, Texas), Jan. 1, 1863; A. J. Fremantle, *Three Months in the Confederate States,* pp. 82, 86.

esting sights—Negro women, their heads wrapped in gaudy bandanas perched high on wagons loaded with chairs, tables, and bedding; stalwart Negro men trudging beside the slow-moving vans; dust-covered, barefooted "pickaninnies," to whom the journey was more of a frolic than a fight, now running along beside the wagons, now stealing a ride on the "perch-pole"—an offense which was apt to call forth a sharp threat from an observant "mammy" that "de conjurer 'll git you for sho."

At night the overseer or owner would halt the party near some convenient creek or spring and unload a few necessary provisions. The men would build a roaring fire, while the women busied themselves with the preparation of supper. After the meal, the Negroes might buoy their spirits and entertain their master with a few spirituals. Then to bed, but not, perhaps, without a prayer by the master for freedom from the "Yankees" accompanied by audible "Amens!" and "Grant it Massa Jesus!" from the members of the dark circle whose secret prayer, in some cases, was for freedom from "massa," whatever that freedom might mean.

Sometimes the planter would move a part of his Negroes into a nearby wood, swamp, or canebrake to await the passing of an invading force. If the Federals lingered in the neighborhood for a long time, or if the invasions became frequent, the party would have to abandon the wood or swamp for places more remote. Some planters were kept moving from place to place in quest of a safe retreat from the seemingly omnipresent "Yankee."

The necessity of "refugeeing" was a hardship for planters and Negroes alike. It often meant the severance of family ties. This hardship was sometimes accentuated by a cold reception in the community chosen for the new home. In the case of the Negroes, sadness resulting from the severing of home ties was sometimes tinged with regret at being farther removed from the "Yankees" and freedom. A Tennessee owner sought to alleviate the unpleasantness incident to removal by calling all his Negroes together and giving them a drink of whiskey immediately before ordering their departure.

So strong was the aversion of Negroes to "refugeeing," that they sometimes openly resisted removal. The announcement by the planter of his intention of moving to the interior often resulted in a wholesale flight of his slaves to the Federal lines. When President Davis issued an order for the removal by the military authorities of slaves in northwestern Mississippi, the State legislature raised a protest that the execution of such an order would "cause the larger portion of the slaves to go to the enemy." So strong was the objection, that the President revoked the order.[5]

Many masters abandoned their slaves rather than move them when the "Yankees" arrived. An editorial in the Charleston *Daily Courier* headed "Onesimus" said that "masters have deserted their servants under panic and surprise, even after full opportunities of preparations, about as often in comparison with the numbers, as servants have designedly left their masters. For such masters, we know or propose no special recompense or sympathy."[6] These fugitive masters," as General Hunter called them, were sometimes held in contempt by their abandoned black subjects; at least, such seems to be the implication of a song said to have been sung by them and attributed to a colored author:

> Say darkeys hab you seen de massa,
> Wid de muffstash on he face,
> Go 'long de road sometime dis mornin'
> Like he gwine leabe de place.
> He see de smoke way up de river
> Whar de Lincum gun-boats lay;
> He took he hat, an' leff berry sudden,
> And I spose he's runned away.
> De massa run, ha, ha!
> De darkey stay, ho, ho!
> It mus' be now de kingdum comin',
> An' de yar ob jubilo.[7]

When the report "Yankees coming!" reached a community, there were many slaves who chose to expedite the advent of freedom by going to meet their deliverers. The question as to approxi-

---

[5] Jefferson Davis, Constitutionalist, *Letters, Papers and Speeches,* Dunbar Rowland, ed., VI, 84, 92; *Laws of Mississippi,* 1863, Nov. Sess., chap. 140, Resolutions. There were exceptions to the slaves opposing removal. The father of Frances Fearn, a Louisiana master, offered his slaves the choice of going with him to Texas or remaining at home until the "Yankees" came. They begged to be taken with him. *Diary of a Refugee,* p. 28. For a similar case see J. F. H. Claiborne's "Reminiscences of the Late War," New Orleans *Daily Picayune,* July 5, 1883. Claiborne's slaves implored him to leave Louisiana and to take them with him. They were "afraid of the jay hawkers, afraid of being impressed into the Confederate army."

[6] Charleston *Daily Courier,* Sept. 17, 1864.

[7] George Cary Eggleston, ed., *American War Ballads,* II, 200. Edmund Kirke (pseudo.), who gives this verse in his *Down in Tennessee,* p. 125, claims to have heard an old Negro grave-digger singing it in a Nashville cemetery after Federal occupation of the town.

mately how many slaves ran away to the Federals during the war cannot be answered. But it can be said with safety that the arrival of Union soldiers in any part of the South marked the beginning of a flow of black humanity toward the Federal camp; and that, in many cases, the flow was so great that it carried away the bulk of the male slave population.

The very close relationship between the approach of the Federals and the flight of the slaves is illustrated by the case of Shirley Plantation on the James River in Virginia. The Federals first came to the vicinity of the plantation on June 30, 1862. There is no evidence in the records of any slaves having run away prior to that time. On July 14, 1862, two weeks after the arrival of the Union force, the journal records that "15 Negro men and boys ran off at different times up to this date." A few days later a woman and two children absconded. In a short time the Federals passed on. On July 13, 1863, the "Yankees" made their second appearance in the vicinity, coming up the river with eight or ten gunboats. In the next three days, fifteen Negro men ran off to them. On April 5, 1864, the Federal fleet again came up the river. This time there were "140 or 150 transports and gunboats." For a while there was no notice of any slaves running away; but evidently preparations were being made. On May 10, the exodus began. From May 10 to May 14, thirty Negroes, principally women and children—most of the men from the place having run away on previous visits of the Federals—went to the fleet. By June 20 seventeen more had departed. This brought the total of the runaways for the three Federal visits to eighty. The records indicate that this was practically the entire slave population of Shirley.[8]

The proportion of slaves running away from Shirley is doubtless exceptional, but an abundance of evidence indicates a close parallel of tendencies in other invaded areas. A Confederate general estimated that a million dollars' worth of Negroes was escaping weekly to the Federals in North Carolina in August 1862.[9] Frontier counties in Virginia were exempted from the impressment act because they had lost such a large proportion of their slave population.[10] William Butler of the United States Christian Commission wrote from Mississippi that "after Pemberton marched out with his army, Vicksburg was looked upon by the Negroes as the very gate of heaven, and

[8] Library of Congress, Shirley Plantation Records.
[9] *O. R.*, Ser. 1, IX, 477.
[10] *Acts of Virginia*, 1863, Called Session, chap. 6.

they came trooping to it as pigeons to their roost at night." [11] On April 20, 1862, Mrs. Betty Herndon Maury noted in her diary that the "full band" of the Federal army across the river from Fredericksburg was playing "Yankee Doodle" and the "Star Spangled Banner." The entries after that date contain numerous references to Negroes running away.

The slaves displayed a considerable degree of ingenuity in effecting their escape through the Confederate lines. They frequently deceived the pickets by telling them that they belonged to "de nex' plantation" and were simply on their way home. The problem of obtaining passes was often solved by getting some intelligent slave to write them. This was more easily accomplished in cities than in rural sections. There seems to have been a sort of "bootleg ring" in Richmond devoted to "running negroes" through the lines, with a white man at its head, who prepared all the passes and furnished a four-horse wagon for transportation. The charge was "from two to three hundred dollars according to the number engaging seats in the wagon." [12]

Drastic steps were taken during the war to prevent the escape of slaves to the Federal lines. Picket lines were "doubled" on the York River in February, 1864, in an effort to stay the Negro exodus to "Yankeedom." The passport system was rigidly applied in frontier regions. In all the Confederate states there were local organizations formed such as "home guards," "independent scouts," and "mounted pickets" to help preserve order and to prevent the escape of slaves. The Georgia legislature passed an act in March, 1865, requiring the governor to "establish a line of mounted pickets of such numbers and at such points as he may deem sufficient for the purpose of arresting and preventing the escape of slaves." [13] The use of small boats by slaves in the coastal regions was greatly restricted or entirely forbidden. Legislation was enacted to tighten the patrol laws in practically all the Confederate states.

Individuals and local organizations also took steps to prevent the escape of Negroes to the Federals. Citizens assembled in public meeting at Hempstead, Texas, in the fall of 1862 adopted a resolu-

---

[11] Mobile *Daily Advertiser and Register,* Nov. 15, 1863, quoting G. W. Elliot.

[12] Richmond *Daily Dispatch,* March 10, 1864. See also Richmond *Enquirer,* Jan. 9, 1864. There are reports of a similar ring operating in Savannah. Fugitives were charged $50 a family; if they lacked the cash they might pay in kind—pork, bacon, etc. Montgomery *Weekly Mail,* Oct. 28, 1863.

[13] *Acts of Georgia,* 1865, Called Sess., Res., no. 30; Brown to Johnston, March 14, 1865, Georgia Archives, Governor Brown's Letter Book, 1861–1865.

tion "that the Legislature be requested at an early day to enact a law making it a capital crime for any slave to desert from his master with the intent of going over to the enemy." That this was not a mere explosive utterance is indicated by the fact that an executive committee was appointed for immediate action, "to try and hang any negro caught in attempting to escape to the enemy." A group of planters in Mississippi petitioned the governor to detail a man conscripted for the Confederate army for special and important service at home; they added the explanation that he was the "owner of a pack of Negro dogs and has devoted a good portion of time to the patrol duty." [14]

Some of the slaves who ran away returned to their masters after a brief sojourn within the Federal lines. Their return, in some instances, was due to homesickness; in others, it was due to the disillusioning influences of hardship or disease in the Federal camps. The action of three Negroes on Magnolia Plantation in Louisiana is probably typical of that of many in other parts of the South. The Negroes ran away on May 26, 1862. On May 30 they returned. The overseer, in making a record of their return, wrote: "They say they have Seen the Eliphant and are glad to get Home." [15]

The attitude of the slaves toward the invading "Yankee" varied from extreme fear and hostility in some cases to unrestrained veneration in others. Instances of genuine fear were much more numerous in isolated and backward communities, where the slave population greatly exceeded the white element. This fear was sometimes due to the impressions which the Negroes had obtained from stories told them by their white masters and mistresses. When the Federals came to Port Royal, South Carolina, in 1861, the Negroes, instead of running to meet them with open arms, in some cases ran the other way. The Union authorities were much perplexed. On investigation they found that the slaves were under the impression that they were going to be seized and sent away to Cuba. Their masters had told them this. It was with great difficulty that confidence was established by the newcomers.

Southerners were not unaware of the wholesome influence which a fear of the "Yankees" would have on the loyalty of their Negroes. This, coupled with the amusement which they derived from

[14] Houston *Tri-Weekly Telegraph,* Oct. 31, 1862. Foster to Pettus, Oct. 20, 1862, Miss. Archives, Ser. E, no. 58.

[15] Magnolia Plantation Records (MS. in the custody of Professor J. de Roulhac Hamilton at the University of North Carolina).

working on the imaginations of their servants, led to the origination and circulation of many stories of the diabolical appearance and the cruel practices of the Federals. Some of these were exaggerated as they were retold by the Negroes. A slave who escaped to the South Atlantic blockading fleet from Georgia in April, 1863, said that his mistress had "told him that as soon as he came to the 'Yankees,' so soon would they put a harness, prepared for the purpose, on him and compel him to drag cannons and wagons about like horses." [16] An old colored woman in Shelby County, Tennessee, said that when she asked her mistress what the "Yankees" looked like, she was told, "They got long horns on their heads and tushes in their mouths and eyes sticking out like a cow. They're mean old things." [17] Georgia owners told their slaves that the Federals threw women and children into the Chattahoochee River, and that when the buildings were burned in Atlanta they filled them with Negroes to be roasted by the flames.[18] With such stories as these in circulation, the observation of one old Negro when he was first told that the newcomers in blue were the "Yankees," "Why dey's folks," and the exclamation of another, "Great dairdy! So Yankees stan'!" are not surprising.[19]

Among the little Negroes the term "Yankee" was a veritable bugbear. Their elders often used the threat "the Yankees'll git you" to hold them to good behavior. When the dusky urchins happened to be the first ones on the place to see the approaching columns, they would run to their "mammies" "with eyes like a full moon," crying "Yankees coming." [20]

There were instances in which the slaves' attitude toward the Union soldiers was characterized more by hostility or contempt than by fear. The ruthlessness with which cabins were ransacked and personal effects taken was highly offensive to the Negroes. In such cases, the "day of jubilo" was turned into a day of sadness.

Some of the Negroes were apparently indifferent to the approach of the Federals. They regarded the newcomers as neither devils nor deliverers, but simply as another group of masters. This is reflected in the assertion of some Port Royal, South Carolina, slaves to a Union official that "the white man do what he pleases with us;

---

[16] Journal of Samuel P. Boyer, entry of April 25, 1863.

[17] Orland Kay Armstrong, *Old Massa's People*, p. 301.

[18] New Orleans *Times*, Jan. 4, 1865, quoting New York *Post*.

[19] *South Carolina Women in the Confederacy*, I, 220, narrative of Margaret Crawford Adams; Elizabeth W. Pearson, ed., *Letters from Port Royal*, p. 217.

[20] Mrs. Rogers, "Reminiscences of a War Time Girl," in M. P. Andrews, ed., *Women of the South in War Times*, p. 300.

we are yours now, massa"; likewise the statement of an old Virginia Negro that she came to the Federals "because others came." [21]

In the majority of cases, the slaves seem to have received the "Yankees" with enthusiasm. But the expression of their joy was often repressed in the presence of their "white folks." Normally they threw off all restraint and gave themselves to shouting and singing and "bressing de Lawd." By some "Mas Linkum" was venerated as a god and his soldiers as divine emissaries. General Sherman's name was mixed "with that of Moses and Simon and other scriptural ones as well as 'Abraham Linkom,' the Great Messiah of 'Dis Jubilee' " by the praying and shouting black hordes at Savannah.[22] His army entered Covington, Georgia, with flags unfurled and the band playing patriotic airs. "The Negroes were simply frantic with joy," Sherman said. "They clustered about my horse, shouted and prayed. . . . I have witnessed hundreds if not thousands of such scenes; and can now see a poor girl in the very ecstasy of the 'Methodist' shout, hugging the banner of one of the regiments and jumping up to the 'feet of Jesus.' " [23]

Closely related to the Negroes' attitude toward the "Yankees" is their conception of the war and its issues. In some isolated communities the slaves may have known practically nothing of the existence of the conflict, much less its causes. An aged Virginia servant, who remembered the War of 1812, on hearing the distant boom of the cannon of the Federal gunboats on the Rappahannock River, is reported to have said, "Well, I 'clare 'fo' Gawd, dere's dem damn Britishers again." [24] Another Virginia slave explained to a group of his companions that the cause of the war was that "somebody from across the water sont a shipload o' money to us cullud folks and somebody stole it; an' now dey gwine fight it out." [25] The degree of ignorance manifested by these two Negroes was exceptional. Many of the slaves knew the issues of the war from its early stages. The majority of them knew that their freedom was at stake after the issuance of the Emancipation Proclamation. There were a

[21] Pierce, *Freedmen of Port Royal,* p. 308; *Report of a Committee of the Representatives of the New York Yearly Meeting of Friends upon the Condition and Wants of the Colored Refugees,* p. 7.

[22] M. A. Howe, ed., *Home Letters of General Sherman,* p. 319, letter of Dec. 25, 1864.

[23] W. T. Sherman, *Memoirs,* II, 180.

[24] Statement of Joseph Christian Bristow, Urbanna, Virginia to the author in 1933. The old slave belonged to Bristow's relatives.

[25] Statement of Anderson Brown, Petersburg, Virginia, ex-slave and ex-Union soldier, to the author in 1933.

number of methods by which they might obtain information. The domestic servants often heard the topics of the day discussed by the whites. Booker T. Washington listened to the conversations about the war as he fanned the flies from the table at the "big house."[26] However, the whites usually avoided commenting on prospects of emancipation in the presence of Negroes. Bishop Isaac Lane of the African Methodist Episcopal Church satisfied his curiosity as to what the "white folks" discussed among themselves by stealing into a closet adjoining the dining room and listening to the conversation. In other cases, slaves listened to war-talk from places of concealment under their masters' houses and in the branches of conveniently situated trees. Some masters took the slaves into their confidence, especially their most trusted ones, and frankly told them that their freedom was one of the basic issues of the war. Body servants were effective agents among the Negroes in the spreading of news of the war. In 1861 a great many servants accompanied the Confederate soldiers to the army. In the camps they were in the war atmosphere; they heard its issues discussed at the mess and around the campfire; some even talked with prisoners. When rations became short in 1862 and 1863, the majority of these servants were sent home. They were usually not hesitant in imparting to their sable brothers the information which they had gained. Negroes who went to exposed areas to work on defenses also had excellent opportunities to hear about and discuss the issues of the war. One of the chief objections offered by the planters in the interior to sending their slaves to work on fortifications was that they brought dangerous ideas back to the plantations, creating dissatisfaction and unrest.

The slaves were ingenious at passing on from one to another the news which came to them. By the use of "keywords" they were able to carry on conversation about the progress of the war even in the presence of their owners. In a certain section of Virginia "grease" was used as a code word, and, according to Robert Russa Moton, "If a slave coming back from town greeted a fellow-servant with the declaration, 'Good mornin' Sam, yo look mighty greasy this mornin',' that meant that he had picked up some fresh information about the prospects of freedom which would be divulged later on."[27] In another locality Negroes who prayed for Abraham Lincoln referred to him as "Old Ride-Up."[28] While the whites were ignorant of the

[26] *Up from Slavery*, p. 10.

[27] Robert Russa Moton, *What the Negro Thinks*, p. 10.

[28] Joseph E. Roy, "Our Indebtedness to the Negroes for their Conduct during the War," *New Englander*, LI (1889), 354.

detailed workings of the "grapevine telegraph," as this secret, informal means of Negro communication was called, they were aware of its existence, and they marveled at its effectiveness.

More than one owner who was complacent in the assurance that his "niggers knew nothing about the war and cared less" would have been startled had he known the extent of their knowledge. He would doubtless have been chagrined had he known the aspirations so effectively concealed behind their deferential smiles and obsequious manners. After the close of the war, when the white people of a certain community had passed a resolution expressing appreciation for the loyal conduct of their slaves, an old Negro made the observation: "They needn't have done that for every now and then we were falling behind a stump or into a corner of the fence and praying for the Union soldiers." [29]

It was not an uncommon thing for slaves to obtain knowledge of military events before their masters. Intelligent domestic servants were frequently sent to get the mail. Those who could read would scan the headlines for the news and pass it on to the Negroes whom they encountered on the way to the "big house." Those who could not read would often pick up scraps of information by lingering at the post office after the issuance of the mail and listening to the reading and discussion of the news by the whites. In several instances masters received their first knowledge of the Emancipation Proclamation from their slaves.

After the Federals came into a community, the Negroes sometimes had more complete information about local and remote events than their masters. The "Yankees" would tell the Negroes of their intention of occupying houses of certain citizens, when they intended to leave the vicinity, and what recent victories had been won. This intelligence, when passed on to the masters, was spoken of by them as "nigger news."

Information concerning the progress of the war was generally received with great interest by the slaves. While they were usually very proficient at affecting unconcern, there were times when their actions and their looks betrayed them. A Chattanooga editor observed that, "the spirits of the colored citizens rise and fall with the ebb and flow of this tide of blue devils, and when they are glad as larks, the whites are depressed and go about the streets like mourners." [30]

Although numerous instances might be cited of Negroes being

[29] Roy, *New Englander,* LI (1889), 354.
[30] Montgomery *Weekly Mail,* Aug. 15, 1863, quoting Chattanooga *Confederate.*

indifferent to the success of the Union army and even of their reject-
ing freedom when it was offered to them, these instances are the
exceptions rather than the rule. It is true that many slaves had very
imperfect ideas of the meaning of freedom. It is probably just as true
that many of them, had they known what freedom entailed, would
have recoiled from it. But the sentiment of the spirituals indicates
that the slaves had been longing for freedom for many years. They
were looking forward to it in 1861. They had no definite idea as to
when it would come; but when the marching of troops and the
beating of drums announced that a war was in progress, it was
natural for them to hope, and even to believe, that it would bring
their liberation. This was demonstrated by an old slave woman on a
plantation in eastern Virginia. On the Sunday of July 21, 1861, she
was in the kitchen cooking dinner. Occasionally the roar of the
cannon at Manassas could be heard. The old "mammy" greeted each
"boom" which came to her ears with a subdued, "ride on Massa
Jesus." [31]

The Negroes' secret longing for freedom during the war is
reflected in their surreptitious prayer meetings. Long after the
occupants of the "big house" had drowned their cares in sleep, a
group of slaves might be assembled in the quarter praying for freedom and the success of the Union cause while one of their number
watched for the "patarollers."

Booker T. Washington said that the first knowledge that he had
of the fact that he was a slave and that the freedom of the Negroes
was being discussed was "early one morning before day when I was
awakened by my mother kneeling over her children and fervently
praying that Lincoln and his armies might be successful and that one
day she and her children might be free." He also said that, though
he was just a child during the war, he later recalled "the many late-
at-night whispered discussions" in which his mother and the other
slaves on the plantation indulged. He expressed the belief that "even
the most ignorant members of my race on the remote plantations
felt in their hearts that the freedom of the slaves would be the one
great result of the war, if the northern armies conquered. . . . I have
never seen one who did not want to be free or one who would
return to slavery." [32]

The early policy of the Union authorities in freeing the Negroes
who came to their lines encouraged the slaves. The issuance of the
Emancipation Proclamation lifted their hopes for freedom still higher

[31] Statement of Anderson Brown, Petersburg, Virginia, to the author in 1933.
[32] *Up from Slavery*, pp. 7–15.

and made them more concerned than ever for the success of the Union army.

The action of the slaves when freedom was brought to them is another indication that they had been looking forward to it with more than a passive interest. Even trusted slaves, those who had helped hide the silver and other valuables, sometimes followed the deliverers when they came. It was not disloyalty, but the lure of freedom, which impelled them to go. The attraction of freedom is demonstrated by the difficulty with which old domestic servants sometimes resisted it. One venerable Negro, after the "Yankees" had passed by the plantation taking most of the Negroes with them, said to his young master, with a note of sadness in his voice: "Well I never expected us to hear freedom come and knock at my door and I refuse it, but that is what me and my family have done." [33] An old cook in the service of a South Carolina family was put on a wage basis in the summer of 1865. After a time, she expressed a desire to go into a town about a mile away to work. The mistress and her family, being anxious to keep one who was such a good cook and who had been with them so long, offered to raise her wages to almost twice the amount she would receive in town. The old slave, after offering one evasive excuse after another, finally said, "No, Miss, I must go. If I stays here I'll never know I'm free." [34] A similar case was that of an old Georgia Negro who, when asked why she left the old plantation, responded, "What fur? 'Joy my freedom." [35]

The ultra-idealistic manner in which the Negroes thought of freedom is vividly illustrated by an incident which took place in Alabama shortly after the termination of the war. A white man riding to his work early one morning observed a group of colored children huddled on the side of the road. Near them in a ditch, he saw a woman stretched out, quite inert. He asked the children who she was. The oldest one replied, "Mammy." The man then asked what her trouble was, adding the remark that she looked as if she might be dead. To this the child responded, "Yassah, massah, she is daid, but she's free." [36]

The slaves often showed great elation on the reception of freedom, even on plantations where their treatment had been exceptionally good. Booker T. Washington says that "there was little if any

---

[33] Elizabeth Allen Coxe, *Memories of a South Carolina Plantation During the War*, p. 47.

[34] W. W. Ball, *The State That Forgot*, p. 128.

[35] Sidney Andrews, *The South Since the War*, p. 353.

[36] Memoirs of J. R. Webster (MS. in private possession).

sleep" the night after word was sent to the slaves' quarters that "something unusual was going to take place at the 'big house' the next morning." After the slaves had assembled and had been told that they were all free, "for some minutes there was great rejoicing . . . and wild scenes of ecstasy." His mother "leaned over and kissed her children while tears of joy ran down her cheeks. She explained to us . . . that this was the day for which she had been so long praying." [37] Even more demonstrative was an old Virginia Negro who when informed of his freedom "went out to the barn and jumped from one stack of straw to another as fast as he could jump," and "screamed and screamed!" [38] After Lee's surrender, Mrs. Roger Pryor, who was staying at her brother's plantation near Petersburg, Virginia, was waked in the middle of the night by a shrill scream, " 'Thank Gawd! Thank Gawd A'Mighty!' Then all was still." The next morning an old colored man explained that "Sis Winny . . . got happy in the middle of the night and Gawd knows what she would have done if Frank hadn't ketched hold of her and pulled her back in the kitchen." [39]

The fact that the slaves' ideas of emancipation had become so exaggerated—a factor in their elation—is suggestive that freedom had long been discussed and idealized. The cases of the Vicksburg Negro who expected his race to assemble in New York after the war and "have white men for niggers," [40] and the South Carolina Negro who, in answer to his master's inquiry as to where he was going replied, "I dunno, Massa; dey dun gi me dis hoss; I suppose I'se gwine to Heben or a better place," [41] are doubtless exceptional; but the association of emancipation with "comin' of de Kingdom" and "de day of Jubilo" indicates the existence for a long time of a deepseated desire for freedom.

While the attitude of the Negroes toward the "Yankees" was characterized by the greatest variations, and while the reactions to freedom ranged from indifference to elation, there can be no doubt that the general effect of Federal invasion upon the institution of slavery was disturbing and disruptive.

[37] *Up from Slavery*, pp. 20–21.

[38] *Nineteenth Annual Report of the American Missionary Association* (1865), p. 17.

[39] *Reminiscences of Peace and War*, p. 385.

[40] T. W. Knox, *Camp-Fire and Cotton-Field*, p. 373.

[41] Narrative of Nettie P. Evans, Anderson County, South Carolina, in *South Carolina Women in the Confederacy*, II, 159.

Suggestions for Additional Reading

General and Bibliographical Works

Bennett, Lerone, Jr. *Before the Mayflower* (Baltimore, 1966).

Franklin, John Hope. *From Slavery to Freedom* (New York, 1967).

Meier, August, and Elliott Rudwick. *From Plantation to Ghetto* (New York, 1966).

Miller, Elizabeth. *The Negro in America: A Bibliography* (Cambridge, 1966).

Salk, Erwin A. *A Layman's Guide to Negro History* (Chicago, 1966).

Welsch, Erwin K. *The Negro in the United States; A Research Guide.* (Bloomington, Ind., 1965).

Work, Monroe. *A Bibliography of the Negro in Africa and America* (New York, 1928).

I. Origins of American Slavery

Ballagh, James. *A History of Slavery in Virginia* (Baltimore, 1902).

Davis, David Brion. *The Problem of Slavery in Western Culture* (Ithaca, N.Y., 1966).

Degler, Carl. "Slavery and the Genesis of American Race Prejudice," *Comparative Studies in Society and History,* II (October 1959).

Gossett, Thomas F. *Race, The History of an Idea in America* (Dallas, 1963).

Handlin, Oscar and Mary. "Origins of the Southern Labor System," *William and Mary Quarterly,* 3d Series, VII (April 1950).

Jordan, Winthrop D. "Modern Tensions and the Origins of American Slavery," *Journal of Southern History,* XXVIII (February 1962).

———. *White over Black: The Development of American Attitudes toward the Negro, 1550–1812* (Chapel Hill, N.C., 1968).

II. The Foreign Slave Trade

Curtin, Philip. *The Atlantic Slave Trade: A Census* (Madison, Wisc., 1969).

Davidson, Basil. *Black Mother: The Years of the African Slave Trade* (Boston, 1961).

DuBois, W. E. B. *Suppression of the African Slave Trade to the United States, 1638–1870* (Cambridge, Mass., 1896).

Duignan, Peter, and Clarence Clendenen. *The United States and the African Slave Trade, 1619–1862* (Stanford, Calif., 1962).
Howard, Warren S. *American Slavers and the Federal Law, 1837–1862* (Berkeley, 1963).
Williams, Eric. *Capitalism and Slavery* (Chapel Hill, N.C., 1944).
Wyndham, H. A. *The Atlantic and Slavery* (London, 1935).

III. Colonial Slavery

Bassett, John Spencer. *Slavery and Servitude in the Colony of North Carolina* (Baltimore, 1896).
Brackett, Jeffrey R. *The Negro in Maryland* (Baltimore, 1904).
Cooley, Henry S. *Slavery in New Jersey* (Baltimore, 1896).
Greene, Lorenzo J. *The Negro in Colonial New England, 1620–1776* (New York, 1942).
Hast, Adele. "The Legal Status of the Negro in Virginia 1705–1765," *Journal of Negro History,* LIV (July 1969).
Jernegan, Marcus W. *Laboring and Dependent Classes in Colonial America, 1607–1783* (Chicago, 1931).
Johnson, Guion G. *Ante-Bellum North Carolina* (Chapel Hill, N.C., 1937).
Klingberg, Frank J. *An Appraisal of the Negro in Colonial South Carolina* (Washington, D.C., 1941).
McColley, Robert. *Slavery and Jeffersonian Virginia* (Urbana, Ill., 1964).
McManus, Edgar J. *A History of Negro Slavery in New York* (Syracuse, 1966).
Morris, Richard B. *Government and Labor in Early America* (New York, 1946).
Phillips, Ulrich B. *American Negro Slavery* (New York, 1918).
Quarles, Benjamin. *The Negro in the American Revolution* (Chapel Hill, N.C., 1961).
Sirmans, M. Eugene. "The Legal Status of the Slave in South Carolina 1670–1740," *Journal of Southern History,* XXVIII (November 1962).
Steiner, Bernard C. *History of Slavery in Connecticut* (Baltimore, 1893).
Tate, Thad. *The Negro in Eighteenth-Century Williamsburg* (Williamsburg, Va., 1965).
Turner, Edward. *The Negro in Pennsylvania* (Washington, D.C., 1911).
Twombly, Richard C., and Robert H. Moore. "Black Puritan: The Negro in Seventeenth-Century Massachusetts," *William and Mary Quarterly,* 3d Series, XXIV (April 1967).

IV. The Life of a Slave

Botkin, B. A. *Lay My Burden Down: A Folk History of Slavery* (Chicago, 1945).
Coleman, J. Winston, Jr. *Slavery Times in Kentucky* (Chapel Hill, N.C., 1940).

Eaton, Clement. "Slave-Hiring in the Upper South: A Step toward Freedom," *Mississippi Valley Historical Review,* XLVI (March 1960).

Mooney, Chase C. *Slavery in Tennessee* (Bloomington, Ind., 1957).

Osofsky, Gilbert, ed. *Puttin' On Ole Massa* (New York, 1969).

Phifer, Edward W. "Slavery in Microcosm: Burke County, North Carolina," *Journal of Southern History,* XXVIII (May 1962).

Phillips, Ulrich B. *American Negro Slavery* (New York, 1918).

———. *Life and Labor in the Old South* (Boston, 1929).

Postell, William Dostite. *The Health of Slaves on Southern Plantations* (Baton Rouge, La., 1951).

Sellers, James B. *Slavery in Alabama* (Tuscaloosa, Ala., 1950).

Stampp, Kenneth. *The Peculiar Institution* (New York, 1956).

Sydnor, Charles S. *Slavery in Mississippi* (New York, 1933).

Taylor, Orville W. *Negro Slavery in Arkansas* (Durham, N.C., 1958).

Wade, Richard. *Slavery in the Cities, The South, 1820–1860* (New York, 1964).

V. The Slave's Response

Aptheker, Herbert. *American Negro Slave Revolts* (New York, 1943).

Frazier, E. Franklin. *The Negro Church in America* (New York, 1963).

Freyre, Gilberto. *The Masters and the Slaves: A Study in the Development of Brazilian Civilization* (New York, 1946).

Gara, Larry. *The Liberty Line: The Legend of the Underground Railroad* (Lexington, Ky., 1961).

Genovese, Eugene. "Rebelliousness and Docility in the Negro Slave: A Critique of the Elkins Thesis," *Civil War History,* XIII (December 1967).

Halasz, Nicholas. *The Rattling Chains: Slave Unrest and Revolt in the Ante-bellum South* (New York, 1966).

Jackson, Luther P. "Religious Development of the Negro in Virginia from 1790 to 1860," *Journal of Negro History,* XVI (April 1931).

Johnson, F. Roy. *The Nat Turner Slave Insurrection* (Murfreesboro, Tenn., 1966).

Klein, Herbert S. *Slavery in the Americas: A Comparison of Cuba and Virginia* (Chicago, 1966).

Lewis, Mary A. "Slavery and Personality: A Further Comment," *American Quarterly,* XIX (Spring 1967).

Perkins, Haven. "Religion for Slaves: Difficulties and Methods," *Church History,* X (September 1941).

Stampp, Kenneth. *The Peculiar Institution: Slavery in the Ante-Bellum South* (New York, 1956), chap. IV.

Tannenbaum, Frank. *Slave and Citizen* (New York, 1947).

Wish, Harvey. "American Slave Insurrections before 1861," *Journal of Negro History,* XXII (July 1937).

Woodson, Carter. *History of the Negro Church* (Washington, 1921).

VI. Slavery and Southern Society

Conrad, Alfred, and John Meyer. "The Economics of Slavery in the Ante-Bellum South," *Journal of Political Economy,* LXVI (April 1958).

Engerman, Stanley. "The Effects of Slavery upon the Southern Economy: A Review of the Recent Debate," *Explorations in Entrepreneurial History,* IV (Winter 1967).

Genovese, Eugene. *The Political Economy of Slavery: Studies in the Economy and Society of the Slave South* (New York, 1965).

————. "The Significance of the Slave Plantation for Southern Economic Development," *Journal of Southern History,* XXVIII (November 1962).

Govan, Thomas. "Was Plantation Slavery Profitable?" *Journal of Southern History,* VIII (November 1942).

Phillips, Ulrich B. "The Economic Cost of Slave-holding in the Cotton Belt," *Political Science Quarterly,* XX (June 1905).

Stampp, Kenneth. *The Peculiar Institution: Slavery in the Ante-Bellum South* (New York, 1956), chap. IX.

Sutch, Richard. "The Profitability of Ante-Bellum Slavery—Revisited," *Southern Economic Journal,* XXXI (April 1965).

Wade, Richard. *Slavery in the Cities: The South, 1820–1860* (New York, 1964), chaps. IV and IX.

Woodman, Harold. "The Profitability of Slavery: A Historical Perennial," *Journal of Southern History,* XXIX (August 1963).

VII. The End of Slavery

Cornish, Dudley T. *The Sable Arm: Negro Troops in the Union Army, 1861–1865* (New York, 1956).

Franklin, John Hope. *The Emancipation Proclamation* (New York, 1963).

McPherson, James, ed. *The Negro's Civil War: How Negroes Felt and Acted during the War for the Union* (New York, 1965).

Quarles, Benjamin. *Lincoln and the Negro* (New York, 1962).

————. *The Negro in the Civil War* (Boston, 1963).

Rose, Willie Lee. *Rehearsal for Reconstruction: The Port Royal Experiment* (Indianapolis, 1964).

Shannon, Fred. "The Federal Government and the Negro Soldier, 1861–1865," *Journal of Negro History,* XI (October 1926).

Wish, Harvey. "Slave Disloyalty under the Confederacy," *Journal of Negro History,* XXIII (October 1938).